SCHELLING: AN INTRODUCTION
TO THE SYSTEM OF FREEDOM

SCHELLING: AN INTRODUCTION TO THE SYSTEM OF FREEDOM

ALAN WHITE

YALE UNIVERSITY PRESS
New Haven and London

Published with assistance from the Louis Stern Memorial Fund.

Designed by Nancy Ovedovitz and set in VIP Palatino type
by P & M Typesetting, Inc.
Printed in the United States of America by Murray Printing
Company, Westford, Mass.

Library of Congress Cataloging in Publication Data
White, Alan, 1951–
    Schelling: an introduction to the system of freedom.

    Bibliography: p.
    Includes index.
    1. Schelling, Friedrich Wilhelm Joseph von, 1775–1854. I. Title.
B2898.W46 1983   193   82-16034
ISBN 0-300-02896-2

10 9 8 7 6 5 4 3 2 1

To my mother, Anne Stelzenmuller White, and to the memory of my father, Locke White, Jr.

Der Philosoph glaubt, der Wert seiner Philosophie liege im Ganzen, im Bau: die Nachwelt findet ihn im Stein, mit dem er baute und mit dem, von da an, noch oft und besser gebaut wird: also darin, daß jener kBau zerstört werden kann und doch noch *als Material Wert hat.*

The philosopher believes that the value of his philosophy lies in the whole, in the building, but those who come after find it in the stone with which he built and with which, from then on, others build often and better; thus, in the fact that the building can be destroyed without ceasing to be valuable as material.

Nietzsche

CONTENTS

PREFACE

This book is a study of the thought of Friedrich Wilhelm Joseph Schelling, a nineteenth-century German philosopher who has become obscure. I have written the book because, for reasons described more fully in my introduction, I believe that Schelling should not be allowed to remain obscure: his influence is too great for that, some of his reflections too profound. This book is intended not only for specialists in the philosophy of German Idealism but also for readers interested in the intellectual transition from Kant to Kierkegaard and Marx, and those seeking to understand the philosophical heritage shared by Marxists and existentialists. I have written the book as an introduction, and I have therefore attempted to include sufficient explanation and background information to make it understandable to anyone willing to read and to think carefully; others are scarcely likely to concern themselves with philosophy books in any case. While my concern with being intelligible to readers who are not specialists in German philosophy has led me to attempt to write clearly, it has not led me, I hope, either to avoid or to oversimplify the fundamental problems that Schelling faces or the solutions to them that he proposes. To be truly introduced to a philosopher's thought is necessarily to be confronted with philosophical problems; for the philosopher, of course, those problems are what make philosophy interesting. I have attempted to describe the problems, then, rather than to avoid them, but I have attempted to describe them clearly enough that their significance will be apparent even to those readers who confront them here for the first time. Discussion of these problems, and especially of Schelling's reactions to them, necessarily involves discussion of several other philosophers whose names are not household words or whose names are little more than words even in many philosophy departments. I hope that those who read this book will find that these names need not have caused any initial feelings of apprehension: I presuppose in the reader no more knowledge of these philosophers than of the problems they consider. Readers are likely to find three sections more difficult than the rest; these are the discussions of Fichte's *Doctrine of Science,* of Schelling's *System of Transcendental Idealism,* and of Schelling's *Of Human Freedom.* Of the works I treat in detail, these alone are available in English translations, and I have therefore chosen to follow the arguments made in them closely enough that readers struggling with the translated primary texts will be truly aided by my discussions of them. This does not mean, I stress again, that I presuppose any knowledge of the original works: it has been my intent to include in this book all that the reader needs to know to understand the book. I hope that all readers will come to some understanding of Schelling and of the problems he faces; readers who can solve those problems should write their own books.

My sincere thanks to my teachers, Stanley Rosen and Thomas Seebohm, for philosophical training and inspiration; to the Pennsylvania State University and the German Academic Exchange Service (D.A.A.D.) for financial assistance during part of the time in which this study was written; and to Maureen MacGrogan and the rest of the superb team at the Yale University Press for allowing me to work with them as they turned my manuscript into this book.

1 SCHELLING AND HIS PROJECT

METAPHYSICS AND ANTHROPOLOGY

In 1809, halfway through his philosophical career, Friedrich Wilhelm Joseph Schelling wrote:

> Man is placed on a peak: he has within himself the capacity for spontaneous movement toward good or toward evil; the bond holding these principles in him is not necessary, it is free. He stands at the point of divergence: whatever he chooses, it will be his deed, but he cannot remain undecided. . . . The essence of man is essentially *his own deed*.[1]

With this insight—which anticipates by over a century Sartre's teachings that human existence precedes human essence and that human existence is grounded in a "primordial choice"— Schelling raised himself to a philosophical peak, he placed himself at the point of divergence between two paths. He could either focus exclusively on human beings as radically free agents confronted throughout their lives with the necessity of making decisions and choosing courses of action, or he could attempt to go beyond the human level, he could strive to uncover the supersensible source that gives rise both to humans and to the good and evil between which they must choose. A step along the former path would have been a step into the twentieth century, the beginning of the existentialist attempt to explain the world in human terms; Schelling did not take that step. Instead, he stepped back into the eighteenth

---

1. F. W. J. Schelling, *Sämmtliche Werke*, 7:347, 385. I will henceforth cite the *Werke* parenthetically, giving first the volume number (1–14) and then the page numbers. The present reference is to *Philosophische Untersuchungen über das Wesen der menschlichen Freiheit und die damit zusammenhängende Gegenstände*, translated by James Gutman as *Of Human Freedom*. Gutman's edition indicates the pagination of the *Werke*. A key to all references to Schelling's works is provided in the Selected Bibliography. Translations from works whose German editions are cited are my own.

century, reviving for the last time the classical attempt to understand all that exists in terms of the transcendent absolute in which it is grounded. In choosing the latter path, Schelling remained true to the metaphysical tradition, but in raising practical and existential questions that earlier philosophers had ignored or avoided, he helped to bring that tradition to its end; he became the last of the classical metaphysicians.

When Schelling was born, in 1775, the German philosophical world was dominated by the metaphysical system of Christian Wolff, a system grounded in the naive assumptions that virtually all human beings share vague notions concerning God and the soul, that these notions are essentially correct, and that the philosopher who states them clearly thereby uncovers the truth. Wolff's world was shattered, during Schelling's childhood, by Kant's *Critique of Pure Reason*. Kant insists that supersensible entities like God and the soul are beyond the ken of human reason, and that when philosophers ignore the limitations of the human intellect, their theories are suspect. Kant's arguments inspired a rising generation of thinkers to search for a better metaphysical doctrine, and Schelling, in his early twenties, was for a time the most influential of those thinkers. Schelling's predominance was short-lived; he was soon surpassed by his former classmate and follower Hegel, who overwhelmed his contemporaries by claiming that he had brought the Western philosophical tradition to its end by attaining—and presenting, in rigorous, scientific fashion—absolute knowledge. Schelling survived Hegel, and by the time he himself died he had, through his critique of Hegel and his reflections on the nature of philosophy, decisively influenced Kierkegaard and Marx; he had thereby helped—albeit inadvertently—to inaugurate a new epoch in Western thought, one based on the radical rejection of the tradition stretching from Plato to Hegel.

Schelling himself never abandoned the metaphysical project, but the efficacy of his attack on Hegel, accompanied by the manifest impotence of his own final system, convinced the most important of his successors that the tradition had exhausted itself. Marx and his followers turned from problems of theory to those of practice, insisting that metaphysicians had sought an abstract, narrowly rational satisfaction that would be inadequate to the real needs even of the few who might be able to appreciate it. The more important task, Marx argues, is to alter political and economic conditions in the world to make comprehensive satisfaction possible for all human beings. Kierkegaard, and after him such thinkers as Heidegger, Jaspers, and Sartre, shifts the focus of philosophy from essence to existence, arguing that metaphysicians, concentrating on the realm of the eternal, the infinite, and the purely rational, had neglected the temporal, finite, and all too irrational world in which human beings are forced to live.

After Schelling's death—and in part as a result of his own philosophical activity—metaphysics lost its traditional status of first philosophy, the highest theoretical discipline; it gave way to various sorts of philosophical anthropologies, various attempts to ground all philosophy in the study of human being rather than in the study of being as such.[2] This development constitutes a revolution that is among the most confusing and most important in philosophy's history, a revolution whose effects are visible in many other intellectual disciplines and even in the political structure of the twentieth-century world. What began with an obscure event of interest only to European philosophers, namely, the rejection of the metaphysical tradition, has developed into movements influencing events and thinkers throughout the world. The importance of Marxism to modern society is obvious, that of existentialism to contemporary literature well known. Moreover, existential reflections have been introduced into clinical psychology by Ludwig Binswanger and Medard Boss—and more recently by their popularizer, Rollo May—and into theology by such thinkers as Rudolf Bultmann, Karl Barth, and Paul Tillich. Tillich, indeed, makes his indebtedness to Schelling explicit and emphasizes Schelling's importance in the history of ideas:

> The influence of my Schelling studies on the whole of my further development is very strong. . . . Decisive confirmation of my own evaluation of Schelling came to me, for the first time, when

---

2. Throughout this study, "anthropology" refers to *philosophical* anthropology in the broadest sense, that is, to philosophical undertakings that accept *human* being as the necessary starting point for philosophy. This "anthropology" should not be confused with the contemporary social science.

I encountered Nietzsche and the philosophy of life, and, next, when I became involved in the philosophy and art of existentialism. Both movements are, to a great extent, dependent upon Schelling.[3]

The revolution Schelling helped to cause, the revolution through which philosophical anthropology replaced metaphysics as the primary concern of thinkers devoted to first philosophy, is a development that may at first appear to be both obscure and, to all save historians of ideas and a few philosophers, irrelevant; yet it has profoundly affected ways of living and thinking in the latter half of the twentieth century. Regardless of the diversity of its effects, however, and regardless of their importance to nonphilosophers, the development itself is a philosophical one, and it can be understood only through the consideration of philosophical texts and issues. The crucial issues are articulated in the works of F.W.J. Schelling.

THE SYSTEM OF FREEDOM

Schelling's thought is profound and intriguing; if it were not, it would not have been so influential in the past. Schelling's works are obscure and enigmatic; if they were not, they would not be so seldom read today. No other modern thinker of comparable importance is so inaccessible, particularly to the English-speaking world; few of Schelling's works have been translated, but even if all were available in English, it would be difficult for most readers to approach them. The significance of the questions and arguments in his early works would be apparent only to those already acquainted with the thought of Spinoza, Leibniz, Kant, and Fichte, and Schelling's later works regularly presuppose conclusions reached—and problems encountered—in the earlier ones. The latter difficulty is particularly great, for Schelling's thought continued to develop throughout the half-century during which he was philosophi-

3. Used as an epigraph for the English translation of Tillich's dissertation, *Mysticism and Guilt-Consciousness in Schelling's Philosophical Development*, trans. Victor Nuovo. The source of the remark is Tillich's *Gesammelte Werke* (Stuttgart: Evangelisches Verlagswerk, 1959), 1:9.

cally active. Many philosophers spend their careers elaborating doctrines that remain essentially the same; readers interested in such thinkers, and professors teaching about them, can select from among their works the less forbidding. That is not possible with Schelling, for he spent his career seeking his position rather than developing it; his search was so widespread that scholars have given him the epithet "the Proteus of German Idealism."

Schelling deserves his epithet in that he often begins from what seem to be different principles and consequently reaches, in his various works, divergent and even contradictory conclusions: he is Protean in that he is responsible for a number of distinct systems. To say that Schelling changed his position several times is not, however, to say that there were not good reasons for his changes. Schelling viewed his development as completely coherent, and his view has been supported by Heidegger, who insists that "seldom has a thinker fought so passionately, from the beginning, for his one sole position."[4] Schelling's fight is more accurately described as a striving, throughout his career, toward the only position that could satisfy his philosophical demands: Schelling struggled for a half-century with a single project. The project, the key to understanding Schelling's development, is first identified in his second publication—which appeared when he was twenty years old—as the production of the "antithesis to Spinoza's *Ethics*" (1:159). In the same year, Schelling characterizes the antithesis in positive terms as the "system of freedom" (1:315). Thirty-two years later, Schelling's goal had not changed: "A system of freedom—as great in scope and at the same time as simple as Spinoza's, its complete antithesis—that would really be the highest" (10:36).

An antithesis to Spinoza, a system of freedom: these phrases reveal at once Schelling's dependence upon the metaphysical tradition and his divergence from it. Schelling expresses respect for the breadth of Spinoza's *Ethics*—a metaphysical work, despite its title—and for the clarity Spinoza achieves

---

4. Martin Heidegger, *Schellings Abhandlung über das Wesen der menschlichen Freiheit*, p. 7.

through adherence to the geometrical method of presentation. Spinoza begins with concise if not always clear definitions and axioms and then uses them in proofs of propositions and corollaries. Starting with God or the absolute, Spinoza develops his system by "explaining the results which must necessarily follow from the essence of God, or of the eternal and infinite being."[5] Throughout his career, Schelling continues to insist that Spinoza was right in beginning with the absolute; because of this insistence, Schelling never ceases to be a metaphysician. Shelling's divergence from Spinoza cannot be so simply described; indeed, this study in its entirety is devoted to that description. One way in which the major epochs in Schelling's development may be distinguished is through identification of what he sees, at a given time, as Spinoza's most serious flaw. One flaw identified as crucial by Schelling both very early and very late in his career is suggested by the passage quoted above: if the finite world in all its temporal determinateness is among the "results which must necessarily follow from the essence of God," if the acts and events that take place in our world are fully predetermined and thus bound by an absolute necessity, then human freedom is a mere illusion. That, Schelling insists, cannot be; it is this insistence that ties Schelling to the existentialists.

To study Schelling's development is to study his attempts to produce the antithesis to Spinoza's *Ethics*, his attempts to reconcile the demands of system with the demands of freedom. Unfortunately perhaps for those who would understand Schelling's attempts, they are often complicated; fortunately, they are also fascinating.

5. Benedict Spinoza, *Ethics*, preface to Part 2.

2 FROM PROJECT TO SYSTEM

SUBJECTIVITY, HUMAN AND ABSOLUTE

A Spinozist Flaw: Ego as Mere Thing

It is in the essay "On the Ego as Principle of Philosophy" (1795) that Schelling first projects his antithesis to Spinoza's *Ethics*. By "antithesis" Schelling does not mean something completely different from Spinoza's system. As Schelling's title suggests, he disagrees with Spinoza concerning what philosophy's principle is, but the context in which the disagreement arises is Spinozist: Schelling shares Spinoza's understanding both of what philosophy is and of what kind of principle philosophy needs. The two agree that philosophy is concerned with all of reality and not with a specific part of it; whereas the herpetologist studies snakes and frogs, the philosopher studies the whole. One consequence of this difference is that the principle or principles of philosophy must be of a different sort from the principles of the special sciences. The principles of the herpetologist—the starting point for his investigations—include the methods shared by all biologists and the scheme of classification according to which reptiles and amphibians are in a different category from birds or insects. Since philosophy is the study of the whole, it lacks a clearly defined subject matter; it also lacks a presupposed method, for it is not a part of a more comprehensive science whose method it could simply adopt. One way of expressing this difference between herpetology and philosophy is to say that the former is a relative science, the latter an absolute one. Herpetology is defined by its relations to the other zoological sciences, such as ornithology and entomology; zoology is defined by its relations to the other biological science, botany; and biology as a whole is defined by its relations to such other sciences as physics and chemistry. Philosophy is not one among many similar sciences, it is not a distinct part of a larger whole; in that its nature is not determined by any relations to other similar endeavors, it is absolute; it stands alone.

If philosophy is to stand alone, Schelling and Spinoza reason, that on which it focuses must also stand alone. The philosopher's account of the whole cannot begin with a part of the whole; it must rather begin with the source or ground of all that is within the whole, it must begin with the absolute. In agreeing with Spinoza that philosophy actually *can* begin with the absolute, Schelling differs from many of his peers. For this reason, his own critique of Spinoza is preceded by a defense of the Spinozist doctrine that philosophy is the rational science of the absolute. The crux of the defense is directed against Kant's arguments, in the *Critique of Pure Reason*, that rational knowledge of the absolute is impossible for human beings.

In the *Critique of Pure Reason*, Kant attempts to distinguish the areas in which human knowledge is possible from those in which it is not; he explores and charts the "land of pure understanding," seeking to ground mathematical and empirical knowledge, and then strives to prove that this land is the sole "land of truth," that it is an island surrounded by a sea of illusion. Those who—like Spinoza—leave the solid ground of science and mathematics in search of supersensible absolutes can encounter nothing more than fogs and icebergs, but they tend to conclude mistakenly that they have discovered new and better worlds. Kant insists that if there is land beyond his land of truth then it is inaccessible to human beings, for it is beyond the bounds of human reason.[1]

In responding to the Kantian objection, Schelling does not teach that there is a third sort of knowledge wholly unrelated to mathematical and empirical knowledge and simply alien to Kant. He argues rather that the forms of knowledge defended by Kant can be grounded only in a sort of knowledge that is distinct from them. Although Kant argues that the limits of the human intellect exclude all save mathematical and empirical

---

1. Immanuel Kant, *Kritik der reinen Vernunft*, A235/B295–96. Henceforth, this work will be cited parenthetically; A identifies page numbers from the first (1871) edition, B those from the second (1878) edition. The best English translation is that of Norman Kemp Smith, *Critique of Pure Reason*; Smith's edition indicates the original pagination.

knowledge, his awareness *of the limits themselves* can be neither empirical nor mathematical; that awareness reveals our access to a third sort of knowledge, termed by Kant *transcendental*, a sort that is developed only through philosophical reflection on human experience as a whole. While Kant uses transcendental knowledge to develop arguments proving that our mathematical and empirical knowledge is reliable, he leaves transcendental knowledge itself ungrounded. Kant's *Critique* thus presupposes principles that it does not examine, and it reveals a stratum of knowledge—and thereby an aspect of the knower—that it does not investigate. Schelling appropriates Kant's nautical metaphor in claiming that while those who accept the *Critique* as a complete account of human knowledge may perhaps believe that they reside secure on solid land, that belief is mere self-deception: they have in fact chosen to cower timorously at anchor rather than setting forth in search of truth. The true philosopher leaves Kant's land of the understanding to follow Spinoza in "risking everything, desiring either the *whole* truth, in its entire magnitude, or no truth at all" (1:152).

Schelling fully approves of Spinoza's attempt to ground his system not on Kant's land of truth—the familiar factical[2] world in which finite subjects are opposed to finite objects—but rather in the absolute, in that which is the source of subjects and objects and even of itself. Having countered the Kantian assertion that we can have no knowledge of the absolute, Schelling next faces the question of what the absolute is. In answering this question, the twenty-year-old Schelling relies on two presuppositions whose validity he begins to doubt only in later years, after they have led him into difficulties. He presupposes, first, that we can say what the absolute is by identifying the fundamental class to which it belongs and, second, that the two fundamental classes of all beings are the class of subjects and that of objects. Schelling's question, then, is whether the absolute is like a person or like a thing, whether it is like the

---

2. "Factical," like "factual," refers to what in fact is; I use the former term for its connotations. Whereas the factual is opposed to the merely apparent, the factical is opposed to the necessary: what is factical exists, but might not have existed. The important connotation is that of contingency.

soul or like the body. In approaching the question, Schelling continues to take his bearings by Spinoza and his critics. According to those critics, Spinoza teaches that the absolute is an object rather than a subject. This, the critics insist, is a contradiction: to be absolute is to be unconditioned, in German *unbedingt*, and to be an object is to be a thing, a *Ding*. The absolute, if an object, would be an *unbedingtes Ding*, an "unbethinged" thing. Yet to be an object, according to the critics, is to be *for* a subject, to be made into an object—"bethinged"—by a subject; a thing can no more be unbethinged than a square can be round.[3]

Schelling agrees with Spinoza's critics that the absolute cannot be an object, but he denies that Spinoza thought of the absolute as such. Spinoza himself does not describe his "absolute substance" as either subject or object; to determine how he understood it, Schelling examines the predicates that characterize it. These include self-identical substantiality, pure being, and unity, none of which, Schelling asserts, can apply to objects: objects change with time, they are made up of distinct parts, and they come into being and pass away. The human soul, the archetypal subject, is often thought to be the unchanging essence of the person, that which makes an individual the *same* individual throughout life or, according to some, throughout many lives or into a life after death. Whether or not the soul is in fact immortal and unchanging, we do not contradict ourselves if we think of it as such, but we do, ac-

3. Schelling does not explain his distinction between subjects and objects. He relies implicitly on two generally familiar aspects of the distinction: first, in a narrower sense, subjects are conscious, thinking beings, and objects are the things they are conscious of or think about. In the broader sense, subjects act, objects are acted upon. The broader sense is reflected in the grammatical distinction between subjects and objects: in "The boy throws the stone," the boy is the subject and the stone is the object, whereas in "The stone breaks the window," the stone is the subject and the window is the object. Schelling's argument concerning the absolute could be restated, albeit not fully adequately, as follows: the absolute cannot be object, for to be object is to be acted on by something and thus to be relative to that something. By a more questionable but perhaps helpful extension, it could be said that the absolute can be subject without being relative to anything because to be subject is to act, and action can be intransitive.

cording to Schelling, fall into contradiction if we think of the body, or of any mere thing, in those terms. Since the predicates Spinoza applies to the absolute can apply to subjects but never to objects, Spinoza does not teach that the absolute is an *unbedingtes Ding*.

In Schelling's view, Spinoza is right to begin with the absolute, and he characterizes the absolute as it must be characterized. Spinoza's crucial error thus cannot be found in his doctrine of the absolute as such; it is found rather in his assumption that the absolute must be completely different from and beyond the human subject, the ego. Given that assumption, Spinoza's system is fully coherent, but the assumption itself is unwarranted and leads finally to absurdity and confusion: if the ego is outside of and heterogenous to the absolute, and the absolute is characterized in terms appropriate to subjects, then the ego must, paradoxically, be determined as an object. If the ego is opposed to the absolute, then it cannot share the self-sufficiency and autonomy of the latter and must be fully dependent; it must be taken to be dependent not only on the absolute but even on the mere things in its world. Spinoza thus reverses the true relation of subject and object, "making the ego non-ego and the non-ego ego" (1:170).

Having presented the ego as dependent, Spinoza is unable to account for the most important attribute of the human subject, namely the faculty of consciousness. Even if it were granted that a purely passive, fully determined entity could have some faculty of awareness, such an entity could be aware at most of impressions such as colored shapes and meaningless sounds. Consciousness of objects as externally existent unities—the kind of consciousness normal for human beings—is possible only for subjects capable of attending now to certain sensations or impressions, now to others, and of synthesizing them into its unitary stream of consciousness. Kant indeed is able to establish that our knowledge of things in the world is reliable only by proving that the subject plays an active role in the production of experience. Schelling accepts this most important part of Kant's teaching and insists that even the "lowest degree of spontaneity in theoretical philosophy," that exhibited in the simplest possible reflection or direction of attention, presupposes the independence of the subject from the object and thus manifests the primordial freedom of the subject as fully as does "the highest [degree of spontaneity] in practical philosophy" (1:205), the spontaneity exhibited in free choice and moral resolution.

The human ego could not be conscious of anything if it were not free, Schelling argues, but if the ego shared none of the properties of the absolute, then it could not be free, for freedom is among those properties:

> Through its concept, an absolute excludes every determination through alien causality; absolute freedom is nothing other than the absolute determination of the unconditioned through the . . . laws of its being, its independence from all laws not determinable through its *essence* itself, from all laws that would posit in it anything not already posited through its mere being, through its positedness in general. [1:235]

Schelling affirms the Spinozist teachings that the absolute is free from all outside influence and that absolute freedom, as action in accordance with essence, is absolute necessity. Those of Spinoza's critics who fault him for not describing the absolute in the terms generally applied to the Christian God, Schelling insists, reveal only that they themselves do not grasp what it means to be absolute. Spinoza is right in placing the absolute beyond truth, goodness, will, virtue, and wisdom; it is beyond all because it is the source of all. This, in Schelling's view is Spinoza's "most sublime idea": the essence of the absolute is the unconditioned power required for purely autonomous action. Those who would reject the idea on the basis of its lack of correspondence to their notions of God—be they Christian or otherwise—reveal thereby only the defectiveness of those notions. Those who would reject Spinoza's idea in favor of a moral god contradict themselves, for a moral god would be one bound by external moral laws and such a being would be no god (1:196, 235). Unlike these critics, who take themselves to be followers of Kant, Spinoza correctly grasped the nature of the absolute; he erred only in insisting that the ego is heterogenous to it.

In so championing Spinoza, Schelling does not intend to oppose Kant: he insists that those who attempt to canonize the teachings of Kant's three Critiques trivialize rather than support the Kantian position. In Schelling's view, it is Fichte who first grasps the spirit of Kant's project without being misled by the letter of his published works: he sees that the Critiques are merely propaedeutic, intended to clear the way for an adequately grounded metaphysical system, and that as such they are presystematic. It is what Schelling takes to be Fichte's path beyond the Kantian Critiques that he first follows in his attempt to discover the antithesis to Spinoza's *Ethics*. He searches for an absolute immanent to the human ego rather than opposed to it, an absolute that can ground an account of human beings as free and conscious subjects.

The Fichtean Alternative: Ego as Absolute

In 1794, a year before the appearance of Schelling's "On the Ego," Fichte's first two major works were published. Like Schelling, Fichte intends to use Kant's critique of dogmatic metaphysics as the basis for a new philosophical system. As the term implies, dogmatists are those who rely on opinion rather than on knowledge, those whose highest authority is— whether they realize it or not—faith rather than reason. According to Kant, all traditional metaphysicians are dogmatists in that they ground their teachings in supersensible absolutes, in principles that are beyond the scope of the human intellect; since nothing can be known about such absolutes, all that is said about them is mere dogma, mere opinion. Knowledge is possible, Kant insists, only with respect to logical and mathematical truths and to the things we perceive with the aid of our senses. The inconsistency of this doctrine is indicated above: in arguing his point Kant affirms that the ego—the human subject—plays an active, constitutive role in the formation of ordinary experience; he also maintains that the ego can know the categories and principles through which it constitutes the objects of its experience. Yet Kant does not acknowledge that his arguments rely on knowledge of the ego that is neither logical nor mathematical nor empirical, nor does he recognize that knowledge of how subject and object interact to produce experience is knowledge that is in a sense absolute: it is absolute in that it is not relative to any particular human subject or to any particular object of experience. Nor, consequently, does Kant recognize that the subject itself, at least on the level where it attains this absolute knowledge, is also in some sense absolute.

Fichte draws from Kant's arguments and their implications two conclusions concerning metaphysics and dogmatism: he concludes that metaphysics is impossible in principle if the absolute is essentially different from the ego, and he concludes that since the ego is in some sense absolute, he should be able to ground a system in it. To distinguish his system from dogmatism, Fichte classes it "critical idealism": the system is to be idealistic (rather than realistic) in that it will present the absolute as subjective[4] rather than objective, critical in that its absolute will be the only absolute that we can know, namely the absolute that each of us somehow is. Fichte christens his system "the doctrine of science" *(Wissenschaftslehre)*. In the first of his major works, "On the Concept of the Doctrine of Science," he presents only his first principles, but in the second, *Foundation of the Entire Doctrine of Science,* he sketches the system in its entirety. It is the latter work that was most influential on the Schelling of "On the Ego."

Fichte's **Wissenschaftslehre** *of 1794*[5] The 1794 *Doctrine* is divided into three parts: "Axioms of the Entire Doctrine of Science," "Foundation of Theoretical Knowledge," and "Foundation of the Science of the Practical." In the first part, Fichte derives and explicates the three axioms purported to ground all knowledge; in the second, he dialectically demonstrates the inadequacy of merely theoretical philosophy; and in the third,

4. "Subjective" is used here to mean "having the nature of a subject" (rather than that of an object); this sense of the term must be kept distinct from the pejorative sense, the sense in which "subjective" refers to something arbitrary, something dependent on the tastes or whims of a specific individual.

5. As is indicated above in the preface, the following discussion is designed to be sufficiently detailed to be of some aid to those struggling with the 1794 *Doctrine* itself. Readers not concerned with Fichte, and who would prefer to avoid the details, may choose not to read this section; the summary that follows, in the section "From Fichte to Schelling," does not presuppose understanding of this analysis.

he outlines the practical teaching that is to satisfy the demands of human reason. The work's entire structure is—as the section titles indicate—determined by Fichte's distinction between theory and practice; that distinction itself derives from his three grounding axioms.

The second and third of his axioms have, according to Fichte, long been known even to dogmatic metaphysicians. In general terms, those axioms state that subject and object are, within the realm of ordinary experience, at once opposed and related: the subject is subject only in having—knowing or acting on—an object, while the object is object only in being objectified by—being known or acted on by—a subject. The first axiom, which grounds the other two, was not recognized by pre-Kantian dogmatists; this most important axiom states that subject and object are both opposed and related only *for* the subject, whose awareness of both itself and the object grounds the relation between the two. The ego, understood as absolute ground, is the principle silently presupposed by Kant's Critiques, the principle from which the critical system must develop; Kant himself does not recognize the ego as this principle, but, Fichte insists, the first Critique fulfills the negative function of showing that no other principle can suffice. Prior to Kant, philosophers had introduced various sorts of principles, but none had fully grasped the fundamental importance of the ego: pre-Kantian metaphysical doctrines are all defective in that all are grounded, at best, in the two subordinate axioms.[6]

In Fichte's view, all earlier metaphysicians share the flaw Schelling attributes to Spinoza: all present the ego as dependent upon and determined by the object. Restated in the confusing terminology peculiar to Fichte, the objection is that the dogmatists present the ego as "theoretical." So used, "theoretical" designates the property—passive dependence—asserted by dogmatists to constitute the essence of the human subject.

6. Johann Gottlieb Fichte, *Grundlage der gesammten Wissenschaftslehre*, in *Sämmtliche Werke*, 1:122. Cited henceforth in the text by page number. The original pagination is indicated in the English translation of Peter Heath and John Lachs, *Science of Knowledge with the First and Second Introductions*.

Within the *Doctrine*, Fichte also uses the term to modify "philosophy." In this latter, traditional sense, "theoretical" identifies teachings that concern what is, as opposed to the "practical" teachings that concern what should be or should be done: in the traditional sense, theoretical philosophy is descriptive, practical philosophy prescriptive. In the peculiarly Fichtean sense, the ego is theoretical if it is determined by its object, practical if it determines its object; an ego beyond all objectivity would be neither theoretical nor practical, but rather absolute. That Fichte uses the terms in the traditional senses as well as in his own can be confusing to the reader who does not distinguish among the senses or who does not note in specific cases which sense is intended; nevertheless, the senses are related. If the subject were merely theoretical—if it were fully determined by the object—then a theoretical account of it, a theoretical philosophy, could be complete, and any practical philosophy would be senseless. Since, however, the ego is practical—since, according to Fichte and Kant, it determines its object—the philosopher who would exhaustively explain it must provide an account of what it should do; since the ego is practical, all merely theoretical accounts of it—all accounts that try to describe simply what it is—will miss its essence.

The 1794 *Doctrine* is, in these terms, an argument intended to prove that the subject is practical rather than merely theoretical or purely absolute, and thereby that philosophy must be practical. That the ego is not merely theoretical—that it is somehow absolute—is posited in Fichte's first axiom; the arguments given for this axiom—and thus for the absoluteness of the ego—are presented as irrefutable, but Fichte acknowledges that they will remain unintelligible to those who lack the "capacity for the freedom of inner intuition" (p. 88), that is, to those who cannot or do not take the reflective step to Kant's transcendental standpoint, from which both subject and object may be considered. The second and third axioms, the only ones known to pre-Kantians, assert that the ego is finite—thus, that it is not absolute—as it appears within the realm of experience; there, it is limited by and inextricably related to the object.

The task of the *Doctrine* as a whole is to reconcile the ego's apparent finitude with its necessary infinitude. The second part of the *Doctrine*—that devoted to the theoretical—contributes to the task in two ways. First, starting from the ego of experience, it attempts to reveal that the ego, even as limited by the object, cannot be simply passive-receptive, that it cannot be theoretical in the Fichtean sense. Second, starting from the ego as absolute, the ego of the first axiom, it attempts to reveal the genesis of the apparent limitation of the ego by the object. The theoretical part of the *Doctrine* thus purports to establish both that the ego cannot be purely finite—simply theoretical—and that, if it is truly infinite or absolute, it will nevertheless come to appear to itself to be finite. Given these results, Fichte attempts in the *Doctrine*'s third part to show how the ego as practical can, while factically limited by the object, attain satisfaction by acting upon it.

In arguing that subjective finitude and infinitude are reconciled within the practical subject, Fichte also attempts to show how his critical doctrine will avoid the defects of dogmatism. The latter is directly considered in the second part of the *Doctrine* as one of the ways in which those who do not recognize the absoluteness of the ego may try, in vain, to make sense of things:

> The essence of *critical* philosophy consists in its presentation of an absolute ego as simply unconditioned and determinable through nothing higher than itself; when this philosophy follows consequently from this axiom, it is the Doctrine of Science. On the other hand, *dogmatic* philosophy opposes something, on the same level, to the ego; this is accomplished with the concept of the [object], purported to be higher than the ego, and at the same time fully arbitrarily presented as that which is simply highest. [p. 119]

This general definition requires a clarification and a qualification. It must be made clear that the dogmatist can posit the object as absolute only because he has not reached the level of the absolute ego; he thus does not teach that the absolute ego is subordinate to the object, but rather that the absolute is objective, and the ego merely finite. The necessary qualification to the general definition, introduced by Fichte only much later in the *Doctrine*, specifies the dogmatism described in the definition as dogmatic *realism;* to it must be opposed a dogmatic *idealism,* a theory of the sort that Schelling attributes to Spinoza, one in which the absolute is presented as a subject, but a subject wholly distinct from the ego of human experience (p. 155). In the *Doctrine,* dogmatism arises not as the direct antithesis to Fichte's criticism, but rather as itself appearing in two opposed forms—realism and idealism—representing the two extremes Fichte intends to avoid.

The development of the theoretical part of the *Doctrine* is, like that of the dogmatist's system, based on the second and third of Fichte's axioms (p. 122). Its task is to discover the ground of unity between the theoretical subject and the object upon which it seems to depend; there must be such a ground, for the two are united in ordinary experience. Fichte's approch to the task is structured by a conceptual-dialectical method designed to result either in success or in proof that failure is inevitable. He begins by identifying the most general concept applicable to both the subject and the object—their first "ground of identity." This concept or ground is *determination:* subject and object are alike in that both are determinate, or, differently stated, consciousness is always consciousness of something, and the something is always determinate. This ground of unity is next examined in terms of its ability to account for the opposition between subject and object; inadequacy is established by the identification of a "ground of difference," a concept applicable to only one of the two and whose one-sided applicability is not explicable through the proposed ground of identity alone. Determination is unable to ground a complete account of the relation of subject and object in that it does not clarify which element is determining and which determined. Since the first ground of unity thus fails, a new one must be discovered, one that can account for the difference that led to the rejection of determination. The dialectical process continues with the search for additional grounds of difference. The process would cease with the discovery of an adequate ground of identity—one that would account for all differences between subject and object—but Fichte claims to reveal the inadequacy of all possible candidates. The theoretical dialectic halts only when subject and object have been determined in such a way that no further synthesis term, no further ground of identity, can be provided (pp. 114–15). At this point, the notion that the finite subject is merely finite must be abandoned, for if it were such, its relation to the object—asserted in the third axiom— would be unintelligible. Reason demands a ground for the unity of subject and object, and since there is no such ground available if the subject is merely theoretical, reason decrees that the subject be taken to be practical. Fichte presents this decree as a cutting of the Gordian knot that theoretical philosophy is unable to untie: reason announces, in effect, that if the ego cannot be understood as simply finite, it must be somehow infinite. With this announcement, the realm of practical philosophy is entered, and dogmatism is left behind (p. 143). If the nature of Fichte's critical alternative is to be understood, however, his rejection of dogmatism must be more closely considered.

Within the theoretical dialectic, the objective and subjective absolutes of dogmatic realist and idealist arise as possible but ultimately inadequate grounds of identity of subject and object. Both fail in that they are unable, in characteristic ways, to account for an important ground of difference, namely the subject's awareness of the object. Fichte argues, as Schelling will in "On the Ego," that the realist's absolute object could not function as ground for the conciousness of the human ego, even if consciousness is erroneously taken to be passive-receptive: the realist cannot explain how the ego could be independent of the object to the extent necessary for awareness of it. The idealist has the reverse difficulty: having presented as ground a purely absolute subject—one that remains infinite and transcendent—he is unable to account for the origin of the finite subject, the subject that finds itself opposed to and limited by finite objects. The dogmatic realist cannot make the step from the absolute object to any sort of subjectivity, and the idealist cannot make the step from the absolute subject to its finite counterpart. For Fichte, as for Schelling, the human ego must be both finite and infinite; since for the realist it can be only the former, for the idealist only the latter, neither sort of dogmatist can account for the subjectivity of the ego.

Fichte avoids the danger of dogmatic realism by insisting

that the absolute is subjective. Having done so, he can avoid dogmatic idealism only by explaining how finitude and infinitude are reconciled in the human ego. His idealism is "not dogmatic, but rather practical, determing not what *is*, but what *shall be*" (p. 156). Because the human ego is neither an unchanging absolute nor a dead object, Fichte cannot explain it by saying simply what it is; he must rather explain how and why it acts, and what it is in the process of becoming. For Fichte, there is no absolute ego existing wholly apart from a purely finite ego; instead, the human ego is both finite and infinite, but it is not such in any static way, in any way that could be directly observed and analytically explained. Rather, it is both only in constantly acting in ways that reveal that it must be both. In Fichte's terms, it is both infinite and finite in that it is practical: its action as infinite must lead to its apparent finitude,[7] and its action as finite must reveal that it has not ceased to be infinite:

> The lessened activity of the ego [as finite] must be explained from the ego [as infinite] itself; the last ground [of the lessening] must be posited in the ego. This is done through the positing of the ego, which in this respect is practical, as that which *shall* contain within itself the ground of existence of the non-ego that reduces the activity of the intelligent [i.e., theoretical] ego: an infinite idea that cannot be thought, which therefore does not explain what is to be explained, but rather shows *that* and *why* it is inexplicable; by which the knot is not untied, but is rather set forth into infinitude [bin die Unendlichkeit hinaus gesetzt]. [p. 156]

7. See Fichte's "Deduction of Representation," pp. 227–46. In translating this title I have followed a practice common among translators of philosophical works and have used "representation" for *Vorstellung*. *Vorstellung* is frequently used in German, even by nonphilosophers, to refer to mental images, ideas, impressions, or notions. "Representation" is not used in the same way in ordinary English, but since many philosophers use *Vorstellung* as a technical term, the translating of it in some cases as "idea," in others as "impression," would lead to confusion. In addition, "idea" is best reserved for *Idee*, "impression" for *Impression* or *Eindruck*. Since there is no better alternative, "representation" is pressed into service for *Vorstellung*. It may be helpful—though it may also be misleading, if taken too literally—to consider how the term could be used in context: rocks and trees exist in the world, and I *represent* them to myself mentally.

Though Fichte earlier speaks of cutting a Gordian knot, he here promises only to displace one; but rather than revealing an inconsistency, the apparent change indicates an important difference between Fichtean theoretical philosophy and Fichtean practical philosophy. The knot that thwarts theoretical reason is a logical one: the ego can be understood neither as finite nor as infinite, but the law of excluded middle decrees that it must be one or the other, and the law of noncontradiction denies that it can be both. Practical reason's decree that the ego is both infinite and finite cuts through the knot tied by the theoretical laws, but it thereby reveals a second knot: if the ego is in essence free, but is everywhere bound by objective chains, the question arises of how it is to overcome its frustration. This is the knot that practical reason cannot cut, the knot that "is not untied, but is rather set forth into infinitude."

Fichte is clear in his insistence that the ego's frustration can be overcome only through action; he is not so clear, however, in indicating what sort of action is required or what degree of satisfaction can be attained. The practical subject arises as the ground of unity between the subject's finite and infinite aspects: it is confronted by objects that limit it, but it is capable of altering those objects and thereby of satisfying its desires. The subject would be completely and continually satisfied only in overcoming objectivity as a whole, that is, in becoming absolute. For the ego as absolute, though, there could be no consciousness, for there would be nothing for the ego to be conscious of: even self-consciousness would be self-objectification and would destroy the ego's absoluteness. In the absolute state, there could be neither content nor determination; thus, the human subject cannot desire to become absolute without thereby "denying reason and demanding its annihilation" (p. 282).

If the subject does not or cannot will its own destruction in absoluteness, then its goal must be somehow determinate. The subject is incapable of projecting anything like a utopic state in which all its desires would be satisfied, precisely because such a state would be beyond all determination; it is unthinkable because it is empty. Thus, the subject can do no more than project finite and realizable alterations of its environment, none of which can lead to complete satisfaction: each state of transitory relief is necessarily followed by one of renewed yearning. At any moment, then, the subject is at best both satisfied and discontent (p. 291). At the level of its own working, the subject approaches, apparently as closely as it ever will, the accomplishment of its task. Whenever the results of an act correspond to the subject's original intention, "the harmony is there, and there arises a feeling of *approval*, which is here a feeling of *contentment*, of fulfillment, of total completion (which lasts however only for a moment, because of the necessarily recurring yearning)" (p. 328).

This mundane and transitory satisfaction is all that human beings can hope for, at least according to the 1794 *Doctrine*. Elsewhere, Fichte promises much more. In a brief address presented at the end of his 1794 lectures, for example, he depicts humankind as continuing to carry out its one grand plan "until all matter bears its stamp, and all spirits constitute with its spirit one spirit" (p. 415). Whereas the *Doctrine* teaches that there is no satisfaction higher than manipulation—the satisfaction resulting from the utilization of contingently encountered objects in the service of arbitrary, temporary desires—the address suggests that human activity can transform the world as a whole so completely that no important desires would remain unsatisfied. The radical difference between the two practical teachings, both presented in the same year, suggests that, however thoroughly Fichte may have considered the principles of his system, he had not, as of 1794, completely thought through all its details. A further omission, crucial with respect to Fichte's ultimate practical teaching, will be revealed by a closer analysis of the argument resulting in the move from theoretical to practical philosophy.

The move from the theoretical to the practical part of the *Doctrine* is accomplished in two steps: Fichte argues first that since the ego is neither theoretical nor absolute, it must be practical, and second, that since the ego is practical, it can attain satisfaction only practically—only by acting upon objects—and not theoretically, not by merely thinking about them. The second step is not described in the *Doctrine*, but Fichte's conclusions reveal that he takes it. Had he attempted to explain it, he doubtless would have realized that it is unwarranted: it seems to follow only if the ambiguity of "practical" is ignored. As a term in the conclusion of the first part of Fichte's argument, "the ego is practical" means that the ego is both finite and infinite, that it is at once confronted by objects and somehow beyond them. Here, "practical" is used in the peculiarly Fichtean sense. In the premise of the second part of the argument, however, "practical" must be taken in its traditional sense and not in the Fichtean one: in the second part of the argument, it signifies *action* as opposed to *thought*. Only if this is its meaning in the premise does Fichte's conclusion follow, but the shift from the Fichtean to the traditional sense is not justified. This is so because both theory and practice in the traditional senses—that is, both thinking and acting—are practical in the Fichtean sense: as Fichte himself argues in the *Doctrine*'s second part, if the ego were simply passive—if it were theoretical in his special sense—then it could not be conscious of objects and, thus, could not be theoretical in the traditional sense: it would be unable to produce theories, for it would be incapable of thought.

The conclusion that the subject is at once finite and infinite only in acting thus contradicts Fichte's own teaching that the subject is both also in thinking. It might be suggested, in support of Fichte, that the subject can think only about objects and thus remains dependent on them; yet, as both Fichte and Schelling take Kant's first Critique to reveal, the philosophizing subject reflects on itself as well as on its object and thus attains the transcendental level, beyond the finite realm of the subject-object opposition. Although Fichte does not recognize it, the *Doctrine* in fact reveals that there are *two* ways in which the ego can potentially attain satisfaction: through activity and through philosophy. In ignoring the latter possibility, Fichte ignores one of the fundamental questions concerning the relation of theory and practice: he does not consider the question whether the subject is better advised to seek satisfaction through acting in the world or through reflecting on it. Near the beginning of the Western philosophical tradition, Aristotle supported the latter position, arguing that the best life is that of contemplation; Marx was among those who, two and a half

millennia later, rejected that tradition, insisting that "the philosophers have only interpreted the world in different ways;
the important thing is to change it!" In the 1794 *Doctrine*, Fichte
ignores the opposition between the theoretical and the practical as ways of life; he thus fails in his attempt to reconcile theory and practice.[8]

From Fichte to Schelling Fichte sent Schelling the first two parts
of the *Doctrine* before the third and final part was published,
and Schelling studied those parts with care; but while he had
no difficulty in acquiring the third part following its appearance, he confesses in a letter written in early 1796 that he has
not yet even read it.[9] This does not mean that he was entirely
ignorant of the practical teachings with which Fichte's system
concludes; although that teaching is presented in full only in
the *Doctrine*'s third part, remarks about it are contained in the
first two parts of the *Doctrine* and also in Fichte's other works.
Schelling was certainly aware of Fichte's insistence that the human ego can attain satisfaction only through action and not
through thought alone; he knew from the *Doctrine*'s second
part that Fichte intended to avoid dogmatism by presenting a
practical idealism, one "determining not what *is*, but what *shall
be*" (Fichte, p. 156). What Schelling likely did not know is that
Fichte, in order to keep his critical idealism distinct from dogmatism, believed himself forced to deny that the ego can completely attain the absoluteness that it strives for, the absoluteness that would bring satisfaction. Indeed, Schelling diverges
from Fichte—though perhaps without knowing that he was
diverging—in insisting that the absolute is fully accessible to
human beings, at least temporarily. A brief reconsideration of
some of Fichte's teachings will reveal that the *Doctrine* itself
opens the way that Schelling chooses to follow.

8. "Theory" and "practice" are used here and in the remainder of this study
in their usual senses; I have used Fichte's peculiar senses only in the analysis
of the 1794 *Doctrine*.

9. Schelling's letter to Niethammer, 22 January 1796; published in Manfred
Frank and Gerhard Kurz, eds., *Materialien zu Schellings philosophischen Anfängen*,
pp. 139–42.

Fichte asserts that the state in which all the subject's desires were permanently satisfied would be a state in which the subject would cease to exist as a subject: as long as the subject is confronted by objects, it desires to overcome them, but if it were to overcome all, nothing would remain for it to act on or even to think about and consciousness would cease. Since the human subject is deprived of this complete satisfaction, its condition is in contradiction with the infinitude it desires; the contradiction is the origin of practical—and of philosophical— yearning. Though Fichte, by suggesting that the subject cannot will its own annihilation, denies that the yearning can be completely satisfied, he also employs ambiguous terms that could be taken to refer to an immediate awareness, on the part of the human subject, of its own infinitude: he refers in the *Doctrine* to "inner intuition" (p. 88) and in an earlier work to "intellectual intuition" (pp. 10, 22). He later explicitly denies that this intuition is to be understood as a pure and immediate self-knowledge, but his clearest denial is included in the third part of the *Doctrine*, the part that Schelling did not read at a time when its influence might have been crucial.

Fichte's doctrine of intellectual intuition need not be clarified here; it is important to Schelling's development, indeed, precisely because its significance is not immediately apparent: its obscurity enabled Schelling to adapt it, possibly inadvertently, to the needs of his own project. The adaptation becomes intelligible if three Fichtean claims are considered in conjunction: Fichte asserts, first, that the subject as fully infinite would be beyond all consciousness and determinate content; second, that full infinitude is the only state in which all the subject's desires would be satisfied; and third, that the subject—at least the philosophizing subject—in some sense transcends its own finitude through the act of intellectual intuition. These doctrines, taken together, suggest a solution to the subject's yearning that Fichte does not directly consider; it is the solution of the mystic, the solution sought by those who have concluded that satisfaction is to be found neither in action in the world nor in reflection upon it, but rather only beyond it, in the empty and ineffable realm of the absolute.

Far from advocating the mystical rejection of the world, Fichte does not, in the 1794 *Doctrine*, even present it as a possibility; yet he does refer to the annihilation of reason in the absolute, and he does not deny that such annihilation is possible. Indeed, the sole barrier between the individual and the absolute would seem to be the individual's will to exist, a will that, according to Fichte, dooms the individual to frustration. For Schelling, who like Spinoza desires "the whole truth or no truth at all," this frustration is unendurable; if the step to the absolute can be taken, Schelling is determined to take it.

The Specter of Mysticism

The first Spinozist flaw identified by Schelling is the absence, in the *Ethics*, of an explanation of the subjectivity of the human subject. In "On the Ego" and in "Philosophical Letters concerning Dogmatism and Criticism" (1795), Schelling seeks to develop the antithesis to Spinoza by overcoming that flaw; he attempts to do so by adopting the Fichtean doctrine that the subject is at once finite and infinite, at once limited by objects and capable of reflecting and acting on them. Schelling views Fichte's doctrine as correct but incomplete; as has been shown, it raises questions that Fichte himself does not consider. The most important of these questions concerns the completeness of satisfaction the subject can attain through philosophizing, through reflecting on all that is rather than through acting on a part of it. Schelling attempts to answer that question, but his answer draws him near to the mystical conclusions merely suggested in Fichte's 1794 *Doctrine:* Schelling discovers that his critical doctrine, like Spinoza's dogmatic one, must present as the goal of the subject annihilation in the absolute. In that both systems reach the same conclusion, neither is ultimately superior; when Schelling realizes that Fichte's way will not take him truly beyond Spinoza—when he realizes that Fichte's is no real alternative—he is forced to reconsider the requirements of a system that will be the complete antithesis to Spinoza, a system that will repeat none of the mistakes of the *Ethics*. The way Schelling is led to that reconsideration must now be examined.

In "On the Ego," Schelling takes the first of two important steps beyond Fichte: he accepts the conclusion, which follows from Fichte's own principles, that the human ego's yearning for full infinitude requires the willing of a contentless state beyond all self-consciousness. Whereas Fichte deemphasizes that conclusion, hesitating to acknowledge that the ego can will the annihilation of reason, Schelling insists that "the final goal of the finite ego and of the non-ego as well, that is, the final goal of the world, is its *annihilation as* a world, that is, as an aggregate [*Inbegriff*] of finitude (of finite ego and non-ego)" (1:200–01). In "On the Ego," Schelling continues to agree with Fichte that the human subject cannot attain this goal, but he sees in the goal itself the basis for a practical solution to humanity's problems that is far more ambitious than the solution given in the 1794 *Doctrine*. The problems that demand solution all result, in Schelling's view, from limitations on the subject's freedom; they will be solved only when that freedom is absolute. For Schelling, "the beginning and end of all philosophy is freedom" (1:177),[10] in that only a free entity could possibly philosophize and in that the highest aim of any free entity must be absolute freedom. The way to the achievement of this aim is through theoretical reflection rather than practical activity: the philosopher must understand the human condition as it is before he can determine how it could or should be altered. Indeed, Schelling asserts that the theoretical teaching alone suffices, that once it is presented, moral and political doctrines follow without difficulty:

> Give man consciousness of what he *is,* and he will soon learn to be what he *should* be: give him *theoretical* respect for himself, and the *practical* will soon follow. . . . the revolution in man must issue from his *consciousness* of his essence, he must be theoretically good in order to become so practically. [1:157]

Human beings normally consider themselves to be distinct individuals with conflicting goals; as long as they retain this self-understanding, Schelling suggests, they can be neither

---

10. In a letter to Hegel from 4 February 1795, Schelling writes, "The alpha and omega of all philosophy is freedom." The letter is published in Frank and Kurz, eds., *Materialien*, pp. 125–27.

good nor free. Philosophy must teach us that we are infinite or absolute as well as finite, and that our finite concerns—those that lead us into conflict—are trivial when viewed from the level of the absolute. Indeed, since the level of the absolute is beyond all limitations of individuality, all human beings are one *in essence* even though, in the empirical situation, we are in constant conflict. When our essential identity is grasped by all, all will come to "obey the same laws of freedom, as one complete person" (1:158). Since these laws are inherent in our essence, the subject who obeys them is absolutely free: that subject determines its own actions from within rather than having them determined for it from without.

In humanity's march toward the goal of acting "as one complete person," the philosopher plays a crucial role, for "all ideas must have been realized in the realm of knowledge before they may be realized in history; and humanity will never be one before its knowledge has developed into unity" (1:159). Human knowledge could develop into unity only with the presentation of a successful philosophical account of the whole; the young Schelling was naive enough to believe that the appearance of such an account was imminent and hubristic enough to hope that, if he hurried, he could be its author.[11] The account would have to be the antithesis to Spinoza's *Ethics*, the system grounded in the subjective absolute with which the human ego is in essence one. In "On the Ego," Schelling remains at a stage of anticipation of the complete account; only in his next work, the "Letters," does the project begin to develop.

In the "Letters," Schelling continues to focus on the problems of the subjective absolute and of its relation to the human ego; but his continued identification of freedom as the essence

---

11. Schelling's conviction that philosophy was on the verge of completion partly explains why his works from 1794 through 1804 were so many and varied. Studying those works sequentially, one gets the feeling that Schelling saw in the teachings of Spinoza, Leibniz, Kant, and Fichte all the pieces he would need to construct his account of the whole. In each work—to continue the metaphor—he tries to fit the pieces together; when one attempt fails, he attempts a rearrangement. Only after 1804 does he realize that there is something seriously wrong with some of the pieces he has been using.

of subjectivity, in conjunction with a second crucial step past Fichte, leads him to some radically non-Fichtean conclusions that, if viewed in isolation from the underlying project, appear to be simply inconsistent with the teachings of "On the Ego." To be correctly understood, these conclusions must be seen in the context of the systematic antithesis to Spinoza which he now calls, for the first time, the "system of freedom" (1:315).

As its title indicates, Schelling's third publication is not presented as a systematically developed essay; it is rather a series of letters. The letters are addressed to one who, for aesthetic reasons, prefers dogmatism to criticism. The recipient's argument, indirectly revealed in Schelling's responses, is that any teaching grounded in the notion of a moral god—as all critical systems are assumed to be—undermines the tragic struggle of the individual against an external order that he is powerless to alter; this critical doctrine thereby undermines art itself, for it is in the struggle of human beings against fate that the aesthetic vision is grounded. In countering this argument, Schelling insists that his correspondent has misunderstood both criticism and dogmatism. He acknowledges that there can be no real tragedy—and therefore no real art—if the world order is guided by a moral god rather than by blind fate, but he denies that critical philosophy is grounded in such a god. At the same time, he denies that dogmatism can satisfy the aesthete's demands: it ultimately teaches submission to fate rather than the tragic struggle against it. Schelling's task in the "Letters" is to reveal the true nature of criticism, as opposed to dogmatism, and to show that only critical philosophy can ground an understanding of humanity that will adequately explain both human freedom and the aesthetic capacity.

Schelling begins by renewing his castigations of those who pervert Kant's teachings by seeking refuge in the idea of a moral god, but his arguments against them are different from those of his earlier works. In "On the Ego," he objects to the subjection of the absolute to external laws, insisting that the absolute can act only in accordance with its own essence; in the "Letters," he asserts that those who consider the determination of the absolute—as moral or otherwise—to be possible reveal thereby that they have not reached the level of the truly absolute: the absolute cannot be related to anything at all, and thus it is beyond all content and determination (1:288; cf. 308). This argument is not entirely new: the emptiness and indeterminacy of the absolute are asserted in Fichte's 1794 *Doctrine* as well as in Schelling's "On the Ego." In both of these works, however, the absolute is nonetheless determined as subjective. By the time he writes the "Letters," Schelling has recognized that that determination cannot be made: to place the absolute in any category is to limit it and thus to destroy its absoluteness. That which is truly absolute, Schelling now insists, is beyond the subjective as well as the objective and therefore cannot be classed as either.[12]

Since, according to the "Letters," the absolute must remain indeterminate, the absolute itself is not the locus of the conflict between dogmatists and critical idealists. Rather, conflict can arise only when the realm of the absolute is forsaken:

> Anyone concerned primarily with settling the conflict among philosophers must start from the point where the philosophical conflict itself, or—and it comes to the same thing—the original conflict in human spirit starts. This point, though, is no other than that of *emergence out of the absolute*; for we would all agree concerning the absolute if we never left its sphere, and if we did not emerge from it, we would have no other realm concerning which we could be in conflict. [1:294]

In the absolute, all is one; the "original conflict in human spirit" starts with the emergence of human individuals from the unity of the absolute—in theological terms, with the creation of the universe—and the philosophical conflict starts when philosophers reflect, not on the absolute itself, but rather on its relation to the world of human experience. Philosophers cannot dispute about the absolute, for they cannot even say anything about the absolute; at the same time, Schelling in-

---

12. Schelling's improved understanding of the nature of the absolute probably resulted from contact with the poet Hölderlin, who shared living quarters with Schelling and Hegel while all were studying in Tübingen in the early 1790s. See my doctoral dissertation, "The End of Philosophy: A Study of Hegel and Schelling," pp. 220–22. For a more complete discussion of Hölderlin's philosophical ideas, see Dieter Henrich, "Hegel und Hölderlin," in *Hegel im Kontext*, pp. 9–40.

sists, philosophers will never cease to dispute about the "emergence out of the absolute." That dispute would cease only if there were arguments proving that a specific account of the emergence was the sole true account; but, according to Schelling, there can be no such arguments. Though Schelling insists in "On the Ego" that rational argumentation can establish critical idealism as the sole tenable doctrine, he argues in the "Letters" that dogmatism and criticism are equally defensible.

Schelling's resurrection of dogmatism is at first perplexing, but closer consideration reveals it to be a rational, if incomplete, development rather than an arbitrary reversal. The development is made necessary by Schelling's recognition that there can be no rationally compelling theory concerning the nature of the absolute. Etymologically, "theory" is closely bound to the notion of seeing; to theorize is to look at something, either physically or with the mind's eye, and to describe or explain what is seen. The absolute is not among the things that may be pointed out in the world of experience; it is for this reason that Kant denies that human knowledge of it is possible. Fichte relies on an intellectual intuition—a mental vision—of the absolute ego, but denies that that vision is tantamount to the attainment of absoluteness. In the "Letters," Schelling goes beyond Fichte in insisting that the intellectually intuiting ego is absolute; in that act or state, if it were permanent, the individual would find complete satisfaction.

The intuiting of the absolute is an experience in which consciousness ceases, for in it there is no awareness of a distinction between the seer and the seen. For this reason, intellectual intuition is a "condition of death," and those for whom it became a permanent state would "go out of time into eternity" (1:325). For human beings, for better or worse, the condition is not permanent; intuition is always followed by reflection, vision is always followed by the attempt to understand what has been seen. Reflection on the absolute poses unique problems, however, for in the vision of the absolute, nothing is seen. It is for this reason that there can be no compelling theory of the absolute: since the absolute is beyond all determination and content, intuition of it leaves nothing on which reason can reflect, and thus there is nothing to explain. This is why, according to Schelling, there can be no philosophical dispute concerning the absolute itself: the absolute is the same for critical idealists, Spinozists, cabalists, Brahmins, and nonsectarian mystics (*see* 1:326). According to Schelling's arguments, the Zen Buddhist who experiences *satori* after years of meditation and asceticism sees nothing different from what the philosopher who reflects on the nature of absoluteness sees: the absolute is beyond all distinctions.

Dispute among those concerned with the absolute begins only with reflection on the absolute, only with the attempt to make sense of the experience of intellectual intuition. In Schelling's view, there are only two ways in which the experience can be understood; since no rational argument can prove the correctness of either, the individual must freely choose the one or the other. It is at this point of decision that Spinoza takes his individual path:

> either he had become identical with the absolute, or it had become identical with him. In the latter case, the intellectual intuition would be of himself—in the former, intuition of an absolute *object*. Spinoza preferred the former. He believed himself to be identical with the absolute object, and lost in its infinitude. [1:319]

Reflection can yield only two interpretations of the experience of intellectual intuition of the absolute: it is an experience either of total self-realization or of total self-negation. The interpretation chosen by a given individual becomes the basis for a practical doctrine designed to aid those heeding it in attaining absoluteness to the fullest extent possible: reason continues to demand that the subject strive for infinitude—nothing else can offer true satisfaction—and the philosopher must provide the teaching that will guide it toward that goal. Spinoza takes the absolute to be the complete absence of all subjectivity and consequently teaches that the individual subject must "strive to become identical with the infinite, to drown in the infinity of the absolute object" (1:315). The demand is for oblivion: "Annihilate yourself through the [objective causal order], or: comport yourself purely passively to-

ward the absolute causality" (1:316). The intensity of Spinoza's
philosophical eros is proved by his willingness to demand his
own negation. This willingness places Spinozist dogmatism beyond refutation, but it is irrefutable only for those who, like
Spinoza, can guide their lives by its fundamental tenet, only
"for one who is able to realize it, *practically*, in himself, one for
whom it is bearable to work for his own annihilation, to remove from himself all free causality, to be the modification of
an object in whose infinitude he will, sooner or later, find his
(moral) downfall" (1:339). The complete coherence of the dogmatist's system is paradoxically grounded in the freedom to
embrace it, a freedom that dogmatists themselves seek to overcome through the "moral downfall" of total quietism, complete
passivity. Yet critical philosophers, those who recognize that
the essence of the subject is freedom, will defend the rigor of
the dogmatic system even more strongly than will its adher-
ents, precisely because its possibility, as a practical project the
individual may embrace, reconfirms the freedom of human
beings:

> To a spirit that has made itself free, and that has only itself to
> thank for *its* philosophy, nothing could be more unbearable than
> the dogmatism of narrow minds that can suffer no other systems
> next to their own. Nothing enrages the philosophical mind more
> than to hear that from now on all philosophy is to lie in the
> bonds of a single system. . . . The entire sublimity of [the philos-
> opher's] science consists in the fact that it can never be com-
> pleted. In the instant in which he believed himself to have com-
> pleted his system, it would become unbearable to him. He would
> cease in that instant to be *creator*, and would be reduced to being
> an instrument of his creation. [1:306]

The critic therefore defends the coherence of the dogmatic
system, but, having himself interpreted intellectual intuition
subjectively, he achieves his own consequence through a completely opposed practical imperative: he is to "realize the absolute in *himself* through unlimited activity."

> If I thus *posit* everything in the *subject*, I thereby *negate* everything
> of the *object*. Absolute causality in me would be the overcoming,
> for me, of all objective causality as *objective*. In expanding the lim-

its of *my* world, I restrict those of the objective. If my world had
no more limits, then all objective causality would be annihilated
by my own. I would be the absolute.—But criticism would be
reduced to the confusion of mysticism if it presented this final
goal even as *attain*able (far more if as attained). It therefore uses
the idea of fulfillment only *practically*, for the determination of
morality. . . .

My *determination* in criticism is, namely: *Strive toward intransient
selfhood, unconditioned freedom, unlimited activity.* [1:335]

Schelling agrees with Fichte that the critical philosopher avoids
mysticism by determining his final goal to be unattainable. Yet
it is not clear what the philosopher should do to approach that
goal. For the mystic, whose goal is annihilation in an absolute
is beyond all individuality and subjectivity, the practical program is clear: sit, meditate, and avoid worldly concerns. Fichte
teaches that the philosopher should seek Schelling's "unconditioned freedom" through manipulation or alteration of finite
objects, but that program is far too modest for Schelling. But
Schelling does not, in the "Letters," provide a clear alternative
to the Fichtean program: the "Letters" do not reveal *how* the
subject can or should strive for "unlimited activity." Schelling
offers no more than two vague suggestions concerning what
the critic should do; we may begin with the one given in the
final consideration of the problem that originally motivated the
writing of the letters.

In the "Letters," it will be remembered, the problem of the
absolute arises in the context of aesthetics rather than—as is
more often the case—in that of metaphysics or of religion.
Schelling's correspondent is concerned with asserting the importance of the aesthetic vision; this concern has led him to
embrace dogmatism while rejecting the sort of criticism that is
grounded in a moral god. Schelling grants that the dogmatism
his correspondent would like to affirm has an aesthetic aspect:
the pure passivity of its intellectual intuition is akin to the aesthete's loss of self in appreciation of the work of art. Having
denied, however, that the tragic struggle against an unyielding
fate can be grounded in dogmatists' quietism, Schelling has
prepared the way for grounding the struggle in critical doctrine. Yet he does not do so. Finally, indeed, rather than de-

fending the tragic vision, Schelling suggests that the notion of an overpowering external necessity—the objective fate crucial to tragedy—should not be allowed to develop:

> As long as man lingers in the realm of nature, he is, in the authentic sense of the word—in the same sense in which he can be *master* of himself—*master* of nature. . . . In *representing* the object to himself, in giving it form and subsistence, he masters it. He has nothing to fear from it, for he himself has posited its limits. But as soon as he removes these limits, so that the object *can no longer be represented*, that is, as soon as he himself has slipped past the limits of representation, he sees himself lost. He is overcome by the terrors of the objective world. [1:337]

Here, Schelling implicitly relies on the Kantian argument that the world of ordinary experience is a human world, a world whose nature is in part dependent upon the human subject's intellectual faculties; Schelling reasons that man, as partly responsible for his world, is master of it, and that the terrors of total subjection arise only when human beings imagine, wrongly, that they inhabit a world whose course is determined independently of them. The critic, who understands this point, sees that there is an alternative to the dogmatist's affirmation of an external absolute necessity; he thereby sees that he need neither capitulate to nor struggle against an insensitive, objective fate. Rather than worrying about such a fate, or about transcendent objects of any sort, the critic is to concern himself with fully understanding—and thereby, perhaps, freeing himself from—objects as they are represented in experience. Having convinced himself that the natural world of experience is the only world—that beyond it is only the emptiness of the absolute—the investigator can turn from philosophy to natural science: "Our spirit feels freer in returning from the condition of speculation to the enjoyment and investigation of nature, without having to fear that it will be led again into the unnatural condition by the ever-returning unrest of its discontented spirit" (1:341).

The critical project suggested by Schelling appears to be merely theoretical, requiring only observation of nature; it is not manipulative, for it does not demand that natural objects be altered. At the same time, though, Schelling does hint that he retains his more ambitious, utopic teaching: at present, he maintains, dogmatism and criticism are equally necessary and equally defensible, but they will remain so only until "all finite beings stand at the same stage of freedom" (1:307). This notion of "stages of freedom" is not developed in the "Letters," nor does any doctrine in that work make it intelligible; Schelling's practical project thus remains vague. This vagueness is but one of several features of the "Letters" that make it an extremely puzzling work. Another is that while Schelling's intention at the beginning seems to be that of grounding the tragic vision, he ends by presenting that vision as superfluous, indeed erroneous; his true interest remains metaphysical rather than aesthetic. Yet even with respect to metaphysics, difficulties remain: Schelling intends to distinguish criticism from dogmatism, but he denies that either is truly superior, and he does not develop the practical doctrine that alone could establish a clear difference between them. While for these reasons the end of the "Letters" appears to be simply inconclusive, it in fact marks the completion of the first stage in Schelling's development. To see why this is so, we must briefly reconsider the difference between philosophy and mysticism.

Intellectual intuition, interpreted dogmatically or mystically as annihilation of the subject in a wholly distinct absolute, appears to be a certain sort of blessedness (Seligkeit), namely, a condition of blissful oblivion. While some may find such a condition appealing, Schelling sides with Lessing in "connecting the idea of an infinite being with the notion of infinite boredom," and in feeling "anxiety and woe" upon imagining becoming such a being. This feeling leads to sympathy with the "blasphemous" exclamation: "For the sake of everything in the world, I would not want to be blessed!" In a footnote to this passage, Schelling adds that he "sees no help in philosophy" for anyone who does not agree with Lessing's sentiment (1:326, 326n). Schelling's remarks suggest that the crucial difference between philosophy and mysticism is visible in the philosopher's rejection of what the mystic most ardently desires; he rejects it "for the sake of everything in the world." He does not reject it for the sake of worldly or physical pleasures, but rather—as the remarks about nature at the end of the "Letters" indicate—for the sake of *understanding* everything in the world. The philosopher, like the mystic, demands the absolute; but whereas for the latter the absolute is the end, for the philosopher it must be the beginning, it must be the starting point from which an account of man and world develops. The mystic feels no need for such an account; the philosopher feels no need for the mystic's bliss.

In the "Letters," Schelling ends a first stage of development by realizing that as long as he focuses solely on the problem of the subject, his criticism will remain complementary to Spinoza's dogmatism; it will not prove itself superior, for it will provide no comprehensive account of the whole. If criticism is to prevail, if it is to overcome the moral quietism of Spinozism and mysticism, it must expand its scope beyond the subject to encompass the truth of nature, of objectivity. Determination of the way in which nature is to be grasped philosophically requires of Schelling development in a direction he has hitherto left largely unexplored.

FROM INFINITE TO FINITE

A Second Spinozist Flaw: No Derivation of Content

The "Letters" close with Schelling's suggestions that a correct understanding of nature is crucial to philosophy and that dogmatism cannot ground such an understanding. The dogmatist's failure in this respect is explained in the first of Schelling's two "Treatises Explicating the Idealism of the Doctrine of Science," published early in 1796; there, Schelling embraces the argument—originally Fichte's—that one central flaw in Spinoza's system is its lack of a true derivation of content within or from the absolute. In the "Letters," Schelling concentrates on philosophy's end or goal, the experience of the absolute in intellectual intuition; he is then unable to assert the ultimate superiority of criticism to dogmatism, for the dogmatist's interpretation of the experience is as defensible as the critic's. In the first of the "Treatises," Schelling reconsiders the problems of the systematic beginning, and the situation changes.

Schelling's account in this treatise begins not with the problem of intellectual intuition, but rather with that of grounding knowledge; the central problem is Kantian rather than Spinozist. Schelling reiterates the argument that the move to the absolute is originally motivated by the lack, on the finite level of ordinary experience, of a ground for the unity of subject and object; the unity must have a ground, for it is an essential condition of experience. The philosopher seeks not the absolute itself—not the absolute as absolute—but rather the fundament of experience—the absolute as ground. In so determining the philosopher's project, Schelling seems to ignore or to have forgotten his earlier arguments concerning the inviolable indeterminacy of the absolute; but his presentation of the absolute as *ground*, in spite of the arguments of the "Letters," reflects more than a simple lapse of memory or attention. In returning in the first treatise to the problem of the systematic beginning, Schelling is confronted with a fundamental paradox: the philosopher demands an absolute that is the unconditioned condition, the groundless ground of all that is; yet the absolute is unconditioned and groundless only if it is indeterminate, and if it is indeterminate, then it can be determined neither as condition nor as ground. The systematic beginning requires, paradoxically, the determination of the indeterminate; the successful beginning must overcome the conflict between absolute as absolute and absolute as ground.

If philosophy must explain the unity of subject and object, Schelling argues, then the dogmatist fails: the unity is inexplicable if the two are taken to be heterogenous; and if both are taken to be objective, consciousness itself cannot be explained. Therefore, the only possibility for explication lies in the demonstration that "spirit, in intuiting objects *at all*, intuits only *itself*" (1:365): knowledge can be explained only through the grounding of subject and object in a subjective, or spiritual, absolute. Schelling envisions a "deduction of representation" far more ambitious than Fichte's: if by starting from the subject as absolute we can derive the necessity of an intuition in which the world appears to us as it in fact does appear to us, then the unity of consciousness will have been explained and the demands of reason satisfied. The success of such a comprehensive derivation would prove, beyond all reasonable doubt, that the unconditioned with which the start was made—the subjective absolute—is indeed the ground of the factical world. The doctrine Schelling would like to establish is that the world is "nothing other than our creating spirit itself in its infinite productions and reproductions" (1:360). The world can be grounded in this spirit—though never in any object, "absolute" or otherwise—because "the essence of spiritual nature [and so, of subjectivity] lies in the fact that there is a primordial conflict in its self-consciousness, out of which an actual world outside of it comes forth in intuition (a creation *ex nihilo*)" (1:358). Spirit is logically prior, but spirit and world are equally necessary: "no world exists unless a *spirit* knows it, and conversely, no spirit exists without a world external to it" (1:358).

In the first treatise, Schelling does not argue that the absolute, as absolute, must posit itself (thereby creating the finite world); he decides instead to consider what would follow *if* the absolute posited itself. Rather than arguing that the absolute as absolute must also be ground, he argues that the absolute as ground would retain its absoluteness. Schelling begins the constructive account in the treatise not with the absolute as such, but with spirit, asserting that "the essence of spiritual nature lies in the presence, in its self-consciousness, of a primordial conflict" (1:358). As self-conscious, spirit is a step removed from the absolute as absolute:

> [Spirit] is only through itself, through its own action.
> Now, that which is (originally) object is as such necessarily also finite. Because spirit is not originally object, it cannot be originally finite, not according to its nature.—Infinite then? But it is *spirit* only insofar as it is object for itself, that is, insofar as it becomes *finite*. Thus, it is not infinite without becoming finite, nor can it become finite (for itself) without being infinite. [1:367]

Schelling's argument may be rephrased as follows. To be object is to be known and/or acted upon, and thus to be limited by the knower or actor; to be limited is, however, to be finite, so objects are finite "according to their nature." To be spirit is to know or to act, and that does not immediately entail limitation and finitude; yet one thing, perhaps the only thing, that spirit must know is itself, for to be spirit is to be self-conscious. In knowing itself, spirit is both infinite (insofar as it is knower) and finite (insofar as it is known); thus, spirit "is not infinite without becoming finite, nor can it become finite (for itself) without being infinite." It is the essence of the spiritual character to be this "most original unity of infinitude and finitude" (1:367); the development of the so-determined spirit as ground is described in the first of Schelling's 1797 publications, *Ideas toward a Philosophy of Nature*.

In the Introduction to the *Ideas*, as in the "Letters," Schelling presents philosophical reflection as leading to a point from which two paths diverge; in the later work, both the point and the paths appear in a new light. Schelling first rejects three theories of objectivity: he denies that the object can be understood as isolated from the subject, as determining the subject, or as providing the matter on which the subject, as formative, works. The object must instead, he concludes, have its origin in spirit; philosophy stands or falls with "the attempt to derive the necessity of the succession of representations from the nature of our spirit, thus of finite spirit in general" (2:35). Philosophy must determine what and how the subject must be in order to be capable of consciousness of a sequence of events—a succession of representations—as at once completely independent from the subject and totally necessary in itself, that is, of nature as a causally ordered whole that functions on its own, without human interference. Surprisingly, Spinoza's "entire philosophy" is now said to be "nothing but this project" (2:35).

> The *first* to fully consciously view spirit and matter as one, thought and extension only as modifications of the same principle, was Spinoza. His system was the first clever projection of a creative imagination that grasped the finite immediately in the idea of the infinite, purely as such, and recognized the former in the latter. [2:20]

Spinoza, grasping "the finite immediately in the idea of the infinite," makes the idea of the infinite prior to that of the finite. He then must acknowledge that neither subject nor object qualifies as infinite: each is conditioned by the other, so neither can be unconditioned. At the same time, there must be a ground of unity for subject and object; otherwise, the subject would be incapable of veridical consciousness of objects external to it. Since neither subject nor object can be the ground, the two must be primordially united in an absolute of which both are mere modifications; Spinoza does not explain how they are united, but argues that they must be united, and that they can be united only in the absolute.

Spinoza's view is, according to Schelling, the only one possible if the idea of the infinite is made prior to that of the finite; yet Spinoza's theory does not solve the problem posed by the existence of the finite, that is, the problem of how it is grounded in the absolute. Schelling's Spinoza is fully aware that there can be no transition from infinite to finite, nothing like an *ex nihilo* creation, but if that relation is ruled out, then Spinoza's absolute must simply be asserted to contain its modifications, and thus finitude, within itself. *That* the absolute grounds both subject and object is simply asserted; *how* it can ground them remains unintelligible (2:36). Spinoza can explain neither why the world is as it is, nor why there is anything at all rather than nothing. The antithesis to the system of the so-interpreted Spinoza must start with the idea of the finite rather than with that of the infinite; it will overcome the dogmatist's defect only if it can show both how and why the absolute is articulated—how and why it includes the finite at all—and, to at least some extent, why it is articulated as it is. To be successful, Schelling's system must solve the problem of the derivation of content.

To overcome the first Spinozist flaw, the lack of a theory of subjectivity, Schelling embraces Fichte's doctrine of the subjective absolute; in seeking to overcome the second flaw by deriving content from that absolute, he remains true to a part of what is, or once was, the Fichtean project. Though the 1794 *Doctrine* contains no derivation of the specifics of the finite realm, Fichte does, in a footnote included in the first (1794) edition of "On the Concept of the Doctrine of Science," assert that,

> strange as it may strike many investigators of nature, in time it will be shown that it is strictly provable that they themselves first put into nature those laws that they take themselves to learn from it through observation, and that these laws, the smallest

and the greatest, the construction of the most trivial blade of grass and the movement of the heavenly bodies, are derivable from the axioms of all human knowledge. [p. 64n]

The derivation of the factical world from the principles inherent in a subjective absolute is thus a project to which Fichte was at least at one time attracted. Nevertheless, the Schelling of the *Ideas*, in developing a similar project, no longer identifies Fichte as his most important predecessor. Rather, the philosopher now presented as first taking the way opposite to that of Spinoza, the only thinker besides Spinoza whose "entire philosophy" consists in the sole truly philosophical project, that of attempting "to derive the necessity of the succession of representations from the nature of our spirit, is Leibniz" (2:20, 35).

The Leibnizian Alternative: Nature from Spirit

The influence of Leibniz is visible already in Schelling's earliest works,[13] but Schelling first focuses on Leibniz in the Introduction to the *Ideas*; there, Leibniz is presented as taking the "opposite path" from Spinoza's. Spinoza's way is that of "grasping the finite immediately in the idea of the infinite, purely as such, and recognizing the former only in the latter." This way leads from the nature of the absolute to the "true" nature of the finite, the nature it must possess, *given* the absoluteness— the lack of determination, the inviolable infinity—of the absolute. Leibniz's opposite path must then lead from finite to infinite, through consideration of what the finite entity must be to be grounded in the absolute. This approach has one immediate advantage over Spinoza's: it starts with the apparent multiplicity of factical entities that appear to themselves, and

---

13. While Schelling's references to Leibniz reveal that he was deeply influenced by the latter (see "The End of Philosophy," pp. 239–41), that influence has not been stressed in the secondary literature. I note in addition that the problems traditionally identified as crucial to Schelling—those of the irrational, of contingency, and of evil, all of which arise as central in the 1809 *Freedom* essay—enter the mainstream of European philosophy with Leibniz; these problems are not thematized by, for example, Descartes or Spinoza. This point is developed in detail by Alfred Baeumler in the excellent and fascinating study, *Das Irrationalitätsproblem in der Aesthetik und Logik des 18. Jahrhunderts bis zur Kritik der Urteilskraft*, pp. 37–45.

to human beings, to be finite. Leibniz must show how these entities are grounded in the absolute, but since the start is made from plurality and determination rather than from the indeterminate unity of the absolute, the former need not be presented as following necessarily from the latter. Spinoza reasons that since factical entities are not absolute, they must ultimately be nothing; he thereby encounters the problem, insoluble within his system, of how that which is fundamentally nothing could or should exist at all. Leibniz starts by insisting that factical entities, as not nothing, must be somehow absolute; his task is that of showing how they retain infinitiude while appearing to be finite.

The finite, according to Schelling's Leibniz, is "not thinkable without something positive to give it reality and something negative to give it limits." Normally, philosophers attempt to account for finitude by separating a positive element or factor from a negative one, determining each in isolation, and then reuniting the two; then, however, the problem necessarily arises of the introduction of negativity into pure positivity—the problem of the transition from infinite to finite—and since, according to Schelling, that transition is impossible, the project is doomed to failure. Leibniz avoids the difficulty by focusing on the individual as such rather than on purportedly isolated factors: in the individual, and nowhere else, are positive and negative elements originally and inseparably united. The fundamental stratum of reality is not an empty, purely positive absolute but rather the multiplicity of individuals or, in Leibnizian terms, of "monads":

> The only things held by Leibniz to be originally real and actual in themselves were representing beings; for in them alone is the original union from which everything else that is called actual develops. . . . External things are not [i.e., do not exist] actually in themselves, but only come to be through the modes of representation of spiritual natures. [2:38]

The monads, as "real and actual in themselves," are "absolutely self-grounding with respect to [their] being and knowledge, and in being at all, they are also what they are, that is, [beings] to whose nature belongs this determinate system of representations of external things" (2:39). Each monad grounds its own specific set of representations. The "external things" thus follow from the "natures" of the monads, but that does not mean that they are arbitrary: the monad, rather, has no being independent of the objects it represents, for it is what it is only as representing precisely those objects. I, as monad, create the contents of my consciousness—though I am not immediately aware of doing so—but I do not do so arbitrarily: I am the individual I am only in being aware of precisely the contents that constitute my consciousness. In addition, most of the objects I create—most of the objects that I am aware of—are shared by other intellects: every monad somehow represents the same real universe, the same succession of "the things themselves," so that "the succession is truly objective" (2:35), is common to all. The objectivity of the external things is evidenced by intersubjective agreement concerning them: those things represented by a given monad not as mere external things—not as dead objects—but rather as, themselves, "representing beings"—as monadic subjects—are all represented as themselves representing a single common world, albeit from different viewpoints and with different degrees of adequacy. Stated in less convoluted terminology: since I am in general agreement with other human beings concerning what there is in the world, I know that that world is not a private fantasy.

Intersubjective agreement is a necessary condition for the objective reality of external objects, but it is not a sufficient condition, for intersubjectivity is itself suspect. If all that enters my consciousness is produced by my consciousness, then I produce even the other human beings with whom I seem to agree concerning the existence of an external world. My world—any monad's world—remains a dream world: that all the characters active within any dream seem to inhabit the same world does nothing to prove that the dream is more than an arbitrary product of the dreamer's imagination. Further arguments for the intersubjective reality of the monad's world are therefore needed. Leibnizian arguments for the point could be adduced, but all would depend on the principle of sufficient reason, which Schelling does not invoke in its full Leibnizian force. A Leibnizian could argue that the existence of other rational subjects is the only possible sufficient reason for my belief that they exist: I can be sure I am not deceived on this point because there could be no sufficient reason for the deception. Schelling, perhaps aware of the vulnerability of this logical argument, relies instead on moral and teleological ones deriving from the teachings of Kant. Schelling argues, first, that I am necessarily conscious of myself as a moral agent and that I can be a moral agent only as a member of a community of beings of my kind; the existence of such beings is, he concludes, beyond doubt (2:53; 1:398). The second argument, influenced by Kant's discussions of internal purposiveness (*Zweckmäβigkeit*), is that all organic entities are necessarily represented as acting in accord with their own ends, and thus as existing independently of their being represented.

If, as Schelling and Leibniz argue, the world is common to all, then it cannot have its origin in the individual as individual. Instead, according to Schelling, the external things known by all "come into being, as though in their own world, by force of the mere laws of our nature, according to an inner principle in us." "Our" nature, common to all beings "of our sort," is proved to exist—like *our* world—by intersubjective agreement: we all "represent the appearances of the world in the same necessary temporal series." The principles determining the specifics of the finite world must therefore be sought in "the essence of finite natures in general" (2:38).[14] From that essence

---

14. Schelling's terminology here can be confusing: *Natur* is used in the plural to indicate that which is particular to individuals *qua* individual and in the singular to denote that which is common to all individuals who "represent the appearances in the same necessary series." Similarly, *Wesen* is used at times, generally in the plural, to refer to the individual or individuals—in which cases I render it as "being" or "beings"—and at times to refer to that which is common to all individuals. In the latter cases, I use "essence," as in "the essence of finite natures." Every representing being is, then, a being (*Wesen*) with its own *Natur*; the essence (*Wesen*) of the individual is the *Natur* shared by all in its species, or even, in a broader extension, by all finite individuals. *Natur* refers also at times to nature in the broadest sense, that is, to the experienced world, which includes representing beings (monads) as well as "experienced things."

follows the one universe represented by all "finite natures"; the individual monads remain distinct in that their views of that universe exhibit differing degrees of confusion.

The doctrine of monads, the teaching that metaphysics must begin with individuals rather than with a unique and transcendent absolute, is for Schelling Leibniz's most important idea. In Schelling's view, though, the Leibnizian schema is not the culmination of a metaphysical system, but rather the beginning. With it is posited the true task of the philosopher:

> If then the entire succession of representations originates in the *nature* of finite spirit, the entire array of our experiences must be derivable from [that nature]. . . . Philosophy is therefore nothing other than a *doctrine of the nature of our spirit* [*Naturlehre unseres Geistes*]. [2:38–39]

The task is practical as well as theoretical; the philosopher is an observer, but he can observe only after initiating a re-creation of the world:

> We observe the system of our representations not in its *being*, but in its *becoming*. Philosophy becomes genetic, that is, it allows the entire necessary array of our representations to come into being and run its course before our very eyes. From now on, there is no separation between experience and speculation. [2:39]

In embracing this project, in claiming that the factical world in all its specificity is derivable—or, better, constructible—Schelling proves himself to be as hubristic as any philosopher who has ever lived. He exhibits far more confidence in his own intellect than Leibniz ever did, Kant's intervening critique of the human mind notwithstanding. In Leibniz's view, the specifics of the experienced world would be derivable only by a god, only by an infinite intellect with full access to the principles ruling the world's development and to the implications of those principles. This would require, first, an awareness of all "possible worlds," that is, all states of affairs that are not contradictory and all configurations of compossible states; such awareness would be tantamount to complete understanding of the implications of the principle of contradiction. The intellect, to be infinite, would also have to be able to determine which unique conjunction of compossibles would have sufficient reason to exist, that is, which would be best; such determination would require complete understanding of the implications of the principle of sufficient reason. The infinite intellect would thereby know all particulars concerning the factical world, but the human intellect, dependent upon its confused and perspectival representations of the world, cannot attain such infinitude. Leibniz himself can therefore speak only generally of the factical world, and is unable to provide specific grounds for specific events.

Schelling denies that Leibniz developed his system to the fullest possible degree. Leibniz establishes, at least to Schelling's satisfaction, that the finite world must be grounded in the intellect—in spirit—but he denies human access to the level at which the intellect is absolute, the level from which the finite world in its specificity would be derivable. Schelling, under the influence of Fichte, is convinced that the absolute *is* accessible, and he reasons that the philosopher must therefore be able to derive content from it. That Fichte never completed—and perhaps never attempted—such a derivation does not deter Schelling, who is convinced also that Fichte's theories were crippled by his defective understanding of nature. For Fichte, whatever his true practical teaching may be, nature remains merely a means for man to use to his own ends, dead matter with which man can work. This conception is, Schelling insists, inadequate as a theoretical explanation of nature. Under the influence of both Leibniz and Kant (Liebniz, who stresses the essential relatedness of human beings to other sorts of natural entities, which differ from humans only in being more confused; Kant, who in the *Critique of Judgment* identifies internal orientation toward ends as the essence of all sorts of organisms) Schelling insists that a "nature" that existed only to be used by humans would be wholly different from the nature we experience. That nature is not adequately characterized as simply "non-ego." It must rather be explained as it is experienced, as having its own existence and coherence, independent of human beings; the philosopher of nature must unite nature's physical reality with its metaphysical ground, he must reconcile Leibniz's metaphysical principles with the specific details of the physical universe, a coherent whole governed not by human beings but, rather, by the mechanical laws discovered by Newton (2:25).

So determined as the reconciliation of Newton and Leibniz, Schelling's projected antithesis to Spinoza is sufficiently concrete to enable Schelling to begin to work on his system. Problems remain, however, with the status of the system based in the Leibnizian project. In the "Letters," it will be remembered, Schelling denies that any one system could be binding on all philosophers, at least until all humans are at the "same stage of freedom." Both the claim and the qualification reveal the influence of Leibniz. Leibniz teaches that intelligent beings differ from one another in viewing the same universe from different standpoints and with different degrees of confusion. If this teaching is accepted, it could be argued that the philosophical system that alone would satisfy less-confused human beings would not explain, to the more-confused ones, the world as they experience it. Only those whose representations were similarly confused would agree concerning the world as a whole; since, for Leibniz, evolution of sophistication— negatively expressed, avoidance of confusion—is grounded in the will of the individual monad, it would make sense to say that those who agree are at the same "stage of freedom": their wills are equally effective. These Leibnizian tenets clarify Schelling's puzzling assertion that no one system will suffice until all humans are at the same stage of freedom. Nevertheless, the individuality of the individual continues to threaten the claims to adequacy of any single system; the problem this poses for the systematic philosopher troubles Schelling in his *System of Transcendental Idealism,* published in 1800.

A second problem left unsolved by the decision to take Leibniz's way from finite to infinite concerns what the young Schelling consistently sees as philosophy's fundamental problem, namely, the step from the level of first principles—in the terminology of the *Ideas,* the level of the "essence of representing being"—to the level of the factical world (*see* 1:175, 294, 320, 369). The step is tantamount to the transition from infinite to finite, to the derivation of content from the absolute; it requires a middle term between the extremes. In Schelling's view, the only such term that can possibly work is the "internal conflict" in the "spiritual nature," the conflict that leads to its free attempt to posit—to think or know—itself. If the absolute is not conceived in terms of a tendency to posit itself, it cannot be thought of as spiritual, it cannot function as a source of content, and the system of freedom is finally indistinguishable from the system of necessity: there is no antithesis to Spinoza. If the subjective absolute is to *be* absolute, it must intuit itself, and, in intuiting itself, it must not cease to be absolutely free. At the same time, a system can result only if nature can be derived from the primal self-intuition.

The task of Schelling's antithesis to Spinoza, as envisioned in 1797, is thus that of derivation of content from the absolute; only through such a derivation—not, as Schelling had earlier believed, simply through presentation of an absolute essentially one with the human ego—could the system of freedom be completed. The new claim, that which grounds the possibility of systematic development, is that the absolute, both as intuiting itself and as intellectually intuited by the finite subject, is *internally unstable*. In earlier works, Schelling's position is that the absolute, even as visible in intellectual intuition, is beyond all determination and content. In the *Ideas*, however, he asserts that if one has "placed oneself in the position of [Spinoza's] infinite substance," the realization must follow that "infinite and finite are originally and inseparably there— without having to come to be there—not outside of us, but in us, and that the nature of our spirit and our entire spiritual existence is based precisely in this original union" (2:36–37). The system of freedom must begin with the subject's free step to the absolute standpoint, taken to be the standpoint of the absolute itself; the absolute must then be visible as active rather than as inert. Just as the absolute's intuition of itself has resulted in the existence of the world, the philosopher's intuition of the absolute must develop into an account of the world.

3 THE SYSTEM OF IDENTITY

Schelling's earliest works prepare the way for his first period of concerted attempts to construct his antithesis to Spinoza; that period covers the years from 1797 through 1804. Schelling begins by developing a philosophy of nature; he complements that part of his system with a philosophy of spirit, but then recognizes that the two parts are not sufficiently united. He attempts to combine them in the system of identity. Between 1800 and 1804, he struggles to make that system both comprehensive and consistent. He ultimately fails, but there is much to be learned from his failure: in seeking to provide fundamental answers, Schelling succeeds rather in uncovering yet more fundamental questions. To understand why philosophers after Schelling turn from metaphysics to philosophical anthropology, it is necessary to see how Schelling's questions arise within the metaphysical endeavor, and why the metaphysician has such difficulty coping with them; it is necessary to follow Schelling's thought to, and beyond, the system of identity.

FIRST ATTEMPTS

Philosophy of Nature

The works written by Schelling from 1794 through 1796 are short and programmatic: none is as long as one hundred pages, and all concentrate on the principles and form of Schelling's projected system rather than on its concrete development. In the following three years, Schelling moves from the programmatic to the systematic and from the general to the specific. He produces three lengthy works, not treating philosophy in general, but rather developing a philosophy of nature: *Ideas toward a Philosophy of Nature* (1797; 2:11–344), whose Introduction has already been considered, is followed by *On the World Soul* (1798; 2:345–583) and *First Outline of a System of Philosophy of Nature* (1799; 3:1–326). Schelling's earlier reflections reveal that to surpass both Spinoza and Fichte, he must present a constructive account, one beginning with first principles and ending with nature as it is experienced. He develops such an account in the *First Outline,* but the constructions in that work are possible only following a series of inductions, which he presents in *On the World Soul.*

Schellingian induction is the process of reasoning from the multiplicity of phenomena to the smallest number of principles that can account for the phenomena; the purpose of induction is to reveal that apparently disparate phenomena share common grounds. Most important for Schelling is the induction revealing that the opposition between subject and object is not absolute, for if it were, then no unified system could account for both. In earlier works, Schelling argues the same point by considering the relation of ego to non-ego in a purely conceptual manner, but his reflections on Fichte and Spinoza indicate that the successful philosopher must grasp nature as it is experienced, not merely as it is abstractly conceived. In *On the World Soul,* Schelling attempts to undermine the absoluteness of the opposition between ego and non-ego by reflecting on real empirical subjects and objects. Such subjects and objects are alike at least in that both are natural. They differ—as *natural* entities—primarily in that the former are organic and the latter inorganic; if the organic and the inorganic can be shown to share a common ground, then one fundamental difference between subject and object would be explained. In addition, the inductive arguments from phenomena to principles should facilitate later constructions of the phenomena from the principles.

In *On the World Soul,* then, Schelling seeks to move from the real to the ideal, from the world as experienced to the only principles that could satisfy reason's demand that that world be intelligible. He is aware that no "artificial [*erkünstelte*] unity of principles" could explain the phenomena in their complexity: "I hate nothing more than the mindless attempt to destroy the multiplicity of natural causes by means of invented [*erdichtete*] identities" (2:347–48). In order to avoid such artificiality, Schelling bases his inductions, not on an abstract conception of nature, but rather on the concrete observations of empirical scientists and on the theories guiding the further experimentation of those scientists; he seeks to establish that observing the natural world as a whole "leads the investigator to a *common principle* that, fluctuating between inorganic and organic nature, contains the first cause of all alterations in the former and the ultimate ground of all activity in the latter" (2:347). The inductions end by showing "that *one and the same principle connects inorganic and organic nature*" (2:350; *see* 2:564).

If the organic and the inorganic share a common principle, then they must be homogeneous; they are, Schelling argues, in that both are dynamic rather than mechanical. Schelling insists—in more familiar terminology—that the final substratum for all of nature is energy rather than matter. Since all of nature is fundamentally dynamic and active rather than mechanical and passive, Schelling reasons, the natural world cannot be adequately conceived as a great machine; it must rather be understood as the manifestation of the primal animate force known to the ancients as the "world soul" (2:381, 569). Schelling's inductions thus support the conclusion to which his purely philosophical reflections lead him in earlier works: the world must be grounded in a subjective absolute. In addition, Schelling's inductions reveal that nature is structured through dynamic polarities: to electrical and magnetic positivity and negativity correspond the organism's capacities to act and to be acted upon. The ubiquity of polarities in nature leads Schelling to conclude:

> Where there are appearances, there are already opposed forces. The doctrine of nature therefore presupposes as immediate principle a universal heterogeneity and, in order to be able to conceive it, a universal homogeneity of matter. Neither the principle of absolute heterogeneity nor that of absolute homogeneity is the true one; the truth lies in the union of the two. [2:390]

Just as any one magnet contains two opposed poles, the absolute—the world soul—must contain within itself the antithesis of finite and infinite. The primal antithesis itself is, however, beyond the scope of the inductive philosophy of nature: "This antithesis is simply postulated by the doctrine of nature. It is subject only to transcendental derivation, not to empirical. Its origin is to be sought in the original duplicity of our spirit, which constructs a finite product only from opposed activities" (2:396).

Schelling's inductions are presented as providing a negative argument for the absoluteness of the world soul: they purport to establish that no other principle could ground the natural world. In the *First Outline*, Schelling admits that those negative arguments are of little value if they are not positively supported by the successful construction, beginning with the highest natural principles, of a world fully correspondent to the world encountered in experience (3:20, 277). Schelling's next task, then, is to "derive *a priori* what [in *On the World Soul*] was proved through induction, that it is one and the same universal dualism that disperses itself in the magnetic polarity, then in electrical appearances, and finally in chemical heterogeneity, and that finally comes to the surface again in organic nature" (3:257–58). The constructive philosophy of nature is more important than the inductions of *On the World Soul;* but, because this philosophy is limited, it is not yet the highest philosophical science. Schelling's philosophy of nature constructs the world starting from the highest natural principle— that is, from the polarity visible in its simplest form in magnetism (3:250, 251n). The constructions are *a priori*, Schelling insists, in that they are fully necessary (3:278–79),[1] but they do not suffice to reconcile Leibnizian metaphysics with Newtonian physics, for they begin with magnetism—the simplest form in which the absolute appears—rather than with the absolute itself. The philosophy of nature thus cannot solve the truly fundamental problem:

The most universal problem, which encompasses all of nature and is thus the *highest* problem, . . . is this: What is the universal source of activity in nature? What cause brought forth in nature the first dynamic separation (of which the mechanical is a mere consequence)? Or what cause first cast into the universal tran-

1. This is not to say that the necessity is apparent. In this section (pp. 50–73), I ignore methodological problems in order to focus on systematic ones; I indicate what Schelling claims to construct, but not how he claims to do it. For discussion of the latter issue, see pp. 75, 78–79, and 170–87, below.

quility of nature the seed of movement, into the universal identity duplicity, into the universal homogeneity of nature the first
sparks of heterogeneity? [3:220]

Schelling remains convinced that only a reflective structure
can explain the introduction of difference into absolute identity: "It is impossible that [the primal unity], unlimited by anything external, transform itself into something finite for intuition save by becoming *object for itself*, that is, becoming finite in
its infinitude" (3:250). Magnetism, and thus all of nature, must
have its origin in the primal self-reflection of the absolute, its
primordial involution (3:261), but this involution cannot be examined by the philosopher of nature. It is an act rather than
an event—it is done, it does not simply happen—and as such
falls within the realm of the philosophy of spirit, of transcendental philosophy. The primal reflective act, the "absolute synthesis," is thus the "turning point of transcendental philosophy and the philosophy of nature" (3:268). The philosophy of
nature is not first philosophy, but rather a subordinate part of
the system. With his philosophy of nature, Schelling attempts
to convince the Fichtean that nature *can* be treated philosophically, albeit only within the larger context of a philosophy of
spirit; he attempts also to convince the natural scientist that
nature *must* be treated philosophically, that even the empirical
scientist who depends solely on experiments for results must
rely on theories for indications of what sorts of experiments
will be valuable. Finally, and most important, Schelling attempts to show scientists and philosophers that the mechanis-
tic conception of the universe is fundamentally mistaken. In
the romantic tradition, Schelling objects to the notion that the
universe is a grand machine in which plants, animals, and human beings can be nothing other, or nothing more, than complicated parts. To the view that matter in motion is reality and
that life and freedom are mere appearance, Schelling opposes
the view that even matter only appears to be dead, that it too
is encompassed in the world soul. Unlike many romantics,
Schelling attempts to establish his view through arguments beginning from concrete scientific observation; he seeks to construct a philosophy of nature, not a poetry of nature. To com-

plete the construction, he must develop in addition a philosophy of spirit; he first attempts to do so in the *System of Transcendental Idealism* of 1800.[2]

Philosophy of Spirit

The *System of Transcendental Idealism* is more ambitious and more comprehensive, but also more precarious, than any other work Schelling ever published. The work's ambitiousness is reflected in its title, which announces the completion of the project initiated by Kant and furthered by Fichte: Kant shows that transcendental idealism is the only alternative to dogmatism, and Fichte clarifies the first principles of the transcendental system, but Schelling, in 1800, is the first to present that system in its entirety (3:330–31). As an entire presentation, the 1800 *System* is comprehensive: it shows how the philosopher attains the level of the absolute and how he then reproduces or reconstructs the process leading to the development of nature; it describes the origin of human beings and identifies the traces of absoluteness visible in the realm of ordinary experience. In a mere three hundred pages, Schelling attempts to cover all of what philosophy must cover; he gives an account of the whole, moving quickly from finite to infinite and then, more slowly, back again to the starting point. Writing the 1800 *System*, Schelling believed he had discovered true land beyond Kant's "land of pure understanding"; he was convinced he had found the land Spinoza had sought in vain. Confident of his success, Schelling moves through that land with the eagerness and haste of the conqueror, not with the patience or care of the explorer. It is not surprising, considering both the immensity of Schelling's subject matter and the relative brevity of his treatment of it, that the *System of Transcendental Idealism* does not solve—or even clearly recognize—all the problems that arise within it. The unsolved problems are what make the *System* precarious, so precarious indeed that Schelling abandons it within a year's time.

2. Peter Heath's translation of the 1800 *System of Transcendental Idealism* indicates the pagination of the *Sämmtliche Werke*.

Nevertheless, the 1800 *System* remains among Schelling's most important works, for he never moves completely beyond it: in it he follows for the first time the path that he is to continue to retrace for the rest of his life, and he begins to discover the fundamental problems that will never cease to plague him. In the *System of Transcendental Idealism*, Schelling emulates the "great thinker" Spinoza in letting his "speculations take the freest flight, in wagering all or nothing, desiring either the whole truth, in its entire magnitude, or no truth at all" (1:152).

System of Transcendental Idealism Schelling introduces the 1800 *System* by strongly distinguishing transcendental philosophy — which is necessarily transcendental idealism—from the philosophy of nature: the former differs from the latter in that it starts with the subject. Following a Fichtean line of reasoning that he has used before, Schelling presents all philosophy as beginning with the reflective act through which subject and object, united in ordinary experience, are distinguished. The philosopher's task is to ground one of the two poles—now called nature and intelligence—in the other, and since the derivation can begin from either, there are two fundamental sciences. The philosophy of nature begins with the side of the object and seeks to prove that the dynamism visible in such phenomena as magnetism and electricity necessarily develops until it manifests itself in organisms and, eventually, in self-conscious intellects. Transcendental philosophy moves in the opposite direction: starting with the subject, it attempts to prove that there must also be, or develop, consciousness of external objects (3:339–42). The task of the transcendental philosopher is "to start with the subjective, as the first and absolute, and to let the objective arise from it" (3:342). Whereas the philosophy of nature starts with what is known in abstraction from the knower, transcendental idealism focuses on the knower in abstraction from the known. It therefore requires a peculiar sort of cognition. In ordinary conscious experience, we concentrate on what we perceive and what we do, without thematizing our perceiving and doing; awareness of the subject is sacrificed to awareness of the object. Through deliberate reflection, the transcendental philosopher allows the objective to disappear in order to make the subjective visible (3:345). In a certain sense, then, the transcendental philosopher produces his subject matter: he intentionally objectifies that which, independent of his reflective act, would never enter consciousness.

The transcendental philosopher seeks to explain the ordinary experience of finite subjects. The finite subject's own understanding of that experience is grounded in one fundamental prejudice: "There exist things outside of us (3:343)." Reflection on this prejudice reveals that it is based on two primordial convictions shared by finite subjects: we are convinced, first, that we know objects—the things that exist outside of us—as they really are (3:346), and, second, that our subjective ideas can attain reality in the objective world, that is, that we can change the world through our action in it (3:347). The fundamental prejudice and the primordial convictions are essential to finite subjectivity, but they are not immediately certain; all are vulnerable to skeptical doubt. The finite subject's most basic beliefs can be protected from doubt only if they can be derived from a conviction that is absolutely certain (3:346), and Schelling agrees with Augustine and Descartes that the only conviction that is immediately indubitable is the absolute prejudice, "I am" (3:344). In ordinary experience, I am convinced that I know objects, yet those objects may not exist, and in cases of mirage and illusion certainly do not exist. I can be certain only that I myself exist, and therefore I can have full faith only in my knowledge of myself: the only form of consciousness that is immediately reliable is self-consciousness. Schelling's task thus becomes that of deriving consciousness of objects from consciousness of self.

In introducing self-consciousness as transcendental philosophy's highest principle, Schelling does not claim to establish it as that principle; only the successful development of a system could prove that it is truly fundamental. Prior to that development, Schelling insists only that transcendental philosophy, as the attempt to ground all knowledge and experience in the subject, can have no principle other than self-consciousness. Some might object that self-consciousness is itself derivative from something higher, but Schelling argues, in effect, that the objection would beg the question of the possibility of transcendental idealism:

> Since I [as transcendental idealist] want to ground my knowledge only *in itself* [rather than in something that cannot be known], I do not ask further concerning the ultimate ground of that first knowledge (that is, of self-consciousness), a ground that, if it existed at all, would necessarily lie *outside* of knowledge. Self-consciousness is the source of light for the entire system of knowledge, but it shines only forward, not backward.[3:357][3]

Schelling's task is to derive, from the absolute prejudice "I am," the fundamental prejudice "There exist things outside of me," along with the theoretical conviction that I know those things as they are and the practical conviction that my actions can affect them. In abstraction from the system itself, no argument could prove that Schelling's project is *the* fundamental philosophical one or that it is not. Rather, "*that* the accomplishment of this task is philosophy can be shown only through the deed itself, in that that accomplishment brings with it the solution to all the problems that philosophers have always attempted to solve" (3:348).

The "I am" with which transcendental philosophy begins is pure self-consciousness. This mode of awareness, free of all traces of objectivity, has no part in ordinary conscious experience; I can attain it only by abstracting from that experience. In so doing, I necessarily abstract from my own individuality: I am who I am, as a unique individual, only as related in specific ways to specific external objects (including other individuals). As transcendental philosopher, I seek to know myself in isolation from those objects; I seek to know myself as subject, not as individual; I seek to discover the essence I share with all other subjects, not the accidents I share with none. As an in-

---

3. "I do not ask further" is a translation of the German "frage ich nicht weiter." The Felix Meiner edition of the *System* reads, "frage ich mich weiter," that is, "I ask myself further." The substitution of *mich* ("me") for *nicht* ("not") is presumably a typographical error: the context of the passage demands *nicht*. Unfortunately, the Heath translation is based on the Meiner edition and reads "I ask myself further."

dividual, I am "a constant transition from representation to representation, but it is in [my] power to interrupt this series through reflection, and with the absolute interruption of that succession all philosophizing begins" (3:396). I begin to philosophize in the highest sense—I begin to reflect on what is absolutely certain—by positing myself as pure subject, with no traces of objectivity and with no connections to objects of any sort; through my positional act, I become pure ego by freeing myself from all that is non-ego. I also recognize that in the course of my temporal experience—my ordinary experience as an individual—I come to be as *pure* subject only through this act in which I posit myself as such. This recognition becomes crucial when it is considered in conjunction with the fundamental assumption that I, as transcendental philosopher, make: namely, the assumption that pure subjectivity is the ground of all objectivity, that the purely subjective is "first and absolute" (3:342).

Since I assume that subjectivity is the absolute ground, and since I can now attain pure subjectivity only through the act of positing myself as such, I conclude—or, to be more cautious, assume—"that I can originally have come to be only through such [an act]" (3:397). I assume that the pure subject can come to be only through an act of self-consciousness; if the pure subject is the absolute ground, then all that is must have resulted from a primal self-conscious act. As a finite individual, I am—according to the hypothesis—a mere part of "all that is," I am caught up in the process issuing from the primal self-reflection; yet it is in my power to break out of that process by reflecting on it, by raising myself eventually to the standpoint of pure subjectivity. If I then posit myself as pure subject, I repeat or imitate the act through which all that is has come to be. I thereby start the process again from the beginning, and since I am fully conscious of what I have done, I can observe the development of the second process, the one I initiate. If it develops into a world indistinguishable from the world of ordinary experience, then all my hypotheses concerning the absolute status of the pure subject are confirmed: "If there is no more and no less in the second process than in the first, then the imitation is perfect, and a true and complete philosophy results" (3:397).

The task of the transcendental philosopher, bluntly expressed, is to postulate a primal act of self-consciousness and then to see what happens. That act must be the absolute beginning point for the system: "Self-consciousness is the source of light for the entire system of knowledge, but it shines only forward, not backward." If transcendental philosophy is to succeed—if Schelling's improvement on Fichte is truly to surpass Spinoza—then the light issuing from self-consciousness must reveal the origin of the finite world in the absolute:

> It can be demonstrated even to the stubbornest dogmatist that the world consists only of representations, but complete conviction arises only when the *mechanism of its development* out of the inner principle of spiritual activity is completely exhibited; for there could be no one who could still find necessary a world independent of the subject after having seen how the objective world, with all its determinations, develops out of pure self-consciousness, without any external affection whatsoever. [3:378]

The philosopher reaches pure self-consciousness, again, by positing the ego as free of all traces of objectivity. Since objects are static and limited, the pure ego must be active and unlimited; as unlimited, it must be the absolute ground of reality, for anything existent outside of it would constitute a limitation (3:380). As unlimited activity, though, the ego is not yet *ego*, for it is not aware of itself, it is not self-conscious. To be ego, it must intuit itself, but in so doing, it necessarily *limits* itself (3:383):

> Only that of me which is limited, so to speak, comes into consciousness; the limiting activity falls outside of all consciousness, precisely because it is the cause of all limitedness. The limitedness must appear to be independent of me because I can see only my limitedness, and not the activity through which it is posited. [3:390]

In limiting itself, the ego comes to be: "being intuited and being are one and the same" (3:390). Yet it does not thus come to be *for itself*: the ego is unlimited activity, but what it has intuited is, by virtue of its being intuited, limited. The philosopher knows—we know—that the ego is responsible for the existence of its object, but the ego itself knows only that object. If the ego is ever to know itself, it must come to be *for itself* precisely what it is for the philosopher, what it is for us (3:389).

The pure ego attempts to become conscious of itself, but it succeeds at first only in becoming conscious of what it takes to be something else: the ego acts, but it sees only the results of its act. Since this is so, the ego's immediate self-consciousness is not adequate: it is conscious of itself—there is nothing else that it could be conscious of—but it does not know that it is conscious of itself. The ego can come to know itself as itself only, if at all, through an infinite series of synthetic acts through which it attempts to comprehend both itself as active and the results of its acts. If the philosopher were to reconstruct all the partial syntheses, "then the entire cohesiveness of the objective world, and all determinations of nature down to the infinitely small, would have to be revealed" (3:398). It is, however, impossible for us to "deduce all the qualities in nature" (3:399), so we must be content with "relating those acts that make epochs in the history of self-consciousness, and with exhibiting their interconnectedness" (3:398). One reason that we are unable to repeat all the acts or all the resulting syntheses is that while for the ego itself they occur simultaneously, our reconstruction is temporal; a comprehensive reconstruction would require an infinite length of time. We are, however, capable of identifying epoch-making acts, for at every stage in the process we know more than the ego itself knows: we can see, for example, that as long as the ego is simply productive, it can know only its products and not itself. We therefore need not retrace all the productive acts, we can describe the most important and then look beyond them toward the reflective act that we know must come if the ego is ever to know itself fully. Since we as philosophers follow consciously the path the ego itself follows unconsciously, we can identify the epochs in the history of self-consciousness and thereby construct an account that, though not comprehensive, satisfies the demands of transcendental philosophy.

The first epoch begins with the ego's unintentional self-limitation in the act of self-consciousness. Through this act, the ego bifurcates itself into two sorts of activity: its original and continuing productivity, and its attempts to know itself as productive. The opposition between these two activities provides the basis for the derivation of content from the absolute:

> Descartes says as physicist: give me matter and motion and from them I will build the universe for you. The transcendental philosopher says: give me a nature of opposed activities one of which proceeds to infinity while the other strives to intuit itself in this infinity, and from them I will have intelligence come into being for you with the entire system of its representations. [3:427]

If there is any limitation at all, Schelling maintains, there will result a universe consisting of substances interconnected in causal relationships (3:481); the fundamental forces of the universe will necessarily derive from the magnetic, the electric, and the chemical and will succeed finally in producing organisms and then self-conscious, rational entities. Thus, everything included in the philosophy of nature is derivable from the fact of limitedness alone. The ego, seeking to know itself, unconsciously produces, but it can know only the products and not the productive acts; its frustrated attempts at self-knowledge result in "the whole manifoldness of the objective world, the products and appearances of consciousness" (3:455).

Though the natural world can be derived from the fact of limitedness alone, the individual finite human being cannot. I, as philosopher, can derive as necessary the fragmentation of the ego into an apparent multiplicity of finite individuals, but I cannot derive the necessity of my being human or of my being the specific human who I am. I am unable to do so because, though I can see that it is necessary that some sort of limitation arise with the ego's primal act of self-consciousness, I cannot derive the nature of the limitation from the fact of limitation. The most fundamental limitation—one shared by all intelligent beings (3:409), and leading all such beings to think according to the same categories and principles—arises with the primal act but is not derivable from that act:

> Both taken together, that the determinate limitedness cannot be determined through limitedness in general, and that it arises,

nevertheless, together with it in the same act, make *this, for philosophy, the inconceivable and inexplicable.* . . . It is not the fact that I *am* limited in a determinate way that is inexplicable, it is rather the *mode* of this limitedness. [3:410]

Schelling frequently refers to the fact of limitation as the first limitation and to the specific nature of the limitation as the second limitation. As is indicated above, he maintains that the essence of all possible natural worlds is derivable from the first limitation alone. He also asserts that all that happens in all actual worlds is determined by the first limitation—the fact of limitation—alone (3:482). The philosopher sees that he, as individual, will inhabit a world that he will comprehend in terms of certain necessary categories and principles. He cannot determine in advance the world he will inhabit; but since the events of that world are prefigured in the absolute synthesis that results from the first limitation, these events, too, are derivable once the nature of the second limitation is recognized:

It thus can be derived [from the first limitation] that there is, in general, a system of our representations, but not that we are limited to this determinate sphere of representations. Of course, if we already presuppose the determinate limitedness, then the limitedness of individual representations can be derived from it. . . . Once we are placed, through the entire synthesis of our consciousness, in this sphere, nothing can come forth within it that would contradict it or would not be necessary. This follows from the original consequence of our spirit, which is so great that every appearance that comes to us even now presupposes this determinate limitedness, and is necessary to the extent that, if any did not occur, the entire system of our representations would be contradictory in itself. [3:410–11]

The results of the second limitation become important as the ego becomes intelligence, that is, as its attempts to know itself as ego saddle it with consciousness of an objective world. The world with which intelligence is confronted is truly objective because, although it is produced by subjective activity, intelligence cannot know that it itself is responsible for the nature and existence of the world. Once the subject has its objective world, it must know itself as intelligence, not as ego (the ego cannot know itself as ego nor can it, having initiated the attempt to know itself, remain ego, but must necessarily become intelligence; adequate self-knowledge must be knowledge of itself as intelligence). The ego, attempting to become aware of itself, becomes aware of a manifold of objects in a specific configuration; since it cannot know that it is responsible for the configuration of the objects, and since it perceives the objects as causally interrelated, it takes their configuration to be the result of their past interactions (3:481–82; cf. 3:465–66). The act of becoming conscious is therefore perceived as occurring in a temporal succession: intelligence is confronted with a real world, and the apparent ground of the present condition of that world is its past condition.

Even after the ego has become intelligence, its activity continues to be productive; intelligence produces and is aware only of its products, not of itself. It thus can come to know itself, if at all, only in its products, that is, only if it produces something that is itself productive, only if it produces organisms. This means that intelligence cannot know itself directly as intelligence; it must know itself as individual, as a single, living entity. This reveals, according to Schelling, that a third limitation, not foreseen by the philosopher, is inherent in the primal act of self-consciousness. It is the third limitation that makes human beings human beings and that makes me the human being who I am. As a unique finite individual, I am a part of the world and am caught up in its causal nexus. As a true subject, however—being still one with the pure ego, despite the limitations that obscure the unity—I am not a mere product of intellectual activity; I must, myself, be active. Since I am conscious, I will also be conscious of my productive activity; that means, however, that I must decide what I will produce, I must choose. Choice is therefore a necessary phenomenon, but choice, according to Schelling, would be impossible if all objects in the world were equally available to me. If I am to choose, my options must be limited, and they can be limited, Schelling insists, only if there are other finite subjects—for me, other human beings—who can limit the sphere in which I can be active. Finite subjectivity, because it entails choice, presupposes intersubjectivity.

Having derived a real world inhabited by finite individual subjects capable of thinking and acting, Schelling would appear to have completed his reconstruction: the ego has become, in effect, what the philosopher was—what we were—prior to the beginning of the transcendental-philosophical reconstruction. Schelling nevertheless continues, in part because the ego whose development we are observing has not yet become philosopher—it has not yet reached the level we are now on—and in part because he has not yet shown that his transcendental idealism solves "all the problems that philosophers have always attempted to solve." The most important problem it has yet to solve is the problem of freedom.

For the transcendental idealist, the essence of pure subjectivity is unlimited activity; since there can be no external source of compulsion for the pure ego, that ego is absolutely free and acts in accordance with its own essence. Since the ego is the principle of Schelling's system, "the beginning and end of this philosophy is *freedom*" (3:376). The beginning of Schelling's system is free in a second sense: the philosopher's act of self-reflection, which makes the pure ego accessible, must be understood as a free act; there is no sort of external compulsion that could force any individual to make it (3:365, 369). Finite individuals must therefore be intellectually free; if they were not, there could be no philosophers. In addition, finite individuals are convinced—primordially convinced—that they are existentially free, that is, that actions following from their free decisions are effective in the objective world. That practical conviction is, however, in conflict with the primordial theoretical conviction that subjective thoughts are determined by external objects; if they were not, finite subjects could not know objects as they are. As an actor, I assume that I determine things; as a knower, I assume that they determine me. There is thus a contradiction between practice and theory: "this contradiction must be overcome if there is to be a philosophy at all—and the solving of this problem . . . is not the *first* task of transcendental philosophy, but it is its *highest* task" (3:348).

Schelling first identifies his highest task as early as the *System*'s Introduction: he there recognizes a contradiction between the two fundamental convictions the philosopher must derive. Yet the complexity of the highest task becomes visible only in the course of the derivation itself. As we have seen, the derivation takes the form of a reconstruction or repetition of the world process issuing from the pure ego's primal act of self-consciousness; the reconstruction is possible only because all steps in the process are fully determined in that primal act. While we know—the philosopher knows—that all events in the objective world are predetermined, the finite subject believes himself able to influence those events, and his belief is reinforced by experience: the subject's decision to eat a given banana is generally followed by the objective disappearance of the fruit. Yet if, as Schelling teaches, complete knowledge of the absolute synthesis would reveal "all determinations of nature down to the infinitely small"; if, as he also teaches, all temporal events are predetermined in that synthesis (3:482); if, in addition, my eating of the banana is as determined in the original synthesis of my consciousness as my depriving others of the banana is in the original syntheses of theirs (3:545–46), then I am completely wrong in assuming that my arbitrary temporal decision to eat the banana is intrinsically related to its disappearance. I am not completely wrong in believing myself free: though as a product of the pure ego's act of self-consciousness I am enmeshed in a web of external causal connections, I must also, as a persona of the pure ego itself, retain some measure of autonomy. Though my actions and their results are objective events and are therefore predetermined, my intellectual decisions may nonetheless be spontaneous subjective acts. If all of this is so, then decision and event are unrelated: I decide to eat the banana, and the banana is consumed by my body, but the former is not the true cause of the latter. The correspondence between decision and event—revealed, for example, in the disappearance of the banana—could then be explained only through a "pre-established harmony" between the two (3:579). The question of how this harmony can be understood takes us to "the point that is highest in the entire investigation" (3:580).

Having approached the investigation's highest point, Schelling does not immediately storm it; he first retreats in order to attack it from a different direction. The task of the individual is to know itself as individual, but to do so adequately it must also know itself as pure ego, that is, as unlimited activity or absolute will. The first step toward this comprehensive self-knowledge is the individual's recognition of its own freedom on the empirical level: the subject must be aware of the freedom to choose between alternatives. It is irrelevant that the objective results of the individual's choice are predetermined: if the entire world process is not to be in vain—as it would be if self-knowledge were never attained—then individuals must retain the illusion that they are existentially free, that is, that their acts are not completely determined by external factors that they cannot control. Schelling next asserts—he does not argue—that the illusion of existential freedom can persist only if political freedom persists (3:582). If the goal of the world process is complete self-knowledge for all individuals (and the world process could have no other goal), then the most important objective development is that of a just organization of states: only through the existence of such an organization will the political freedom of individuals be guaranteed, only if individuals are politically free will they remain convinced that they are existentially free, and only if they do remain so convinced can they take the first step toward recognition of the absolute autonomy of the subjective (3:593; see 582–92). Since it is essential to the success of the world process as a whole, the development of the just organization of states is the holiest of holies, and, Schelling insists, "the holiest cannot be entrusted to chance" (3:582). There can, however, be no natural necessity for this development, nor can any individual believe it to be a probable (much less a necessary) result of the interactions of the results of countless individual acts of will (3:593–94). Once again, we see the necessity of a pre-established harmony between the objective situation and the conditions necessary for subjective self-knowledge. The question of how this harmony— now seen as some sort of superhuman and supernatural guidance for the world process—is to be understood brings us back to the highest problem of transcendental philosophy (3:594).

History must be guided by a necessity beyond the human

and the natural; some individuals attribute this necessity—
which all have recognized—to the providence of an absolute
subject, others to blind objective destiny (3:594). But we as philosophers know that the higher necessity that binds subjective
and objective can itself be "neither subject nor object, and not
both at once, but only the *absolute identity* in which there is no
duplicity at all, and which for that reason—because duplicity
is the condition for all consciousness—can never enter consciousness." This absolute identity precedes all subjectivity; it
is the being "that divides itself already in the first act of consciousness, and that produces the entire system of finitude
through this division" (3:600). This absolute is not directly accessible, and thus cannot be immediately known as ground;
yet if it is the ground of all finitude, then its traces should be
visible in the course of history (3:601), which itself could only
be the progressive revelation of the absolute (3:603). Complete
revelation of the absolute would require three historical periods. In the first, the necessity governing the world process
would be seen as blind destiny; the second would begin when
the natural laws ruling objective events began to become visible. Schelling sees both periods in human history; he locates
the transition between them at roughly the time of the found-
ing of the Roman republic. The third period has not yet begun;
in that period, the providence guiding history will be fully
manifest to all. Then and only then will God exist, for only
then will the absolute know itself in and through finite individuals (3:604).

Transcendental philosophy's highest problem leads us to an
absolute that cannot be directly investigated, an absolute
whose revelation is not yet complete. The historical revelation,
as incomplete, cannot solve our problem, and the problem
must be approached again, now from a third direction. Our
previous considerations have shown that the phenomenon of
human action is intelligible only as a unification of freedom
and necessity: my thought is free but while my acts appear to
me to be free, they are, as events in the world, fully predetermined. In another sense, however, all events are determined
by "my" acts in that they are determined by the primal act of
the pure ego, of whom I am an avatar. They are determined by

preconscious acts on the level of the pure ego, but not by conscious acts on the level of individual human beings. This means, however, that the harmony between decisions and events, between thought and action, is a harmony between conscious and unconscious activity: my conscious activity results in decisions, "my"—the pure ego's—unconscious activity results in actions and events that correspond to those decisions. We as philosophers know this, but the ego that is the product of our repetition of the world process—the ego that is our object—does not yet know it. If that ego is to reach our philosophical standpoint, according to Schelling, it must see in the world objects that could result only from productive activity that is at once conscious and unconscious. Since my conscious activity is always directed toward specific ends, the identifying characteristic of its products is that they serve purposes. In that all natural things serve purposes for other natural things, nature itself is visible as the product of conscious activity; yet since natural things do not appear to result from purposive activity, they appear at the same time to result from unconscious productivity. Reconsideration of the purposivity visible in nature would therefore provide a partial solution to our problem (3:606), but the solution would be merely partial because it is not apparent, from the observation of nature, that the ground of nature lies in any way in individuals (3:610).

The complete solution to transcendental idealism's highest problem is to be found, not in observation of nature, but only in observation of the work of art (3:611). For the purposes of the philosopher, art is superior to nature in two ways. First, the true art work surpasses the artist's intentions without ceasing to result from those intentions; the art work is the result of activity of the individual artist that is at once conscious and unconscious. Second, the work of art succeeds in revealing the absolute itself: "Only the work of art reflects for me that which is reflected through nothing else, that absolute identical that has already divided itself in the ego; that which the philosopher allows to divide itself already in the first act of consciousness; that which is inaccessible to any other form of intuition: it shines forth out of its own products through the work of art" (3:625). Art "succeeds in the impossible, namely in overcoming an infinite opposition in a finite product" (3:626). With the philosophy of art, then, Schelling's system comes full circle, returning to the principle, the "primordial ground of all harmony of the subjective and objective," with which it began; "our object, the ego itself, has gradually been led to the point where we ourselves stood when we began to philosophize" (3:628–29). The philosopher's activity thus comes to an end; all has been explained that can be explained, and, it would appear, the philosopher has nothing left to think about and nothing to do save to wait for the third period of history, the period of providence, which will be mediated by the highest work of art, a universal mythology (3:629).

From Transcendental Idealism to the System of Identity Though Schelling presents the completion of the system of transcendental idealism as the completion of philosophy itself, he does not cease, in 1800, to philosophize; indeed, he publishes the beginning of a new system within a year. To understand why Schelling so soon feels compelled to make a fresh start, we must consider some of the fundamental problems that are obscured by the impressive superficial coherence of the 1800 *System*. One such problem concerns the relation of transcendental philosophy to the philosophy of nature. In the 1800 *System's* Introduction, and especially in its Foreword, Schelling presents the two as opposed but equally necessary sciences; since the philosophy of nature is actually included as a part of transcendental philosophy, however (see pp. 62–63, above), the *System* itself belies the distinction drawn in its opening sections.

If the philosophy of nature is included within transcendental philosophy, then the 1800 *System* delivers far more than it promises: it is all of philosophy rather than a mere part, and its principle must be the principle of all philosophy. But what is the principle of transcendental idealism? Early in the system, it appears to be the subject, as opposed to the object; it appears to be pure self-consciousness. In introducing that principle, Schelling acknowledges that reflection on the absolute as absolute does not lead to the pure ego, but he insists that only the pure ego can be the absolute ground: "Self-consciousness is the source of light for the entire system, but it shines only

forward, not backward." Much later, the light of self-consciousness nevertheless does shine backward, at least in that it
reveals that the pure ego is not the highest ground; that
ground is absolute identity, which becomes ego by dividing itself in the primal act of self-consciousness. Thus, the principle
to which transcendental philosophy returns is not the principle
with which it begins.

According to the 1800 *System*, absolute identity is prior to
pure subjectivity; it is therefore more fundamental. It cannot,
however, function as a more fundamental principle, for it cannot be a "source of light for the entire system." It is not even
clear that it can be a source of light for itself, that is, that it can
be directly known. Schelling at first maintains that absolute
identity is visible only in the work of art, but in an epilogue to
the system, he qualifies his original assertion: while for most
human beings the absolute is accessible only in aesthetic intuition—in the appreciation of art works—the success of the
derivations in the *System* proves that the absolute is accessible
to the philosopher in intellectual intuition (3:630). Even in the
epilogue, however, Schelling continues to insist that the philosopher cannot know anything of absolute identity because it
is prior to the self-reflective act: "What the identical is in abstraction from—and thus before—this act is a question that
cannot be asked at all. For it is that which can reveal itself *only*
through self-consciousness and which cannot be separated
from this act at all" (3:631). The *System of Transcendental Idealism*, regardless of the success of any of its derivations, does not
yet provide a solution for the problem of the conflict between
absolute as absolute and absolute as ground.

Two further points of difficulty in the 1800 *System* become
visible when the success of the work is gauged by its self-set
criteria. Half-way through the work, Schelling describes his
task as follows:

> Anyone can consider *himself* to be the object of these investiga-
> tions. In order, however, to explain himself, he must first over-
> come all individuality in himself, because that is what is to be
> explained. If all of the limitations of individuality are taken away,
> nothing remains save absolute intelligence. If the limits of intel-
> ligence are then overcome, nothing remains save the absolute

ego. The task then is this: to explain absolute intelligence through an act of the absolute ego, and then to explain, from an act of absolute intelligence, the entire system of limitedness that constitutes my individuality. [3:483]

Despite this description of his task, Schelling never attempts to derive the "entire system of limitedness" that constitutes his own individuality. If such a derivation were possible, it would be valid only for Schelling himself; every philosopher would have to reconstruct the unique process leading to his own existence. The derivation, however, is not possible, for neither the second nor the third limitation can be reconstructed. Since this is so, the "second process," the one initiated by the philosopher, cannot contain "no more and no less than the first process," and "a true and complete philosophy" cannot result; Schelling's system must fail to satisfy one of his own basic criteria. Schelling must, in the system of identity, reject the criterion, for it cannot be met.

A second criterion identified by Schelling is that his system must "solve all the problems that philosophers have always attempted to solve." The 1800 *System* fails to meet this requirement, at least in that it does not consider ethical questions at all: "How the original limitedness—according to which, for example, it is impossible that a man attain during his life a certain degree of excellence, or that he outgrow the guardianship of another—how this limitedness can be brought into harmony with freedom in the case of moral actions, that is a matter with which transcendental philosophy need not be concerned, for it must, in general, merely deduce phenomena, and freedom is for it nothing other than a necessary phenomenon whose conditions must have the same degree of necessity [as those of other necessary phenomena]" (3:551).

Schelling here excludes from the realm of transcendental philosophy the simpler form of a problem that has a more serious form: he considers freedom only as a phenomenon, an appearance; he attempts to avoid the question of its reality. Nevertheless, that question is raised by the doctrines of the *System*. In the passage quoted above, Schelling indicates that there is a difficulty in using the same moral standards to judge both potential saints and those who are by nature vicious. Yet if either saints or sinners are to be morally judged at all, they must be responsible in some degree for their actions. Schelling's system leaves no room for personal responsibility; it cannot, for if all did not follow of necessity from the primal synthesis, then philosophical reconstruction would be impossible: we can reason from principles to results only when the principles fully determine their results. Schelling attempts to retain a freedom of thought and decision—thought not of action—but he cannot consistently do so: if my physical consumption of the banana is necessitated by the objective, natural order, then my decision to eat the banana cannot be my own. Schelling attempts to provide for the possibility of human freedom by strongly distinguishing nature from intelligence—by distinguishing the ego's products from its avatars—but then he offers no better explanation for the experiential unity of subject and object than a vague, pre-established harmony grounded in an ineffable absolute. The 1800 *System* does not solve transcendental philosophy's highest problem; it cannot, for there is an unavoidable conflict between the conditions for the possibility of Schellingian construction and the conditions for the possibility of human freedom. The conflict is present in the *System of Transcendental Idealism*, but it is far beneath the surface of the work; it comes to the surface for the first time in Schelling's works of 1804, and it is directly confronted only in the *Freedom* essay of 1809. Immediately following 1800, in the system of identity, Schelling concentrates on the other fundamental conflict that we have seen arise, namely, the conflict between absolute as absolute and absolute as ground.

STRICT SCIENCE

In three works written between 1801 and 1804, Schelling makes a concerted, even single-minded attempt to be a complete rationalist, to banish from his system the specter of mysticism. The works are devoted to the system of identity, of which, according to Schelling, both the earlier works on the philosophy of nature and the *System of Transcendental Idealism* are partial and preliminary versions. As partial and preliminary, the early works are neither completely clear nor completely rigorous: they are not sufficiently scientific. The demands of science require the use of Spinoza's deductive, geometrical form of development, the form allowing "the greatest concision of exhibition and the most determinate evaluation of the evidence used in proofs" (4:113). Schelling uses that form in *Exhibition of My System of Philosophy* (1801; 4:105–212), in *Further Exhibitions from the System of Philosophy* (1802; 4:333–510), and in *System of All Philosophy and of the Philosophy of Nature in Particular* (6:131–574), which was written in 1804 but published only posthumously.

The system of identity, in its entirety, was to have had three parts: a treatment of the system's first principles, its "general grounds," was to have been followed by accounts of nature and of spirit. In the published scientific works, Schelling does not present the entire system: in the *Exhibition,* he reaches only the stage of the organism (the transition from nature to spirit); in the *Further Exhibitions,* which might have been expected to take up where the previous work left off, Schelling once again devotes much space to the first principles and, in the constructions that follow, provides additional detail on inorganic nature, especially on the organization of the solar system, but he does not even reach the level of the organism.

That Schelling never published the system of identity in its entirety suggests that the system is fatally flawed; examination of the system confirms the truth of what the publication record suggests. Schelling is ultimately forced to acknowledge that the specter of mysticism has been ignored by his "strict science," not truly exorcised from it. Schelling's strict science ultimately fails in that there are fundamental problems that it can neither avoid nor solve; the major goal of the following analysis is to reveal those problems, for they determine the further course of Schelling's development.

Of the three strictly scientific works, Schelling himself consistently presents the first, the *Exhibition,* as the most authoritative. The title's flagrant use of the personal pronoun indicates that, as of 1801, he takes that work to be truer to his own thought than are any of his earlier ones; in the following years, he continues to stress the *Exhibition*'s value. In 1806, he acknowledges that he has improved and expanded many of the specific details of the work's presentation of the philosophy of nature, but he adds:

> The general grounds, however, as they are there presented, have been reconfirmed in all my further investigations, even those aspects that had come to me at the time more through divination than through conscious knowledge: the wrath of the rabid masses who viewed this teaching as a bone of contention cast before them has not, in my opinion, made a single one of its sentences even dubious, much less proved any to be false; and my sole intent is to further maintain and present, in every possible light, the whole and all as it is there presented.[7:144]

As this passage indicates, Schelling's peers—the "rabid masses"—did not give the *Exhibition* the reception its author thought it deserved. Schelling himself never ceases to defend the work; in a lecture presented twenty years after the *Exhibition*'s publication, Schelling insists that that work is, among the several presentations of the philosophy of identity, "the only one that its author has, from the beginning, recognized as strictly scientific" (10:147; *cf.* 7:334).

Schelling's comments suggest that anyone wishing to understand the system of identity should concentrate on the *Exhibition*, yet, as has been indicated, that work does not present the system in its entirety. In addition, the presentations it does make are written in abstract and ambiguous terms; even the most sympathetic of Schelling's recent commentators, Xavier Tilliette, concludes that the work is "questionable, it is falsely rigorous; it extricates itself from the prickly problem of the beginning, performs acrobatics with abstractions, and superbly ignores the origin of the finite." Tilliette sees Schelling's continuing defense of the work as motivated by "the sort of affection one feels for a sickly child."[4] My own suspicion is that Schelling was able to continue to defend the work only because it is so vague; in it, he does not explicitly draw the conclusions that he draws in later works—especially the 1804 *System*—though these conclusions are entailed by the system's own principles. Be that as it may, because the *Exhibition* is both incomplete and needlessly obscure, it is not the proper focus

4. Xavier Tilliette, *Schelling. Une philosophie en devenir*, 1:263.

for those who would understand why the system of identity fails. The more important text is the complete, though unpublished, *System* of 1804; the following analysis concentrates on that text, after introducing a few important but problematic teachings from the *Exhibition* and from *Further Exhibitions*.

Exhibition and *Further Exhibitions*

The opening section of the *Exhibition* reveals the two most important differences between the system of identity and the *System of Transcendental Idealism*. First, the system of identity begins with the announcement of its principle, not with an argument establishing the principle. There are good reasons for forsaking the latter: in the 1800 *System*, Schelling's presystematic arguments can establish no principle higher than the pure ego. Contradiction arises when the systematic constructions reveal that the true principle is not the ego, but rather absolute identity. In the *Exhibition*, Schelling omits the presystematic arguments; if his constructions are successful, he reasons, they alone will suffice to prove that his is the true principle, and any presystematic arguments would be superfluous. As long as Schelling sees the presystematic arguments as necessary, he is forced to begin with the pure ego; as soon as he sees that those arguments are expendable, he is free to begin with absolute identity.

In beginning with absolute identity, the system of identity begins beyond the level of the ego and the finite; that system's second fundamental difference from the 1800 *System* is that, throughout, it must remain beyond the level of the finite, that it does not descend to the level of the factical world. This change, like the first, is motivated by a problem that arises in the 1800 *System:* there, Schelling is faced with the problematic task of deriving his own individuality, and his derivations are limited by inscrutable "limitations," which cannot be reconstructed. In the system of identity, the constructions cannot descend from level to level; they must rather remain throughout on the level of the absolute.

The central problem with construction of content within the absolute is that such construction appears to be impossible in principle: if the absolute contains distinctions and negations, then it is not, according to Schelling, truly absolute. For just this reason, Hegel later ridicules the Schellingian absolute by calling it a "night in which all cows are black." As Tilliette indicates, the *Exhibition* "superbly ignores the origin of the finite" rather than explaining it; yet the work does contain passages that indicate how Schelling later attacks the problem.

In the *Exhibition*, Schelling suggests that there are no real differences or distinctions; the absolute itself is as homogeneous and undifferentiated as the Parmenidean one. Therefore, distinctions cannot *be*, they can merely *appear*, and they can only appear to an arbitrarily reflecting subject (4:126). How the existence of arbitrarily reflecting subjects is possible is not indicated in the *Exhibition*, but only they, Schelling suggests, can be responsible for multiplicity. In addition, the *Exhibition* indicates that finite subjects—subjects capable of arbitrary reflection—may somehow be responsible even for their own finitude: distinctions and oppositions are visible "only to one who has separated himself from totality, and only to the extent that he so separates himself" (4:128). This separation from the absolute, as the source of all opposition, is the source of all error; all that results from it is simply false from the standpoint of reason and unworthy of philosophical consideration (4:127–28).

While opposition is thus beneath the system of identity, differentiation cannot be, or no system would be possible, for there could be no systematic content. Yet if the absolute exists at all, Schelling insists, there must be content: while the essence of the absolute is undifferentiated identity, the form in which the absolute exists is an identity of distinct elements; the absolute exists as identity only if it is the identity *of* something (4:120–21). Since disparate elements can be unified only in knowledge, Schelling concludes that "the totality of what is is in itself—that is, according to its essence—absolute identity itself, but it is also—according to the form of its being—the self-knowledge of absolute identity in its identity" (4:122).

The claim that the absolute exists only as knowing itself and as being known by itself—the claim that the absolute exists as self-reflective—leads Schelling to the problem of what the absolute knows. Since the absolute is beyond all limitation, "the self-knowledge of absolute identity in its identity is infinite" (4:122), and "absolute identity cannot know itself infinitely without positing itself infinitely as subject and object" (4:123). It can do so only by initiating a dialectical process, in which moments of apparent disparity are resolved into increasingly comprehensive identities. In Schelling's terms, the absolute knows itself as a series of developing "powers" of subjectivity and objectivity. The process begins with the primal self-reflection: the absolute as subject (A) objectifies itself (as B). The result of this first act may be symbolized as $A = B$. The sign of equality is appropriate, for A and B do not differ in content: A knows only B, and B is precisely as it is known by A. Nevertheless, the moment is one of merely relative identity, since A (as subject) knows, while B (as object) is known. Because of this distinction the moment is, as one of relative identity, also one of relative difference: B has been posited by A, but A remains unposited. The moment becomes one of relative totality only when it is posited as a whole, as $A = B$, by the higher (more comprehensive) subjective power A^2. A and B are then posited as identical—they are known to be identical—but the totality that is achieved is merely relative in that it does not include one of its components, A^2. The complex now present is $A^2 = (A = B)$, but that is a new moment of merely relative identity, and as such can become a totality only by being objectified by a higher power of subjectivity (4:140–42, 149).

At every moment in Schelling's process, identity is retained in that every objective moment that arises is known by a subjective moment that fully corresponds to it in complexity. If $A = B$ is compared with $A^2 = (A = B)$, the two may appear to be essentially different, but the comparison itself is the work of "arbitrary reflection." Philosophical speculation is concerned not with such merely apparent differences, but with the whole, the entire range of developing identities, of various powers of subjectivity and objectivity. Thus, where the reflective subject—the subject on Fichte's level—will see the plant as relatively defective in "knowing" less than the animal and will see the world of the animal as less complete than that of the human, the philosopher of identity will see instead that the world grasped by the plant is in perfect harmony with the needs and capacities of the plant, and that the same is true for all subjects and for all of objectivity. At the same time, though, most subjects are not absolutely united with their objects because most do not objectify themselves; the identities and totalities remain relative. The process of development of increasingly articulated identities must therefore continue until there arises a subject that is fully self-reflexive or self-conscious, one that grasps itself along with its object; this would be "the form of absolute self-knowledge" (4:141).

Schelling's As and Bs suggest the form of his dialectic, but not its contents. According to Schelling, since the absolute is not a dead object, it must be unlimited activity, an unlimited force of expansion. It is as such that it first objectifies itself, but the objectification is itself a limitation: the attempt at self-knowledge works as a force of contraction. The expansive and contractive forces are, respectively, the dialectic's first objective (B) and subjective (A) powers. As the combination of expansion and contraction, the absolute remains undifferentiated, but no longer unlimited; it is held stable in its limitation, according to Schelling, as prime matter, the first $A = B$. The subjective moment that illuminates prime matter, the first A^2, is primal light (4:142–51).

If the opening developments of Schelling's dialectic are initially unconvincing, that should come as no surprise: to deduce the universe in all its complexity from the empty idea of the absolute is, after all, as likely to be impossible as is any project ever undertaken by any philosopher, however essential the project may have appeared to Schelling. But be the difficulties as they may, Schelling perseveres. Although he never published a complete construction of nature, he sees in his general view of nature the correction of one of the fundamental errors of modernity, the theory, put forth most influentially by Descartes, that nature is static and thus subject only to and fully explicable by mechanical laws (*see* 7:215*n*). He continues to stress that this is among the most serious of Fichte's misconceptions (4:359; 6:17–19; 7:17). Schelling takes the mechanical view to be erroneous in itself and to hinder scientific progress severely by encouraging theorizing that is merely empirical:

"Whenever empirical science attempts to express something universal, it can always expect only to be refuted by later experience, whereas the theory that is derived—mediately or immediately, and more or less consciously—from ideas or from construction can always only be confirmed by experience" (4:473). Schelling sees proof of the superiority of his mode of theorizing in his prediction of the existence of the "planet" Pallas (now commonly called an asteroid), whose discovery shocked empirical astronomers: "It is well known to those with whom I have communicated my ideas over the years or who have attended my lectures that I maintained, on grounds taken from my doctrine of cohesion in the system of the planets, not only the existence of a planet between Mars and Jupiter, but even characterized this position as the point of greatest density in the system of planets" (4:473). Schelling took the discovery of Pallas as a dramatic confirmation of his most complete construction, that of the solar system. His account of that construction concludes:

> If the simple and unforced agreement of all appearances in general can serve as test of a principle and of the theory that is grounded in it, then it must at least be granted that our principle—which of course derives its confirmation from higher grounds—does not fail to pass. There are admittedly a few determinations that are still lacking within the circle sketched here, but they also will enter in the future, e.g., the determinations of the distances of the planets from each other and from the center. [4:507]

The only criticism of his natural constructions that Schelling seems seriously concerned to counter is that his constructions are limited to those phenomena already discovered empirically. He presents his prediction of Pallas's existence as one counterexample, and later, when Fichte reasserts the old criticism, Schelling points out that at a time when magnetism was for empirical physicists no more than "the property of a single metal," he had already presented it as the "necessary category of matter" that later experiments—performed by a French physicist ignorant of Schelling's teachings—clearly confirm it to be (7:108).

The question of whether Schelling's satisfaction with his philosophy of nature is in any way justified cannot be considered here. While modern scientists, more concerned with black holes and quarks than with magnetism and galvanism, might find it naive and implausible, at least some among them would respect Schelling's attempts to produce a unified science. However that may be, even if Schelling's philosophy of nature were completely unobjectionable, its constructions alone could not confirm his principles or satisfy his project. The constructions are confirmed only through correspondence to the factical world as it is experienced, and whereas increasing fullness of detail with respect to inorganic nature would lend increasing plausibility to the undertaking, Schelling's project requires the construction of consciousness, and thus an account of the human subject (4:257, 282). Schelling undertakes that part of the project in the *System of Transcendental Idealism*, but his presentation there is inadequate, in part because he grounds finite subjectivity in limitations, placed on the absolute, whose precise natures cannot be derived. The *Exhibition* partially avoids the 1800 *System*'s problem by denying the possibility that the absolute be limited, but having done so, it does not indicate how the human realm is to be incorporated into the system of identity. That incorporation is attempted only in the *System* of 1804.

From Nature to Spirit: The *System* of 1804

The sole scientific work covering the system of identity in its entirety, the *System of All Philosophy and of the Philosophy of Nature in Particular*, was not published by Schelling himself; according to his son, it was completed in 1804. Since Schelling was not hesitant to publish in his early years, his failure to publish the 1804 *System* is *prima facie* evidence that he was seriously dissatisfied with it. At the very least, by 1804 Schelling has lost faith in his "scientific" form of presentation; while he uses that form in the 1804 *System* itself, he asserts in "Philosophy and Religion," also written and indeed published in 1804, that the dialogue is the form best suited to philosophy (6:13). Yet Schelling does not forsake strict science for purely formal reasons. An additional motive for his turn to dialogue—and for his decision not to publish the 1804 *System*—relates to content: serious contentual difficulties inherent in the system of identity are visible in all the scientific works, but they are most clearly visible in the most comprehensive of these, the 1804 *System*.

Like the other scientifically structured works, the 1804 *System* begins by presenting the absolute, now also termed God, in such a way that, it would seem, it could not possibly function as ground for determinate being, real or ideal. As in the other works, the basis for the development of determination is a primal self-reflection: "God is only insofar as he affirms himself and is affirmed by himself" (6:161), only insofar as he attempts to know himself (6:168). With the divine self-affirmation, determinate forms—now termed *ideas*—arise, but, as in the *Exhibition*, they arise only as unified in the absolute's infinitude; from this, Schelling reasons that "from the standpoint of reason there is no finitude at all, that, therefore, no question can be raised concerning the origin of this finitude in God, for only the infinite emanates from God; that, moreover, to consider things as finite is not to consider them as they are in themselves" (6:161). Philosophy therefore remains throughout on the level of the absolute, of reason, but it is nonetheless comprehensive: "Philosophy is the exhibition of God's self-affirmation in the infinite fecundity of its consequences, thus the exhibition of the One as the All. Again, it is as such the exhibition of the universe as it issues immediately from God's self-affirmation, as his eternal unity" (6:176–77).

The content inherent in God's affirmation is the realm of ideas, the idea being "the primordial form, the essence in things, thus the heart of things" (6:183). Yet the things constituting the finite world are no longer presented, as they are in the *Exhibition*, as resulting from human beings' "arbitrary reflection" on the ideas; they are rather presented as imperfect copies of the ideas, as differing from the ideas in exhibiting them incompletely (6:184). The merely finite things—the defective copies—are, it first appears, of no concern to philosophy: "If then the essences of things as grounded in God's eternity are ideas, then philosophy, as the science of the things in themselves, is necessarily the science of ideas, the science that itself is, throughout, in the identity of the universal and the particular" (6:185). Schelling's general presentation of the ideas suggests that he conceives of them as perfect paradigms of the various types of finite things; individual plants, for example, are imperfect copies of the idea "plant." But he also presents the ideas themselves, at least insofar as they are distinct, as imperfect copies of God (6:184). The status of the ideas is made no clearer in the 1804 *System* than in the *Exhibition*, nor does Schelling explain in the later work how the ideas can be at once unified and distinct on the absolute level. Rather than offering such an explanation, Schelling proceeds directly to the origin of finite appearances.

As is indicated above, Schelling continues in the 1804 *System* to deny that there is a direct emergence or emanation of the finite from God. Nevertheless, the *System* does present the finite as emerging from God rather than as produced by human reflection; the finite emerges from God, but only indirectly. The argument, present only in the 1804 *System*, is that the positing of the ideas as united in the absolute is at the same time the nonpositing of them as separate, and that the positing of them as being only in themselves, in the absolute, is necessarily the positing of them as not being for themselves, outside of the absolute. Relative to the absolute, the ideas *qua* separate from each other are nothing; but "a relative nonbeing includes, as such, a relative being within itself. That which, relative to something—here, the absolute—is *absolutely* not, cannot, *not* so related, be absolutely not, for otherwise it would have to be, in the relation, absolutely" (6:190).

This obscure assertion—among the most obscure ever made by Schelling—is based on two unexpressed assumptions. The more general is the converse of a famous Spinozist dictum: for Spinoza, all determination is negation, but for Schelling, at least in the passage under consideration, all negation is determination. As applied by Schelling, the assumption is that anything subject even to negative predication must somehow exist. Schelling's second assumption is that nothing can be the same both as related to and as independent from the absolute. The second assumption is problematic: if, first, anything is related to the absolute, then the absolute is brought into a relation and is no longer absolute. In addition, if, as Schelling insists, the absolute is comprehensive, then it would seem that nothing could be separate from or beyond it anyway. Schelling's first assumption, applied directly to the absolute, adds to the difficulties. Spinoza's dictum holds for the realm of determinate being: determination is negation in that, for example, to be red is to be nonblue. Schelling's converse—all negation is determination—also makes sense with respect to determinate being in that, normally, to say that something is not blue is to imply that it is some other color. If, however, Schelling's rule is applied to the ideas in themselves, then the absolute, as containing them, must contain negation and finitude; Schelling of course insists that it can contain neither. Yet Schelling's argument can account for the origin of finitude only if the negation he invokes is indeed determinate negation of ideas that are already specific: the claim is not that anything that does not exist within the absolute must exist beyond it, but rather that all that is in the absolute as *in*distinct or *in*different must be, as distinct, beyond it.

Schelling's argument that finite determinate forms are indirectly or negatively posited along with God's direct and positive self-affirmation does not adequately account for the origin of the finite; but by relating finite appearances to the absolute, it grants them a dignity not before recognized, thereby revealing them to be worthy of philosophical consideration:

> Now, it is however the *infinite* affirmation of God, and *in* its infinitude, i.e., the position of the universe *as* universe and thus of the universe itself, it is this position through which the particular in its particularity is posited as nonbeing. . . . Since then it is the position of the universe . . . through which the particular is posited as mere nonbeing, this nonbeing, *as* nonbeing, and precisely in *that* it is nonbeing, is itself *expression* of the universe, the universe is knowable in it, not immediately but mediately, that is through reflex, through a reflected illumination [*Widerschein*]— and thus the whole significance of *appearance* is expressed for the first time. [6:197]

Though Schelling does not point out the change, what began as the "science of ideas" has become a science of appearances.

The change is necessary for, since Schelling's doctrine of the ideas entails their ineffability, the only possible science of them is an indirect science; there is no science if there is nothing to describe or discuss. Schelling's system therefore focuses on the particular; specifically, on the two particular realms of nature and spirit.

The accounts of nature and spirit are structured by the *Exhibition*'s dialectic of subjective and objective powers. The dialectic of the 1804 *System* differs, however, from that of the *Exhibition* in not beginning with the primal act of the absolute. That act has as its immediate result only the ideas in their indistinguishable, ineffable unity. Philosophical construction in the 1804 *System* begins, as in the *System of Transcendental Idealism*, with the absolute synthesis, but all synthesis is now located in the realm of nonbeing. The location of synthesis is revealed in Schelling's description of the relation of appearances to absolute identity, a relation so important that "whoever does not understand it can understand nothing else in philosophy":

> The infinite substance produces, in infinite fashion, only the absolute *thesis*, just as it itself is only absolute thesis. This, however, shines forth again in the particular, whose being is not the same as its essence. . . . The immediate replica of absolute identity in it is the indifference in which [being and essence] fully merge, obscuring each other in the interpenetration (because it is only relative penetration, not absolute identity), thereby producing that impenetrable phantasm or idol of true reality that we call matter. Instead of the thesis, the synthesis is produced, and what is first in the absolute or in itself is third in the replica; this is the universal law of all reflex. [6:228–29]

Philosophy as discursive science is now presented as possible and necessary because of the finitude of the human intellect; in both the 1800 *System* and the *Exhibition* it is the continuing infinitude of the human intellect that, by allowing complete repetition of the process following from the primal self-position, grounds the step beyond Fichte to the absolute as real ground. Within the new framework, that based on the finitude of the intellect, construction remains possible because all follows with absolute necessity from the first synthesis—

which we can reproduce—and because what follows from the synthesis, unlike what follows immediately from the absolute thesis, is articulated. The stress on unity or balance of powers is also retained, for speculative cognition is distinguished from ordinary consciousness by its capacity for grasping things as synthesized rather than as antithetical.

Though Schelling's system is now presented as the work of finite rather than of absolute intellect, it does not develop differently. Schelling's dialectic that issues from the absolute synthesis does not differ essentially from that which issues, in the *Exhibition*, from the primal thesis: in each case, it is one of increasing articulation through successive reflective steps. What is completely new in the 1804 *System* is the continuation of the system of identity into the realm of spirit.

Schelling begins the specific treatment of spirit by insisting that the step from natural entities to spiritual ones is not discontinuous; he does so by explicitly denying the existential freedom that would negate full dependence upon and determination by the natural order. Whereas the younger Schelling argues that such freedom is a precondition for consciousness, the writer of the 1804 *System* recognizes absolute freedom—action in accordance with essence—as the only freedom, and this freedom is completely attributable only to the absolute itself. Since the acts of human beings, like all other finite occurrences, follow (albeit indirectly) from the absolute thesis, even "the individual acts of will in the soul are always necessarily determined, and therefore not free, not absolute" (6:538). The notion of existential freedom and the problems, such as that of the origin of evil, that arise with it result from the same sort of arbitrary reflection that, according to the *Exhibition*, gives rise to finitude as such, the sort of thought "that has borne into science all errors, all one-sided and false systems" (6:541). The fundamental error is made when things are considered not as they are in themselves—that is, not as necessary elements in the progression issuing from the absolute synthesis—but rather as individual items that may differ in specifiable ways from paradigms. It might seem that the ideas would make such comparisons possible, especially since Schelling claims that even in perception what is given is the idea plus a degree of imperfection that, as negation, is "nothing" (6:184). Be that as it may, in his philosophy of spirit Schelling insists that it is a mistake—indeed, the most fundamental mistake—to compare individuals in order to determine degrees of completeness or perfection.

The possibility of comparison of finite beings arises only after the beings exist as finite, so, only beneath the level of the ideas; the ideas themselves are the basis for the indirect position of finite beings, including the humans capable of arbitrary reflection. Each finite being is a necessary part within the coherent whole that results indirectly from the primal thesis, but the finite intellect is capable of grouping the things according to its whims and of abstracting universal concepts from the arbitrarily formed groups. The concepts are produced by the understanding, but since they are produced arbitrarily, they have no veridical relation to the things—or the ideas—themselves. The understanding may form, for example, a concept of the human being and include within the concept the capacity of sight as a human attribute; blindness is then taken to be a privation or defect. Schelling objects that such reasoning should also lead to the conclusion that the square is defective in not being round; that view would be reached if squares and circles were compared with respect to perfection, but it would wholly miss the truth of the square *qua* square. The situations are, according to Schelling, essentially the same: "as necessarily as it belongs to the essence of the square not to be round, just so necessarily does it belong . . . to the essence of the blind person that he does not see; for if his seeing were compatible with the order of nature, then he would actually see" (6:543).

This doctrine seems to make the essence unique to the individual, and thereby suggests that to each individual corresponds a unique idea. This raises the question whether Schelling's guiding notion is Platonic or Aristotelian. The Platonic notion is that a single form or idea is shared by many individuals; the Aristotelian notion is that the form—the primary substance—is unique to the individual. In earlier works, Schelling has endorsed Leibniz's version of Aristotelianism, according to which each form is a unique monad, and each monad, pre-

cisely as it is, is a necessary part within the whole. The doctrine of ideas from the system of identity, however, is not
clear. On the one hand, the constructive method relies on a
Platonic view, for Schelling can dialectically derive only types
of things, not individuals; on the other hand, Schelling's explanation of error—and thus of the merely apparent reality of human freedom—relies on a Leibnizian view. It is not surprising,
then, that Schelling tends to treat the ideas in Platonic fashion
at the beginning of his account and in Leibnizian fashion in the
later parts. In the part devoted to the philosophy of spirit, indeed, Schelling acknowledges his debt to Leibniz, but adds
that Leibniz did not fully understand his own teaching; if he
had, he would not have been concerned with the problem of
evil. Since all follows necessarily from the primal thesis—
since, in Leibnizian terms, all monads, with their perspectives,
are equally necessary within the whole—there is, in fact, no
evil in the world:

> So, for example, the desire and intention of harming others is
> considered, in man, to be *evil*, or something evil. But considered
> *in itself*, and if we look only to what is positive in the act, to the
> activity visible therein and so forth, in a word, if we consider the
> act *absolutely*, not in its relation to the subject, i.e., comparing
> the latter with a universal concept, or with other men, then we
> will perceive therein a sort of completeness, in no way an incom-
> pleteness. Even the fact that this activity is expressed only in
> what harms others is, considered in itself, no privation, for it be-
> longs to the nature of this man just as necessarily as its opposite
> does not. [6:544]

Schelling recognizes that his teaching seems to entail the denial of all moral distinctions. Since all things are perfect in
themselves, none would seem to be better or worse than any
others:

> Since God does not create things by comparing them to each
> other, but each for itself in a particular world, since he does not
> create them through common definitions, nothing is, before
> God, incomplete, and it may be said that the relatively lesser de-
> gree of completeness expressed by, for example, the stone in re-
> lation to the plant, the plant in relation to the animal, the animal
> in relation to the human, the worse human in relation to the bet-

ter, this relatively lesser degree of completeness is, with respect to the stone, the plant, the animal, the less noble man, precisely its completeness, precisely that through which it takes its place within creation and through which it can be an integrated part of it; that through which it is. [6:546–47]

Though in one sense degrees of completeness vanish, distinctions in the adequacy with which the absolute can know itself through different individuals—distinctions in the degrees of completeness of monads' representations—remain. With respect to human beings, the distinction is in terms of degrees of awareness of the world process as necessary and as a whole. Those who do not recognize what is right in the process, or who do not act in accordance with their knowledge of what is right, "comport themselves, to use Spinoza's expression, as tools in the hand of the artist, serving without knowing it, and being used up and worn out in serving. Those who act rightly, however, consciously do what is right and become, through serving, more complete" (6:547). Humans may thus be distinguished in terms of moral perfection, but the distinctions are not to be used as bases for judgment or reprobation, nor does justice require that they be so used; the latter is, according to Schelling, automatic:

For the one who acts wrongly, the lesser degree of reality expressed in him is itself the punishment. Absolutely considered, even he is necessary as a part of the world, and as such is not punishable, is even excusable. But the stone is also excusable for not being human, but is nonetheless damned to be stone and to suffer what a stone suffers. [6:547]

Schelling's doctrine thus purports to retain distinctions of good and evil, but it does so in such a way that the individual is freed from the burden of making moral decisions. The result, for the philosopher, is stoic equanimity, though, given that "the individual acts of will in the soul are always necessarily determined," it is not clear how the choice for stoicism could be made. However that may be, stoicism is both better and more admirable than the consternation that results from trying to obey, and to force others to obey, external and objective moral laws. Schelling's doctrine grounds "the true patience for thinking all things as contained within totality, and respecting all in their places." It does not ground "the desire to force all to submit to one law or to force the manifold of the divine creation, as exceptionally revealed in humanity, under a formula called moral law; this latter is the greatest possible madness, leading not to the calmness and peace that come from our doctrine, but rather either to dissatisfaction and futile struggles, such as those of our self-styled educators and improvers of the world, or else, finally, to indictment of the creator, whose infinite fullness is revealed in all degrees of perfection" (6:548).

Having thus denied all human freedom and, inconsistently, having taught that satisfaction is to be attained only through acceptance of that denial, Schelling proceeds almost immediately with what appears to be a retraction: the finitude of human beings as individuals, earlier asserted to be an indirect result of the absolute thesis and to be necessary to the revelation of the fullness of divine infinitude, is now said to result from a fall or defection from the absolute, from the primal sin of taking the finite realm to be the highest reality (6:552; *cf.* 3:589). The ground of possibility for this defection is not revealed, but the fall itself is presented as volitional and thus presupposes a sort of freedom at least prior to the fall. The new doctrine may be merely an attempt to provide a better account of the origin of finitude than that provided by the "indirect position" doctrine, but the fall doctrine could potentially develop into a treatment of human freedom.

As has been indicated, Schelling is in need of a doctrine of human freedom. Indeed, without such a doctrine his system must end by making his own philosophical activity senseless. The presentation of philosophical argument—or any other kind of argument—makes sense only on the presupposition that those who encounter the argument may be convinced by it, not that they be caused to change their minds by predetermined necessity, but that they be led to do so by the cogency of the argument itself. Schelling seeks to convince those who teach that the absolute must be a moral god, and especially those who might otherwise be misled by such charlatans, that his is the true teaching; he thus assumes a sort of freedom in his audience that his system itself denies. The fall doctrine could be the basis for development of an account of such freedom, but it is not so used in the 1804 *System,* and Schelling continues, having introduced it, to insist upon full determination within the human realm.

As has been shown, Schelling denies that any conscious or willful attempt to act morally can lead to truly moral behavior, because such attempts are in essence perverse, resulting at best in the subjugation of spirit—in itself subordinate to nothing—to the moral law. The highest moral attitude, true religiosity or heroism, requires no such law:

> *Religion* is higher than devotion or feeling. The first signification of this often misused word is conscientiousness; it is the expression of the highest unity of knowing and doing, which makes impossible any contradiction between knowing and acting. A man for whom this is impossible not humanly, psychically, or psychologically, but rather divinely, is called religious or conscientious in the highest sense of the word. He is not conscientious who, for example, must first hold the command of duty before himself and determine himself to act rightly only through respect for the law. He who is conscientious does not need this; it is for him not *possible* to act in a way other than the right way. Religiosity means, according to the term's origin, a boundness of action, in no way a choice between opposed options, such as that which is assumed in the case of free will; not an *aequilibrium arbitrii,* as it is called, but rather the highest determination for the right, without choice. [6:558]

Insofar as it is suggested at all in the 1804 *System,* existential freedom is purely negative, for it implies an acting that is not correspondent to knowing: knowing, in the true sense, can be only of the eternal or divine, and action in accord with such knowledge is always right. As in "On the Ego," Schelling teaches that theory is prior to practice insofar as ethical goodness is concerned. To know the truth is to be unable to act badly. The individual thus achieves completeness through knowledge, but the absolute knows itself in the whole, not in the individual as such. The *System* closes with the assertion, minimally developed, that the highest point for the whole is the perfect state, incorporating the three realms in which the absolute fully expresses itself, those of art, religion, and science (6:575).

In the 1804 *System* Schelling reaches a point of systematic culmination, but he does not reach it through compelling or even consistent argumentation. The problem of the development of finitude, presented as early as 1797 as unavoidable and as demanding solution, is not only not solved, but is treated in three irreconcilable ways. Schelling first teaches that the finite is indirectly posited through necessary determinate negation of the infinite, but he later attributes responsibility to the ideas themselves: they are capable of "falling from grace." In a final twist near the end of the text, a third creation doctrine enters, one attributing direct responsibility for the finite to God himself: "This is the greatest secret of the universe, that the finite *as finite* can and should become like the infinite; God gives the ideas of the things that are in him over into finitude so that they can, through eternal reconciliation, be eternally in him *as* self-sufficient, as having life in themselves" (6:575). This passage recalls also the second crucial difficulty arising in the 1804 *System*, the problem of freedom. The moral "can and should" applied by Schelling to finite entities is truly applicable to them only if they are free, only if they are capable of choosing to act either as they should or otherwise. Schelling, who in his youth presents freedom as "the beginning and end of philosophy," as a condition for the possibility of human consciousness itself, as equally necessary to theory and to practice, comes to deny that man is free at all, without developing the implications that denial has for the philosophical endeavor itself. Yet he is not ignorant of those implications; his awareness of the problem of freedom, even as he worked on the strictly scientific presentation of the system of identity, is revealed in the dialogic works composed during the same period. It is to them that we must now turn.

4 FROM SYSTEM TO PROJECT

While working on his scientifically structured expositions of the system of identity, Schelling wrote other works that, while not as methodologically rigorous, were designed to communicate more effectively the system's central teachings. Most important among the nonscientific works are the dialogic works *Bruno* (1802; 4:213–332), "Philosophy and Religion" (1804; 6:11–70), and *Philosophical Investigations concerning the Essence of Human Freedom and Related Subjects* (1809; 7:331–416). Though only the first of these is presented as a discussion among individuals, Schelling asserts that "Philosophy and Religion" is a sequel to *Bruno* and that it would be more intelligible had he had time to put it into dialogue form (6:13); he also maintains that the *Freedom* essay, which develops "conversationally," is a dialogue in essence if not in superficial form (7:410*n*). These three "dialogues" thus constitute a series that is in at least formal opposition to the three strictly scientific works. A second difference between the two groups of writings is revealed in Schelling's retrospective evaluations of them. He clearly believes that the scientific works are progressively worse than one another, for he consistently presents the first, the *Exhibition*, as the best; he rarely mentions the *Further Exhibitions* in later works; and he never even published the 1804 *System*. While Schelling thus takes the quality of the scientific works to diminish, he sees each dialogic work as improving upon its predecessor. He presents the last, the *Freedom* essay, as the first truly authoritative exposition of the ideal part of the system of identity; according to the *Freedom* essay, the only previous work to have treated similar problems is "Philosophy and Religion," which is described as formally obscure and consequently ineffective (7:333–34). The *Freedom* essay is the explicit sequel to "Philosophy and Religion," and the latter is the sequel to *Bruno*; but the *Freedom* essay contains no reference to *Bruno*. While there are threads that may be picked up in the first two dialogic works, then, Schelling teaches that we should expect to see where those threads lead only in the essay on human freedom.

BRUNO AND "PHILOSOPHY AND RELIGION"

One central flaw preventing Schelling's strictly scientific works from fulfilling his project is their failure to provide an unequivocal and defensible account of the "descent from infinite to finite." In the 1804 *System,* three conflicting creation doctrines are introduced but not compared; two of these, the teachings that the finite results indirectly from the divine positing of the ideas and that the finite is created by God so that it may become infinite through its own efforts, are introduced for the first time in the *System.* The third, according to which the finite is itself responsible for its fall from the absolute, is suggested in the *System of Transcendental Idealism* (3:589) and is not in conflict with the undeveloped suggestion in the *Exhibition* that it is man as finite who is responsible for apparent finitude. A variant of this teaching is developed in the dialogic works, starting with *Bruno*:

> In that highest unity, which we take to be the holy abyss from which all proceeds and into which all returns, with respect to which essence is also form, form also essence, we posit first, to be sure, absolute infinitude and—not opposed to it, but simply correspondent, sufficient, not limiting the infinitude and not limited by it—the timelessly present and infinite finite, both as one thing, itself distinguishable and distinct only in what appears, in truth fully one but conceptually different, like thinking and being, ideal and real. . . .
>
> Because however the finite, although *really* fully like the infinite, nevertheless does not cease to be *ideally* finite, there is in that unity itself the difference of all forms, in themselves not separate from the indifference, and thus with respect to themselves not distinguishable, yet contained in such a way that *each can take for itself its own life and,* to be sure ideally, *can go over into a separate existence.* [4:258; italics added]

As he does in the scientific works, Schelling insists that the absolute contains a multiplicity of forms, but that the forms are therein indifferentiable. Yet with the positing of the forms as infinite, the possibility of finitude also arises. If the move from this possibility to factical actuality is to be a narrowing, that is, if mere possibility is not to be the sufficient condition for actuality (as it would be, for example, according to the "indirect position" teaching), then there must be a further factor determining which of the possibilities are actualized. In *Bruno*, the additional factor is the volition of the potentially finite: "everything that seems to emerge or free itself from [the absolute] is, in it, determined with respect to its possibility of being for itself, but the actuality of its separate existence lies only in itself, and takes place merely ideally,[1] and as ideal only to the extent that a thing, in accord with its mode of being in the absolute, is made capable of being, itself, unity" (4:282). As is suggested above in the consideration of the 1804 *System*, this account has the advantage of providing the basis for a doctrine of human freedom. However, it thereby introduces an element of indeterminacy into the process and thus endangers the enterprise of philosophical construction: if there is a multiplicity of ideas, each of which may or may not "turn away" from the absolute and thereby enter into a finite temporal process, then it would seem to be impossible to construct *a priori* the movement from infinite to finite or the movement within the finite realm itself. The problem is one that arises in the 1800 *System*; there, Schelling claims that divine self-reflection is tantamount to self-limitation, but also that some of the specifics of the limitation are determinable only after the fact. A similar threat to the constructive project arises in *Bruno*, and the threat must arise with

1. Schelling's distinction between real and ideal is not consistently drawn. He uses it at times as if it were parallel to that between object and subject, at other times to that between nature and spirit, and at others to that between being and thinking. In *Bruno*, especially in the cited passages from 4:258 and 4:282, the sense of the terms is as follows: "real" refers to the highest reality, that of the absolute and of the ideas, whereas "ideal" refers to finite or merely apparent existence. Since, according to Bruno, the finite exists only because of the activity of the subject, of finite spirit, and since its apparent reality results from the way it is thought, its designation as "ideal" does not contradict Schelling's other uses of the term. While all of Schelling's uses of the ideal-real distinction are related, they are not all identical; to understand what Schelling means by the terms in any given case, the reader must consider the specific context.

any creation doctrine teaching that there is a narrowing from infinite possibility to finite actuality; if the factor responsible for the narrowing is inaccessible to the philosopher, then the step cannot be reconstructed.

The threat to the constructive project is not recognized in *Bruno*. Indeed, Bruno (who represents Schelling in the dialogue) fully convinces his interlocutor, Lucian (a follower of Fichte),[2] that the construction is completely successful; Lucian is led to reject his earlier Fichteanism. Following Lucian's conversion, Bruno leads him to admit that even a system satisfying the demands of the Fichtean project would fail to satisfy the demands of philosophy; Lucian agrees that "a philosophy grounded in [knowledge on Fichte's level] will completely exhibit the contents [*Inbegriff*] of common consciousness, and be totally in accord with it, without—for just that reason—being philosophy at all" (4:327). Schelling here charges, through Bruno, that the truths of Fichte's system, although unobjectionable on their own terms, provide only a relative knowledge. That system is, according to Schelling, grounded in the insight that to be is to be for a conscious subject. Since the subject is then a necessary condition for any and everything, it is a ground, but since it takes itself to be dependent upon external entities, it is not immediately aware of itself as absolute. If in addition the assumption is made that no more fundamental ground is accessible—and Lucian, as a Fichtean, had made this assumption—then absoluteness is a practical demand for the subject, not a theoretical reality. The philosopher seeking the absolute must thus attempt to subordinate all to the empirical subject, making the non-ego mere means to the ego's ends and thereby presenting a false view of nature (6:326). Since, moreover, the grounding subject in Fichte's system is the thinking individual, it is not absolute (4:325): the practical doctrine that truly follows from Fichte's principles is that each subject should demand subordination of all to himself, each

2. Lucian's phrasing identifies him as a Fichtean: in 1794, Fichte criticizes Spinoza for taking the unjustified step "beyond the pure consciousness that is given in grounded consciousness" (p. 101). Lucian uses the same phrase (4:253), and Schelling later repeats the phrase when criticizing Fichte (*see* 4:353–55).

should strive to become a tyrant. Schelling rejects these results, basing his rejection on the argument that philosophy's
fundamental principle must ground a doctrine that is fully defensible against charges of relativism. He would acknowledge
as satisfying this demand only a system deriving the world as
experienced from an indeterminate absolute by means of a
fully *a priori* construction. Such a construction would have to
begin with the descent from infinite to finite and, although Lucian accepts Bruno's account of the descent, that account
seems to rule out the possibility of any subsequent construction.

In the essay "Philosophy and Religion," which is presented
as the sequel to *Bruno*, the dialogue's teaching concerning the
descent from infinite to finite is explicitly reaffirmed (6:28–29).
That teaching, according to which the absolute grounds the
possibility of the finite while the latter grounds its own actuality, is, however, presented as fully intelligible only within the
realm of practical philosophy. This indicates that the published
scientific works cannot have adequately explained Schelling's
true creation doctrine because, as he notes, those works cover
only the theoretical, the philosophy of nature. Schelling promises to present his true teaching in "Philosophy and Religion"
(6:29).

In the essay, Schelling continues to rely generally on the
principles of the *Exhibition* and the other scientific works: the
world process is to be grasped as resulting from "the self-sufficient self-knowing of the simply ideal"; since self-knowing is
self-objectification, every ideal act of the absolute has a real—
objective—product, such that there is an "eternal transforma-
tion of pure ideality into reality" (6:34). The process would be
completed only if the posited reality were fully like the positing ideality. If such likeness is to result, Schelling now asserts,
the absolute's products, the ideas, must possess the fundamental characteristic of the absolute itself, they must be capable of spontaneously objectifying themselves: "The absolute
would not be truly objective in [the ideas] if it did not communicate to [them] the power of transforming [their own] ideality into reality and objectifying [themselves] in particular
forms" (6:35). The ideas are themselves generative, and there
results a "transcendental theogony," a process resulting from

a creation in which what is created or generated "is dependent upon the generator, but nevertheless self-sufficient" (6:35), capable of independent—and thus free—generative activity. At first, Schelling asserts that the process can be one only of "theogony": only infinite beings, only additional ideas, can develop within it. Since it cannot lead directly to the finite, the latter can result neither from emanation nor from direct or indirect position; rather,

> the origin of the world of the senses is thinkable only as a complete breaking off from absoluteness through a leap. . . . The absolute is the only reality, the finite things are not real; their ground thus cannot lie in a communication [*Mitteilung*] of reality from the absolute to them or to their substrate, it can lie only in a *distancing*, in a *fall* from the absolute.[6:38]

Since this teaching becomes crucial in a work titled "Philosophy and Religion," and since the notion of a fall of man is often associated with Judeo-Christian doctrines, it must be stressed that Schelling considers himself to be following not that religious tradition, but rather the philosophical teachings of Plato and the pagan religion of the Eleusinian mysteries. He compares his God to the divine artificer of Plato's *Timaeus* who, being good, is not envious, and who therefore attempts to make his products as much like himself as possible. Schelling differs from Plato in explicitly insisting that the "products" are therefore created so as to be capable of autonomous activity, so as to be free; he distances himself further from the *Timaeus* by criticizing Plato's reliance in that dialogue on a preexistent matter, which resists the formative workings of the artificer, to explain the imperfections visible in the finite realm. According to Schelling, this sort of dualism represents the "rawest attempt" to explain the origin of the finite and does not express Plato's true teaching, the doctrine that the soul falls from the ideal realm; this true teaching is presented in the "more authentically Platonic works, the *Phaedo*, the *Republic*, etc." (6:36). It is noteworthy that the "indirect position" doctrine presented in the *System* of 1804—the year in which "Philosophy and Religion" was published—relies in part on the Timaean sort of

raw metaphysics. There, Schelling asserts that "infinite substance beams its essence into nothingness or the *me on;* but because of the *impotentia recipiendi Deum,* absolute identity can
appear in it only in the form of indifference or of synthesis"
(6:229).

In "Philosophy and Religion," the autonomy of the ideas
takes the place of the inability of nothingness to perfectly reflect God. The divergence from the fundamental teachings of
the 1804 *System* is profound:

> The peculiarity exclusive to the absolute is that it endows its an-
> tithesis [the ideas] with its own self-sufficiency along with its
> own essence. This being-in-itself, this authentic and true reality
> of what is first intuited, is *freedom,* and from that first self-suffi-
> ciency of the antithesis flows forth what appears again in the
> world of appearance as freedom, there as the last trace and at the
> same time the seal of divinity visible in the fallen world. The an-
> tithesis, as an absolute that has all properties in common with
> the first, would not be truly absolute and in itself were it not able
> to grasp itself in its selfhood, in order truly to be the *other* abso-
> lute. But it cannot be as the *other* absolute without thereby sepa-
> rating itself from the true absolute, or falling from it. [6:39–40]

The ideas, as created by the absolute, are an "other absolute"
in that they are perfectly unified in their infinitude; but they
exist as absolute only to the extent that they act as the absolute
itself has acted, that is, only insofar as they are creative. Despite his earlier insistence that the ideas can produce only
ideas, and thus that they do not forsake the infinite realm
(6:35), Schelling now asserts that the idea's attempt to create is
necessarily a turning away from the first absolute, a negation
of it, and thus a fall. It is the fallen realm that, he now claims,
is the locus of the dialectical development of powers; the highest power is visible in the ego.

As the most complete development of otherness, the ego is
at the furthest remove from the absolute itself, but at the same
time, precisely because it is the most complete development, it
contains the possibility for complete transfiguration into a
new, fully articulated absoluteness. It is through the ego,

through the ego's move from understanding to reason, that the absolute can finally come to know itself (6:42):

> Reason and selfhood [*Ichheit*], in their *true* absoluteness, are one and the same, and while this is the point at which the replica [of the absolute] reaches its highest being for itself, it is at the same time the point where, *within* the fallen world itself, the original produces itself, where those celestial forces, the ideas, are reconciled and let themselves down into temporality in science, art, and the ethical activity of mankind. The great intent of the universe and of its history is nothing other than the complete reconciliation, reabsorption into absoluteness. [6:43]

Although this doctrine is at best vaguely suggested in the *Exhibition*'s teaching that human reflection is responsible for finitude but also capable of rising above it, Schelling hints that it has guided him, at least implicitly, all along: "The significance of a philosophy that makes the principle of the sinful fall, expressed in its highest universality, its own principle, even if it does so unconsciously, cannot be overvalued" (6:43).

The consideration of the fallen world is a part of the philosopher's task, but that consideration does not immediately yield the truth; rather, it provides for the individual a *via negativa* to the ideas themselves. The consideration of the finite "can have only a negative philosophy as its result, but much is won when the negative, the realm of nothingness, is distinguished from the realm of reality and the sole positivity by a clear boundary, since the latter can beam forth again only after the separation" (6:43). The philosopher has access to the ideas, not immediately, but only through the "negation of the negation" of the merely finite (6:45). Though the immediate results of the fall are negative, the fall itself is necessary to the divine self-revelation:

> Just as the final intention of history is the reconciliation of the fallen, so too, the fall itself can now be viewed in a more positive light. For the first selfhood of the ideas flowed forth from the immediate effect of God: the selfhood and absoluteness that they introduce through the reconciliation is however *self-given*, so that they are self-sufficiently in the absolute, irrespective of its absoluteness; in this way, the fall becomes the means to the *complete* manifestation of God. [6:63]

"Philosophy and Religion" attributes to the finite an essential role in the process of divine self-revelation and establishes the potential for a science of the finite; yet that science is merely "negative." The highest science would have to be of the ideas, but Schelling has yet to indicate how such a science might be possible. Even in his account of their function in the whole, Schelling contradicts himself, asserting first that ideas can create only ideas, but later making them responsible for finitude. Further, in asserting now that we have access to the ideas only through the "negation of the negation" of finitude, he seems to make knowledge of them posterior to philosophical understanding of the finite. Finally, in insisting now that created beings must necessarily be free, Schelling makes the *a priori* reconstruction of the finite realm, at least in its historical totality, impossible: entities that are free are known only through what they do, not through what they are. For these reasons, neither of Schelling's sciences is clearly grounded: it is not clear how there could be a science of the ideas in their ineffable infinitude, and it is not clear how events resulting from free choices could be reconstructed *a priori*.

The difficulties visible in each of Schelling's two major works of 1804—even independent of the difficulties that arise when the two are compared—reveal that the system of identity cannot be completed. Yet Schelling does not acknowledge immediately that the difficulties are inherent in the system and, in the five years that separate "Philosophy and Religion" from the *Freedom* essay, he publishes works in which the conflict between his demands for freedom and for necessity continues to grow. In a polemic directed against Fichte, he insists upon the importance of his "speculative theory of freedom," which is grounded in a "true Platonic fall," and accuses Fichte of plagiarizing that theory (7:82–83). But he does not cease to insist that all follows from God: "If (*per impossibile*) no nature existed for me, or if I could posit it as negated, and if I then thought God truly and with living clarity, then, in the same instant, I would have to be impregnated with the actual world (this is the sense of the oft-misunderstood identity of the ideal and the real)" (7:31). In an aphorism, he goes even further in asserting that all in the finite realm is predetermined:

Rational knowing strives to resolve all that is, as individual, in the clarity and evidence of $A = A$. To the normal mode of consideration of things, the sentence, for example, "The air is dissolving into rain [die Luft löst sich eben in Regen auf; i.e., it is just beginning to rain]," would have to be seen as expressing the most contingent possible connection. I can never derive the concept of water from that of air, nor the concept of its now raining from that of the present moment. Therefore, it is said, the sentence is synthetic. But if we observe this condition of nature not abstractly, but rather in its relation to the unity of substance and to its life in the whole of the world, then we conceive in general how even it follows therefrom, and if we were able to see the whole from our standpoint, then we would certainly see that, for example, if it were not now raining, the harmony of the universe would be disturbed, the $A = A$ would have been destroyed. [7:219–20]

The development through which the conflict between freedom and necessity becomes the central one in Schelling's system has now been considered in some detail. A brief summary of that development will insure that the detail has not served finally to obscure. The complex of problems centers on the individual human subject. In Schelling's first gropings toward a well-defined project, it will be recalled, central to his concern is the subjectivity of the subject: it is by presenting the individual as free that Schelling first hopes to surpass Spinoza. Insistence on the importance of the individual *qua* individual, especially in the period when Leibniz's influence leads Schelling to distinguish individuals in terms of their equally necessary perspectives on the whole, leads to the doctrine that there must be a multiplicity of philosophical systems. Were this the case, then of course Schelling's system could be no absolute improvement on that of Spinoza. Indeed, Schelling realizes, his system will be significantly distinguishable from Spinoza's only if he can succeed in deriving content from the absolute. When Leibniz and Fichte then suggest to him a way in which the derivation could be accomplished, the derivation replaces the account of the individual as the focal point of the system. And since the derivation or construction must be claimed to be, if valid at all, universally valid, Schelling concludes that there can be but one philosophical system, and that the uniqueness of the individual's perceptions produces error rather than idiosyncratic truth (see 5:4, 106; 6:140; 7:42). The true system, the *one* true system, will be the universally valid system of identity.

Within the system of identity, the individual as such—not merely the human individual—arises again as problematic in a different way. Only to the extent that an individual, in the specifics of its individuality, is necessary to the whole can it be constructed by the philosopher within the whole. At the same time, no individual can be immediately necessary *qua* individual, or the absolute would be relative to the individual or dependent on it and would thus cease to be absolute. Recognizing the danger, Schelling usually attempts to mediate finite and infinite by introducing the ideas, which he presents as inseparable within the absolute yet somehow distinguishable to those who have no access to the absolute itself. Problems continue to arise concerning the relations of the individuals to the ideas and of the ideas among themselves. The individuals are at times presented as imperfect copies of the ideas (see 6:184); at other times, since "God does not create according to universal concepts," they are perfect in themselves (7:160, 182, 187–88, 220). The ideas are generally presented as complete in themselves, but Schelling suggests at least once that they would be empty if there were no individuals (7:56). Even if the mediating role of the ideas were fully explained, the problem of human freedom would remain. While the constructive method assumes that there is no freedom, the constructive project makes sense as a chosen alternative only if human freedom is real. Perhaps more important, if Schelling denies the reality of freedom, he thereby repeats what he once saw as Spinoza's fundamental error. The problem of freedom, along with the others listed here, necessarily arises within the system of identity, but it at least remains insoluble within it. The problems are serious enough that they should force Schelling to reconsider the requirements of producing an antithesis to Spinoza; they should force him to reconsider his project.

Excursus: The Impact of Hegel's "Phenomenology of Spirit" of 1807 All the works considered so far were written within the twelve-year period from 1794 through 1806. Following 1806, Schelling ceases to publish almost entirely: the only major work still to appear in his lifetime is the ninety-page *Freedom* essay of 1809. In that essay, Schelling draws attention to most of the problems that develop within the system of identity. My account of their development is intended to lend credence to the thesis that there are good philosophical grounds for Schelling's abandonment of the system of identity, and thus for his ensuing silence. Since, however, Schelling's cessation of publication is roughly contemporaneous with the appearance of Hegel's *Phenomenology of Spirit* of 1807, and since the Preface of that work is taken by many to contain a critique that demolishes the system of identity, the *Phenomenology* is often presented as responsible for Schelling's silence. That responsibility is questionable: Hegel's critique is indirect, and Schelling never acknowledges its effectiveness. When the *Phenomenology* was published, Hegel sent a copy to Schelling, with whom he had resumed correspondence shortly before. In his accompanying letter, Hegel notes that the passages that seem to refer obliquely to Schelling—none mention him by name—are aimed at those who have misinterpreted the system of identity and not at Schelling's own teachings. In his response—his final letter to Hegel, one that was never answered—Schelling acknowledges and agrees with Hegel's admission that nothing in the *Phenomenology*'s Preface threatens his own system, but he also notes that it might have been better had Hegel gone to the trouble of mentioning the fact publicly, in the *Phenomenology* itself, rather than merely in the private letter.[3] Regardless of what Hegel and Schelling wrote in their letters, of course, it could be that both actually saw in Hegel's arguments an effective critique of the system of identity. To determine the extent of the critique's influence on Schelling, then, we must consider its main points.

Hegel first suggests that Schelling's development is formal-

3. *Briefe von und an Hegel*, vol. 1. Hegel's letter to Schelling is on pp. 159–62; Schelling's response is on p. 194.

istic,[4] but, while some of Schelling's discussions of his *A*s and *B*s give the impression that he will apply them to any and all contents, Schelling never admits that his method is formalistic, and he never alters it so as to make it less vulnerable to that charge. Whether or not the charge is justified, then, it never had any influence on Schelling. Hegel next ridicules the presentation of the absolute as "the night in which all cows are black," but since Schelling himself often characterizes the absolute, in itself, as night (see 2:66; 4:278; 6:154) and is seriously concerned with its relation to light and to determination, Hegel's remark would likely have struck him as superficial: it refers to a problem long recognized by Schelling and taken by him to demand solution rather than avoidance. Again, Hegel's remark cannot have influenced Schelling significantly, for the latter never changes his treatment of the absolute in such a way that it would have ceased to be, for Hegel, darkest night. Hegel's own suggestion for better understanding the absolute follows immediately after the "all cows are black" statement in the famous programmatic demand that philosophy's highest principle be recognized as "subject as well as substance."[5] This would not have appeared to Schelling as an advance beyond his own position: "subject and substance" simply reformulates "subject-object," and it is by presenting the absolute as subject-object that Schelling attempts to avoid the problems inherent in Fichte's purely subjective principle.

That the passages in Hegel's Preface apparently directed at Schelling did not greatly influence the latter is indicated by the fact that Schelling never changes his doctrines to protect them from Hegel's objections. Nor is the project of the *Phenomenology* itself likely to have seemed to Schelling to make his system of identity obsolete: the *Phenomenology* ends with the absolute, and if the *Phenomenology* is merely propaedeutic to the science of the absolute—and Hegel insists that it is—then it falls in a class of arguments none of which, Schelling is convinced, can be either unique or compelling (5:215; 6:154, 199). Though He-

4. G.W.F. Hegel, *Phänomenologie des Geistes*, pp. 18, 41–42. Translated by A.V. Miller as *Phenomenology of Spirit*, pp. 8–9, 29–30.

5. *Phänomenologie*, p. 19 (*Phenomenology*, p. 10).

gel suggests that Schelling introduces his absolute too abruptly—it appears "as though from a pistol"[6]—Schelling remains convinced, as in the "Letters," that "we would all agree concerning the absolute if we never left its sphere," that only with the move beyond the absolute can philosophical conflict begin (1:294). The question here is not whether Hegel is right in his criticisms, but whether he thereby influenced Schelling; Schelling's own career provides evidence that he did not. The importance of the *Phenomenology* as a cause of Schelling's rejection of the system of identity must thus be taken to be minimal. Sufficient ground for that rejection is contained in the system's own conflicting doctrines.[7]

THE *FREEDOM* ESSAY

In presenting an essay entitled *Philosophical Investigations concerning the Essence of Human Freedom and Related Subjects*, Schelling appears to have forsaken the system of identity entirely. According to the strictly scientific 1804 *System*, human freedom is an illusion and is therefore not worthy of serious philosophical treatment. Nevertheless, Schelling presents the *Freedom* essay as the first authoritative account of the philosophy of spirit, the final part of the system of identity. Since the 1804 *System* had not been published, Schelling could assert that his only previous work treating spirit from the standpoint of the system of identity was "Philosophy and Religion," a piece whose formal obscurity hinders its full appreciation (7:333–34; cf. 7:409n2). Schelling insists that the systematic standpoint is also the standpoint of the *Freedom* essay: the essay is neither a rejection nor even an unforeseen development of the original project, but is rather the part that Schelling has always known would complete the whole. Only external circumstances—

6. *Phänomenologie*, p. 26 (*Phenomenology*, p. 16).

7. Hegel considers Schelling's early teachings in much more detail in his *Lectures on the History of Philosophy*. His treatment there is generally fair, though he presents Schelling's *Freedom* essay as a narrow analysis of a limited problem, rather than as the reflection on first philosophy that it actually is. Heidegger notes this shortcoming in *Schellings Abhandlung*, p. 15.

which are not explained—prevented the earlier publication of the essay's teachings.

Schelling presents the *Freedom* essay as an essential part of the system of identity: it not only completes the system, but it also reveals the system's highest level and thereby clarifies the account of the absolute and the philosophy of nature, neither of which, Schelling admits, is fully intelligible in isolation from it. The *Freedom* essay is a "piece of the whole," in harmony with the earlier scientific works, yet it also "transfigures" those works and reveals their true significance (7:333–35). The essay transfigures the system by revealing its fundamental difficulty. The earlier systematic writings overcome a preliminary difficulty: by establishing the essential identity of subject and object, they overcome the opposition between nature and spirit, and thereby show natural scientists the way to dynamic physics. While the overcoming of the nature-spirit opposition thus solves a problem for the physicist, it reveals to the philosopher a more basic problem, indeed, the most basic problem: "It is time that the higher or, better, the authentic opposition step forth, that of necessity and freedom; with this opposition, the innermost central point of philosophy first comes into view" (7:333).

Schelling presents the *Freedom* essay as a part of the system of identity, yet he introduces it as the treatment of a problem that the system of identity cannot recognize. He also indirectly criticizes the form of his strictly scientific works by describing the Spinozist form of presentation as "insensitive" (7:349). From the beginning of the essay, there is tension between it and the scientific works, and though Schelling does not acknowledge that tension, that is not to say that he was not aware of it. Professing to be disturbed by misinterpretations of his earlier works, Schelling practices, in the *Freedom* essay, conscious esotericism: much could be more clearly expressed, he admits, but he would rather be unintelligible than be misunderstood (7:409n2; *cf.* 7:334). While the essay's title may make the work attractive to general readers, the obscurity of its doctrines—an intentional obscurity—makes the text itself forbidding. Its inaccessibility is increased by the absence (unusual in a work by Schelling) of titled or numbered sections. The structure of the work is therefore not immediately apparent, but remarks within the text indicate that it contains two major sections: the "real investigation" of freedom is presented in the final three-fourths of the essay (7:357–416), following an introduction devoted to the clarification of some crucial concepts that Schelling claims are often misunderstood (7:357).

The Introduction

Schelling begins his introduction by asserting that the problem of freedom can be treated neither in isolation from nor as subordinate to any other philosophical issue: if freedom is worthy of philosophical treatment at all, that is, if it is real, then it must be "one of the ruling central points of the system" (7:336). Yet, according to a common belief, there can be a philosophical system only if the world itself is a system so complete and closed as to leave no room for anything as essentially indeterminate as freedom. Schelling asserts that the problem is not insoluble: an infinite intellect would be able to account for freedom systematically. He insists also that even if human reason, in its finitude, cannot develop the absolute knowledge in which freedom and necessity are reconciled, no argument will ever overcome the philosophical desire for such knowledge (7:337):

> The connection of the concept of freedom with the entirety of a world view will certainly remain the object of a necessary task, without solution to which the concept of freedom itself would be tenuous, and philosophy wholly worthless. For it is this great task alone that is the unconscious and invisible impetus for all striving for knowledge, from the lowest to the highest; without the contradiction of necessity and freedom, not only philosophy but every higher willing of spirit would sink into the death found in those sciences in which it has no application. [7:338]

In this final work treating the system of identity, Schelling thus resurrects one of his earliest and longest-abandoned teachings: the successful system must account for freedom, for it must not deny the subjectivity of the human subject. To deny either freedom or system—and with it, necessarily, reason—or to affirm one without the other is, Schelling now insists, to ignore rather than to solve the problem.

If the problem of freedom is to be faced, Schelling continues, it must first be more clearly stated. He clarifies it in terms suggested by Friedrich Schlegel but which express a common opinion: "the only rational system that is possible is pantheism, which is, unavoidably, fatalism" (7:338); all can be explained only if all is predetermined. Through consideration of various possible significations of "pantheism"—various sorts of doctrines teaching "the immanence of things in God"—Schelling develops the argument that the problem is common to all systems, that it is not restricted to those that are pantheistic in any narrow sense. The problem of fatalism arises not with pantheism, but rather with misinterpretation of the law of identity—presented in the *Exhibition* as the basic law for all things as they truly are—and of the function of the copula in judgments. Statements of the form "*S* is *P*" do not, according to Schelling, express either full oneness or even immediate connection of subject and predicate. The true signification of such statements is revealed in six examples, for each of which the incorrect as well as the correct reading is given. First to be considered is the trivial and contingent assertion "This body is blue." According to Schelling, this example presents no difficulties: no one would be likely to insist that it means "In and through what makes it body, the body is also blue" rather than, correctly, "That which is the body is, although not in the same respect, also blue." The principle clearly visible in this first example is not, Schelling continues, so apparent in sentences of other sorts, where the complexity of content introduces the danger of misinterpretation. "The complete is the incomplete," the second example, would be taken by most of Schelling's contemporaries to express the indifferentiability of subject and predicate and, by extension, the sameness of "the worst and the best, foolishness and wisdom." In fact, the judgment states that "The incomplete is, not through itself, but rather through the completeness that is in it." Similarly, "The good is the evil" expresses, not a negation or denial of the distinction between the two, but rather the fact that "The evil does not have the power of being through itself; that in it which is, is (considered in and for itself) the good" (7:342).

Schelling's fourth and fifth examples are not given in the "S is P" form, but are said to be nonetheless identities subject to the two opposed sorts of reading that have become visible. The examples are judgments that express the oneness of the necessary and the free and of the body and the soul. Misinterpreted, the former may seem to state that freedom, like all other phenomena, is subject to the laws of mechanical causality; similarly, the latter, improperly read, seems to say that the soul is nothing more than an amalgam of such material parts as air, ether, and neural fluids. In either case, it would make as much logical sense to reverse the relationship and reduce necessity to freedom and body to soul; but this, according to Schelling, is not often done. Be that as it may, it is true that "the essence of the ethical world is also the essence of nature" and, we may assume, that in essence body and soul are one. Schelling's final example is the apparent tautology "The body is body." If anything at all is hereby expressed, or even thought, it is not mere sameness, but rather the difference between the body as unity (subject) and its many parts and properties (predicate).

In each of his examples, Schelling insists—and takes himself to be true to the logic of the Greeks in so doing—that the subject is related to the predicate as antecedent is to consequent or as the implicit or involute is to the explicit or developed. Yet the logical illustrations serve, typically, more to obscure than to support the point Schelling seeks to make. The conclusion needed for the larger argument of the essay is that identity entails duplicity, and Schelling attempts to establish this by showing that all judgments, including apparent tautologies, actually express relations of ground to consequent. That alone would be difficult to prove, but Schelling makes matters worse by identifying ground with subject and consequent with predicate; these identifications are impossible even with his own examples. The problems are clearest with the structurally identical fourth and fifth examples. If put into judgmental form, either would require two or perhaps three terms; the fourth would require "body," "soul," and perhaps also "one." If only the two terms are used, then the judgment is, in Schelling's final analysis, false: "The body is the soul" would illicitly ground soul in body, whereas the converse would as one-sidedly ground body in soul. "One is soul and body" would meet the requirements of Schellingian analysis, whereas the grammatically correct "Soul and body are one" would not. What Schelling takes to be the true relation of soul and body is expressible in a simple judgment only if the judgment is analyzed according to the principle Schelling identifies in his first example; that principle would allow the reading, "That which is soul is, although not in the same respect, also body." Here, however, the true Schellingian subject—the ground that the predicate explicates—is not named at all: it is the presumed "essence" in which body and soul are one, that which is in one respect soul, in another, body. Correspondingly, neither soul nor body is ground, neither is antecedent, neither is explicated.

If Schelling recognizes that his logical analysis of the judgmental form is problematical, he does not express his misgivings. Rather, he takes the analysis to reveal the truth of the law or principle of identity: "This principle does not express a unity that merely revolves within a sphere of self-sameness, one that would not be progressive and therefore would be itself insensitive and inanimate. The unity of this law is immediately generative" (7:345). Were this logical conclusion taken in the broadest possible sense, such that it asserted merely that even tautologous judgments distinguish subject from predicate, it would perhaps be unobjectionable. Schelling, however, moves immediately and without visible warrant from the stronger and unsupported logical claim to a metaphysical assertion; he reasons from the logical principle, "The law of ground is as primordial as that of identity," to the metaphysical tenet, "The eternal must be, as itself, also ground" (7:346).

Having proceeded in the course of his terminological clarifications from the notion of identity to that of ground, Schelling next considers the nature of grounding as such. He reasserts a teaching introduced but not fully explained in "Philosophy and Religion": the grounded is dependent upon the ground, but it may be dependent in one way while self-sufficient in others: "[Dependence] does not determine essence; it says only that the dependent, whatever it might be, can only be as following from that upon which it depends; it does not say what it is and what it is not" (7:346; *cf.* pp. 97–99 above). Schelling's argument for this interpretation of grounding is analogical rather than analytic, presenting four cases purported to exhibit, in different ways, dependents that are not entirely subordinated to that upon which they depend. First, he notes that in cases of organic generation the offspring are dependent upon their parents for their existence, but are nonetheless separate individuals; if they were not, there would be a dependency with no dependent, and no real generation. Schelling identifies the same sort of relation between parts and whole in any organic body: the eye, for example, can be eye only within the body, but its partial independence is proved by its susceptibility to isolated illness. The third example is drawn from one of Schelling's own metaphysical doctrines rather than from the realm of observable phenomena; as such, it is questionable as evidence but important to the essay's development. According to this third example, "the emergence of things from God is a self-manifestation of God. God can however be manifest only in what is similar to himself, in free beings that can act on their own: beings for whose being there is no ground save God, but that are, just as God is [die aber sind, sowie Gott ist]" (7:347). The final example is in itself unobjectionable and clarifying: thoughts are engendered within the mind, but once they have arisen, they can attain an independence; they can come to dominate the soul. This example is introduced to clarify the relation of dependent to ground, but it is then developed metaphysically: "The divine representations can only be self-sufficient beings; for what limits our representations save the fact that we see things that are not self-sufficient? God intuits the things in themselves" (7:347).

The analogical argument concerning grounding is far superior to the analytic one concerning identity: the former is expository and suggestive, functioning as intended, whereas the latter is based in a misconception, at best an oversimplification. The analytic argument is flawed, but it would be imprudent to assume that Schelling was wholly unaware of its flaws. We know that, in the *Freedom* essay, he intends to protect his teachings from misinterpretation, and that he attempts to do so by obscuring them. But what could he intend to express by inserting metaphysical tenets into fallacious logical analyses? To answer this question, we must consider how different readers are likely to respond to his presentations. The least careful readers might well accept the metaphysical doctrines introduced as mere logical examples, without noticing that the doctrines are not supported by arguments; readers who are more careful but analytically dogmatic will recognize the logical flaws in Schelling's doctrine of the judgment and, failing to acknowledge the potential cogency or importance of any sort of argument save the strictly analytical, may well close the book before reaching the "real investigation" of freedom. With readers in this second group, Schelling's intended esotericism will have succeeded completely: they will not understand the *Freedom* essay, but since they will remain wholly ignorant of Schelling's positive teachings, they will be unable to misinterpret them. Readers in a third group, finally, will recognize vagaries in Schelling's arguments but will continue to read, realizing that the vagaries could be intentional and seeking to determine what the vagaries might be intended to communicate; only readers approaching the text in this manner are in a position to learn from Schelling, or even to learn whether there is anything to be learned from Schelling. Such readers will note Schelling's insistence that the *Freedom* essay is carefully written and will reason that, if it is worthy of being read at all, it is worthy of being read carefully. If we intend to read carefully, we should be hesitant to conclude that Schelling is simply an incompetent logician. A prudent reading of the text must note the possibility that Schelling intentionally presents inadequate logical arguments, perhaps in order to indicate, to readers intelligent or careful or sympathetic enough to grasp the point, that purely analytical reasoning is inappropriate, even misleading, in philosophy; one can imagine Schelling arguing that such reasoning is too closely related to the merely mechanical.[8]

8. For a fuller treatment of the problem of intentional esotericism, see Leo Strauss, *Persecution and the Art of Writing*, pp. 22–37.

Schelling's introduction purports merely to clarify his terminology; yet Schelling takes his considerations of identity, ground, and dependence to reveal a fundamental truth: "the concept of a derived absoluteness or divinity is so little contradictory that it is in fact the central concept of all philosophy" (7:347). How could such an assertion follow from terminological explanations? To grasp Schelling's general line of thought, we may begin with the tautology "The absolute is absolute," that is, the absolute is self-identical. Through his analysis of judgmental form and the function of the copula, Schelling seeks to establish that identity is always the unity of ground and grounded. While the analysis does not succeed in establishing this conclusion, it does reveal that duplicity need not destroy identity. This means that the absolute could be articulated without thereby ceasing to be self-identical. Given that the absolute is absolute, it could not be dependent upon any articulations it might contain, but neither could the articulations be independent of it; in either case, the absolute would cease to be absolute. Thus, the articulations—if there are any—must be dependent upon the absolute.

Whereas Schelling's explicit but invalid argument is "Identity entails grounding, so the absolute, as self-identical, must be ground (for something nonabsolute)," the successful, implicit argument is "Identity does not exclude duplicity, and if there is duplicity, then the absolute, as absolute, must be its ground." This brings us to Schelling's consideration of grounding as such. Here, Schelling's analogical argument successfully reveals that groundedness or dependence does not entail complete determination. Thus, it is an error—and one that arises from the misunderstanding of the relevant terms—to reason that all that is grounded in the absolute must be predetermined by the absolute. Rather, there is no contradiction in the assertion that the absolute could be the ground for existence of free beings; as grounded in the absolute, these beings would be dependent upon it, but, as free, they would themselves be absolute. Now, given that the fundamental philosophical opposition is that between freedom and necessity, thus, that the fundamental philosophical problem is that of explaining how necessity of existence and freedom of action can be united—

as they seem to be in human beings—Schelling's conclusion is intelligible: "the concept of a derived absoluteness or divinity is so little contradictory that it is in fact the central concept of all philosophy" (7:347). The conclusion is intelligible, at least to the careful reader, but Schelling acknowledges that his arguments for it have been too general to be compelling; all that he claims to have established is "that the denial of formal freedom [or the denial of the theoretical possibility of freedom] is not necessarily bound to pantheism" (7:347), that is, that things may be "immanent in God" or grounded in the absolute, but at the same time, to some degree, free.

In the course of his consideration of the argument equating pantheism with fatalism, Schelling also exposes the functional middle term in that argument (in its most common form): the general belief is that pantheism is reducible to Spinozism, and that Spinozism is necessarily fatalism. According to Schelling, however, Spinoza's fatalism is independent of his pantheism: "The error in his system by no means lies in his positing of things in *God*; it lies rather in the fact that *things* are posited" (7:349). This interpretation is a development of that introduced over a decade earlier in "On the Ego": if God and man are heterogenous, then man must be mere thing, for God cannot be. In the *Freedom* essay, Schelling criticizes Spinoza for presenting all of finitude as mechanically ordered; he corrects Spinoza's error in his own works, especially those dealing with the philosophy of nature. In idealism generally, and dynamic physics in particular, Schelling has animated Spinozism: he has demonstrated that nature is not a lifeless mechanism. Yet the works on nature, as originally presented, are not completely intelligible, because they do not reach the true ground. They therefore depend upon the ideal part of the system (whose publication was prevented only by external circumstances); this part transfigures nature, revealing its truly fundamental form:

> There is, in the last and highest instance, simply no being other than will. Will is primordial being, and only to it do all the predicates of the latter apply: groundlessness, eternity, independence from time, self-affirmation. The entirety of philosophy strives only to find will's highest expression. [7:350]

The idealistic movement has made will fundamental, but idealism retains two flaws: Fichtean idealism can seem to subordinate all to the whims of a given individual—thus making the individual human ego absolute—rather than interrelate all through a primal willing; second, all previously developed forms of idealism provide only for formal or theoretical freedom, not for real freedom (7:351). Idealism has not yet revealed what characterizes freedom in its particularly human form: "Idealism gives, namely, on the one hand only the most general, on the other the merely formal concept of freedom. The real and vital concept is, however, that it is a capacity for good and for evil" (7:352).

The introduction of the problem of evil reveals the most important of the "subjects related to the essence of human freedom" alluded to in the essay's title: "This is the point of deepest difficulty within the entire doctrine of freedom; it has always been sensed and is relevant not only to this or that system but, more or less, to all" (7:352). The problem is not solved by the denial of the reality of evil: if freedom is indeed the capacity for good and evil, then if there is no evil there can be no freedom. Yet if evil is not denied, then the philosophical problem of grounding is complicated, for the absolute must be shown to be the source not only of free and independent entities, but of something within the world—or within those entities—that is at times malignant rather than benign or even indifferent. The dilemma is clearest if put in theological terms: God must be both omnipotent and benevolent, but if he cannot overcome evil he is not the former and if he does not choose to overcome evil he is not the latter. The basic question, neutrally stated, is this: How can the world process as a whole be rationally ordered if it is determined by the interplay of opposed forces striving toward incompatible goals?

According to Schelling, all previous attempts to answer the question by accounting for real evil have failed; explicitly included is the attempt of Spinoza—who follows Augustine—to differentiate evil from good in terms of "degrees of reality" or of completeness. (Schelling does not mention that he made the same attempt in the unpublished 1804 *System*.) Schelling grants that idealism has made some progress with the problem of freedom, but he insists that it finally fails because of its inability to overcome the general prejudice of modern philosophy against the real—the same prejudice that has led to the conception of nature as merely mechanical. The problem of evil can be solved only within a system grounded in reality, in a philosophy of nature such as Schelling's, in which the real is properly evaluated in its relation to the ideal: "Only from the axioms of a true philosophy of nature can there develop the view that will fully satisfy the task that has here arisen" (7:357). In revealing that nature is dynamic rather than mechanical, Schelling's philosophy of nature reveals the affinity of nature and will; in revealing that the natural order culminates with human beings, the philosophy of nature prepares us to see man as the most perfect embodiment of the absolute will.

With the reference back to the philosophy of nature, Schelling's introduction ends. It purports to do no more than clarify certain concepts, most important among them "pantheism," "identity," "ground," and "freedom." Through his clarifications, Schelling intends to rule out in advance two possible objections to his doctrine of freedom. The first would arise when readers identified "pantheistic" tenets in his account; some would see such tenets as proof that the doctrine must finally be fatalistic. The second sort of objection foreseen by Schelling would arise when readers concluded from his having introduced natural relations into the account that the final doctrine must be limited to the mechanical or must reduce the spiritual to the natural. To the extent that Schelling's conceptual analyses illuminate the prematurity of such external criticisms, they are unobjectionable. As has been shown, however, Schelling also introduces metaphysical doctrines that he does not directly support. He claims that since the absolute is self-identical, it must function as ground and must ground free beings. He also asserts that "real" freedom is the capacity for good and evil, but he does not establish that no other concept is satisfactory. Nor does he prove the importance of the philosophy of nature: there is an incomplete negative argument intended to indicate that previous attempts to account for evil have all failed, but even if that argument were complete it would do no more than emphasize the philosophical relevance of Schelling's attempt. It would at best show that Schelling's path is the only one that remains open, but it could not show that that path will lead to the desired goal. This is no damning criticism: it is not generally the purpose of Schelling's introductions to prove in advance that the accounts that follow them must be successful; the introductions seek rather to insure, to the extent possible, that the approach taken will appear promising and the problem developed important, so that the reader will be encouraged to follow the account to the end. In the *Freedom* essay's introduction, the careful reader finds ample encouragement.

The Investigation

Ground and Existence Schelling's "real investigation" of freedom begins with the introduction of a distinction intended to make possible the avoidance of Spinoza's errors and thereby allow the solution of the problems of freedom and evil. The distinction is between "essence [*Wesen*] insofar as it exists, and insofar as it is merely ground of existence" (7:357). The distinction is of utmost importance when applied to God: "Since nothing is prior to or outside of God, he must have the ground of his existence in himself" (7:357). This is a truth that, according to Schelling, no philosopher would deny, but one that most would pervert by presenting the divine ground as "mere concept," not as something "real and actual" (7:358). If, however, the divine ground is real, Schelling argues, the ground-existence distinction explains how things can be "immanent in" God (or, in nonpantheistic terms, grounded in the absolute) without thereby being fatalistically determined by him: "the things have their ground in that which in God is not *himself*, i.e., in that which is ground of his existence" (7:359).

In Schelling's technical sense, God "exists" only following his primal act of self-reflection; prior to that act, God is not nothing (if he were, he could not act), but since he is fully undeveloped, he does not yet "stand out" *(ex-sistere)*. Prior to the self-reflection, God is pure potential, pure, unarticulated ground. Schelling attempts to clarify this primordial condition not with the abstractions of the system of identity, but with mystical terms drawn from the theosophical tradition of Jakob Böhme. In these terms, God as ground is "a yearning to bear himself," a willing of unity that itself is not unity and that, as a yearning whose object is not fully determined, is without understanding; the will that is primordial being is a pure, blind will. Understanding enters only with the self-reflection in which God distinguishes himself from the yearning by objectifying it. Through this reflection, God comes to "see his mirror image," "the word" is spoken, and love and understanding come into existence. Understanding works to separate all that is implicit in the divine ground, while love works to hold together the elements that are thereby distinguished.

God thus acts as willing, as understanding, and as loving; each act corresponds to a real aspect of the divine nature. Since the moment of will or yearning—the ground moment—is real, it is resistant to the efforts of understanding to fully grasp it; for this reason, all that is implicit within the ground—as all that can be is (7:361)—can be unfolded by the moment or power of understanding only in a series of dialectically ordered steps. According to an 1810 lecture, "Were there not something entirely opposed to the light and to thought, something not to be grasped, then there would be no creation at all, everything would be unravelled in mere thought" (7:447).

In the *Freedom* essay, Schelling continues to understand dialectic as a process of increasing articulation. This superficial similarity to his earlier dialectic, however, disguises a much more important difference. In the system of identity, the subjective moment (the moment of understanding) is presented as the source of content: content develops as the subject incorporates its own reflective acts into what it has already objectified. In the *Freedom* essay, the ground as such is said to have all content within it and to resist being grasped or explained by the power of understanding, to resist revealing itself in actual existence; at every stage of dialectical development, the ground is forced to expose more of itself than the power of understanding has previously grasped. In the *Freedom* essay, the source of content is obscurity and darkness rather than clarity and light; this difference from the system of identity destroys the possibility of metaphysical construction, for reasons that will become clearer below.

Since the principle of ground or will resists the principle of existence or understanding, the two are truly opposed, and they are present, as opposed, at every stage of the development of nature and spirit:

> The first principle is that through which [the things] are different from God, through which they are merely in the ground; since, however, there is an original unity between what is typified in the ground and what is typified in the understanding, and since the process of creation aims only at an inner transmutation or transfiguration of the originally dark principle into the light (because the understanding or the light posited in nature seeks in the ground only the introverted light that is akin to it), for these reasons the principle that is dark according to its nature is precisely that which is transfigured into light, and both are, though only in a determinate degree, one in every natural being. [7:362–63]

As the process continues, the subjective principle increases in complexity as it comes more fully to understand, while the obscurities inherent in the objective principle are brought to light as that principle is more fully understood. Throughout the natural process, the order is dialectically fixed, but at the spiritual peak of the development, the principles are in a state of equilibrium: "There is in man the entire might of the dark principle and at the same time the entire force of light. There is in him the deepest abyss and the highest heaven, or both centers" (7:363). In the fullness and balance of the opposition is grounded the possibility of real freedom: "Were the identity of the two principles as indissoluble in the spirit of man as in God, then there would be no distinction, i.e., God would not be manifest as spirit. The same unity that is inseparable in God must be separable in man—and this makes possible good and evil" (7:364).

The Possibility of Evil In the divine order and in the purely natural realm, the development is dialectically fixed, but the element of necessity vanishes when there develops a subject that, like God, can objectify itself along with the "dark principle" in its developed complexity. When the subjective power reaches full development, becoming aware of itself as itself, it is no longer a mere link in the dialectical chain. Within nature, there is a predetermined interplay between the two principles; as far as we know, only human beings are fully conscious of the principles themselves, and thus only with human beings does there arise the possibility of action not determined by the principles. Differently stated: human beings are aware of the multiplicity of finite entities and of their own various drives and desires; at the same time they at least can be aware of themselves as uniting all that they are aware of. Since human individuals are self-conscious, they are parts that contain the whole; as such, they are truly in God's image. This unique status, visible to us in human beings alone, is what makes evil, and thus real freedom, possible. The human being, like God, is a comprehensive unity, therefore called "spirit" or, in the case of the individual, "soul." But the human, as person, is also an entity in the world, capable of opposing himself to the world and of subordinating the rest of the world to his own idiosyncratic needs and desires. Human beings can choose to be guided by the principle of understanding that is common to all, and thus to recognize that they are parts in a balanced whole; or they can choose to be guided by the principle of will that manifests itself uniquely in every individual, and thus to attempt to use other equally essential parts of the whole as means to private ends. Those who choose the latter course upset the balance of principles in their souls by perverting the natural order of subordination of will to understanding; the result is evil, the spiritual counterpart to illness in the body.

Schelling insists that his is "the only correct concept of evil"; no other explanation is acceptable either to the understanding or to ethical consciousness, for all either deny evil or attempt to explain it as imperfection. To do either is however to be "in conflict with the authentic nature of evil. For even the simple consideration that it is man alone, the most perfect of all visible creatures, who is capable of evil shows that its ground can in no way lie in lack or privation" (7:368). The argument that only the absolute itself is perfect could explain at best the finitude of the individual, but finitude as such is not evil (7:370); indeed, finitude is necessary to God's manifestation. "The separation of forces is not in itself disharmony; [disharmony is] the false unity of them, which can be called a separation only when compared to the true [unity]" (7:371). The true unity is the unity of all in God, a unity preserved at every stage of the dialectic of the world process. The false unity cannot arise naturally, nor can it result from chance; it can result only through an autonomous act, and the autonomous act can be performed only by the most perfect creation, the human soul (7:370).

The Actuality of Evil and of Freedom: The "Most Important" Part of the Question Following the derivation of the possibility of evil from the "highest grounds," Schelling turns to the "most important part of the question" (*größte Teil der Frage*), that concerning evil's actuality as a force within the world, a force that can induce the individual to forsake divine harmony. He reiterates the necessity that the principles be separable in man if God's manifestation is to be complete: "any being [*Wesen*] can be manifest only in its opposite" (7:373). Evil must be actualized, for its unrealized possibility would not suffice to reveal, by contrast, its utter absence from God; consequently, human beings are necessarily tempted:

> Man is placed on a peak: he has within himself the capacity for spontaneous movement toward good or toward evil; the bond holding these principles in him is not necessary, it is free. He stands at the point of divergence: whatever he chooses, it will be his deed, but he cannot remain undecided.

This passage, as cited, could have been written by a twentieth-century existentialist; it asserts that human existence precedes human essence, that human beings become what they are only through their deeds. Yet Schelling's continuation of the passage emphasizes a metaphysical grounding alien to existentialists: man cannot remain in indecision "because God must necessarily reveal himself, and because nothing in creation may remain ambiguous" (7:347).

The individual must somehow choose between good and evil, but that means that both options must be visible. Evil cannot exist as such prior to its actualization in the human individual but, according to Schelling, since the ground principle—

the principle of will—always resists the efforts of the principle of understanding to make all intelligible, there are selfish or willful beings throughout the natural realm, beings that defy inclusion in rational explanations of the whole. The whole indeed becomes articulated, and thus explicable, only as a result of the striving of the will to retain its independence from the understanding:

> The irrational and contingent that shows itself to be bound up with the necessary in the formation of beings, especially organic ones, proves that it is not a mere geometrical necessity that has been at work here, but that freedom, spirit, and willfullness are also factors. . . . There are in nature contingent determinations that can be explained only through arousal, in the very first creation, of the irrational or dark principle of creatures—ones that can be explained only through activated selfhood. [7:376]

Omens of evil are visible not only in nature; they are also present in the general course of human history, and though Schelling's summary of the latter is obscure, the principle it purports to establish is clearly stated: "It is the will of God to universalize everything . . . ; it is the will of the ground to particularize everything" (7:381). Given both the nature of God's will and the individuality of the individual, human temptation is fully understandable:

> Even in itself, the combination of the universal will with a particular will in man seems to be a contradiction: the unification seems difficult if not impossible. The anxiety of life itself drives man from the center in which he was created, in that [the center], as the purest essence of all will, is for the particular will the all-consuming fire; if [the individual] is to live in it, all of his peculiarity must die out; for this reason it is almost necessary that the individual try to leave the center for the periphery, in order to seek there a place of rest for selfhood. [7:381]

Since the individual's desire for preservation of its own individuality—as opposed to absorption in the transindividual absolute—is tantamount to temptation, the call of evil is heard by all individuals; nevertheless, Schelling insists, "the evil remains always man's own choice . . . every creature falls through its own fault" (7:382). The origin of evil, as actual, is in the decision of the individual; how this decision is to be understood—that is, how freedom is to be formally or theoretically grasped—is the next problem Schelling considers.

The Possibility of Freedom Schelling begins his treatment of formal freedom—his treatment of how freedom is possible in principle—by denying that freedom can be adequately grasped if it is taken to be a manifestation either of indifference or of contingency: freedom cannot be reduced to chance. Those who attempt that reduction use "a generally bad type of proof, wherein it is concluded, from the fact that the determining ground is not known, that that ground does not exist" (7:382). According to Schelling, theories reducing freedom to indifference are no better than those that deny it altogether: the two are equally myopic, in that "equally unknown to both is that higher necessity that is equally far removed from contingency and from force or external determination, that which is rather an inner necessity flowing forth from the essence of the acting subject itself" (7:383). Schelling here reaffirms the importance of both the freedom first attributed to the absolute in "On the Ego" and the "inner necessity," grounded in the essence of the individual, that is the basis for the Leibnizian construction project foreseen in the *Ideas*. Schelling credits Kant with recognizing that the subject, regardless of how it appears empirically, must be taken to be in itself or in essence beyond the realm of mechanical causality, and thus free; but Kant does not clearly show how the transition from this realm of essence to the finite world and to concrete acts is possible. In Schelling's view, Kant is confronted with difficulties only because he takes the human essence—which alone is free—to be transindividual; if the essence is individual—and according to Aristotle and Leibniz, it is—then it is determinate and can be the source of determinate acts. "As certainly as the intelligible essence acts simply freely and absolutely, so certainly must it act in accordance with its inner nature, or the act can follow from this nature only according to the law of identity and with absolute necessity, which alone is absolute freedom; for that is free which acts only in accordance with the laws of its own essence and which is determined by nothing else within it or outside of it" (7:384).

I am free, then, in that—or to the extent that—I am autonomous; I am autonomous if—or when—my acts are determined not solely by external situations or events in conjunction with my contingent needs and desires, but rather, to some degree, by the principles or laws inherent in me as a moral agent, those that make me the individual who I am. To be free is to act in accordance with essence. This first characterization of formal freedom is accurate, but it is not complete, for "*whatever* a man chooses, it will be his deed": the essence of the individual must therefore itself be chosen by the individual and can follow neither from the absolute nor from the ideas. The individual's essence must follow from the individual:

> Were the essence a dead being merely given to the human being, then, since action must follow from it with necessity, all responsibility and freedom would be impossible. But just that inner necessity is itself freedom, the essence of man is essentially *his own deed*; necessity and freedom stand together as one essence, which appears as the one or the other when viewed from different sides; in itself freedom, it is formally necessity. [7:385]

Schelling recognizes that this conception seems strange, but he asserts that its truth is indirectly confirmed in mental experience: "Incomprehensible as this idea may appear to the normal human way of thinking, there is nonetheless in every human being a feeling that corresponds to it, the feeling that he has been what he is from all eternity, that he has not become so only in time" (7:386).

As a human individual, I have determined my own essence; I have come to be an individual in a self-constitutive act of decision for good or evil. The act itself cannot enter consciousness, for it is a precondition for consciousness: to be conscious is to choose, and choices are guided, albeit generally unconsciously, by principles; one who "has no principles" subordinates all to the desire for self-gratification, but that too reveals a principle. While the primal choosing of principles—in Schelling's terms, the primal choice for good or evil—cannot enter consciousness and is thus independent of the individual

qua conscious, it remains, Schelling insists, the responsibility of
the individual:

> That Judas betrayed Christ could be altered neither by himself
> nor by any other creature, and yet he was not forced into be-
> trayal, but rather did it willingly and with complete freedom. . . .
> In consciousness, . . . that free act that becomes necessity clearly
> cannot come forth, for it, as the essence, precedes [conscious-
> ness], makes it; but that does not mean that it is an act of which
> no consciousness at all remains; in that he who says (in order to
> excuse himself for an unjust act) "That is just the way I am"
> knows full well that he is so through his own fault, even though
> he is right when he says that it is impossible for him to act oth-
> erwise. [7:386]

Schelling's doctrine of freedom grounds a unique sort of predetermined necessity: "as a man acts here, so has he acted
from eternity, and already in the beginning of creation"
(7:387). Schelling recognizes one possible objection to his doctrine: it seems to exclude the possibility of conversion within
this life, the possibility of evil individuals becoming good or
vice versa. Without considering the point in detail, Schelling
suggests the possibility of primordial decisions that, although
tending toward the good or the evil, do not exclude the alternative. Individuals making such decisions can be led, by God
or by other individuals, to change or strengthen their commitments (7:389).

In suggesting that the primal decision, the choice of essence,
need not be binding, Schelling seems to introduce the possibility of existential freedom. The freedom on which he concentrates in the essay is not existential; rather, it is absolute in that
it is equivalent to absolute necessity, and it is transcendental in
that the free decision is made on a level that is inevitably forsaken when the decision is made. The effects of the decision
are visible only within the factical world where, were the decision fully binding, freedom of choice would have to be denied. Yet some freedom of choice is demanded by Schelling's
own teachings. Generally, he maintains that true goodness is
to be found only in the innocence of "religiosity" or "heroism," that is, in the ignorance of evil and the consequent automatic doing of good. Elsewhere, however, he suggests that

good and evil are dialectically related in such a way that positive goodness is the virtue that follows only from the recognition and overcoming of evil; since those deaf to the call of evil
have no need to develop the strength required for persistent
goodness, the highest good is virtue rather than innocence: it
develops only through confrontation with the deepest evil
(7:400; cf. 8:174).

Even if this is the true teaching, even if true goodness requires the choosing of good rather than evil, the choice cannot
be a choice of a familiar, everyday sort. Normally, conscious
choices are made between recognized alternatives, yet good
and evil are not so clearly visible as to make such a choice possible for most people. The choice must therefore be made on
the transcendental level rather than on the level of ordinary
experience: the truly good are those who have, on the level of
the primal decision, seen the lure of evil but totally banished it
in favor of the good. Yet even admitting for the moment the
possibility of such commitments, and of equally strong commitments to evil, these cannot be the only options. Schelling
does assert that the decision must be made for the one or the
other—from that peak on which man is placed, "he cannot remain in indecision"—but it would be difficult, as Schelling realizes, to identify perfectly good or evil human beings; most if
not all seem to remain, in fact, in indecision. Schelling's recognition of the situation is evidenced by his acknowledgment
of the possibility of conversion and by his distinction of true
evil from mere weakness and incapacity. The point is made
more clearly in a work from 1810: "Man, in the state in which
he is now normally to be found, is too bad even for the devil;
the *bad* is *mixed;* sheer evil is in its own right something pure"
(7:480). Despite the normalcy of the mixed state, Schelling is
concerned in the *Freedom* essay with the pure ones. Why this
is his chief concern is not immediately apparent; no more apparent is the relation of the primordial decision for good or evil
to ordinary decisions for specific acts in concrete situations.
These obscurities must be clarified, but they can be clarified
only if they are considered within the context of the essay as a
whole.

In the first half of the "real investigation" of freedom, which has now been considered, Schelling treats the "beginning and origin of evil to the point where it is actualized in individual human beings"; this "seems to leave nothing to do save to describe its appearance in man" (7:389). Much of that description—which, as it turns out, does not cover all that is left to be done—is reiteration. Evil appears in individuals who invert the principles and thereby make "selfhood organ rather than basis," who subordinate spirituality or understanding to selfhood or will (7:389), and thereby form a false and unstable unity: "There is in the evil the self-consuming and always annihilating contradiction that it strives to become creature by destroying the bond that makes it creature and, through the arrogance of wanting to be all, it falls to nothingness" (7:390–91). It is the destructive aspect of evil that makes it abhorrent in a way in which mere weakness or incapacity is not. Nor is there in true goodness anything of weakness, incapacity, or, despite its necessity, compulsion. It is here that Schelling, appropriating a passage from the 1804 *System*, presents true goodness as the religiosity that makes unjust action impossible: the truly good man is not subjugated by duty or law, because he is deaf to the call of evil to the extent that duty and law are unnecessary (7:392; *cf.* 6:558).

God and Evil: The "Highest Question" of the Investigation With the treatment of the difference between good and evil individuals, "we have considered, to the extent possible, the origin of the opposition of good and evil, and how both work through each other in creation." There remains "the highest question of this entire investigation," that of the ethical relation of God to his manifestation: since evil exists, must not God—or the absolute—be evil (7:394)? With this question, emphasis returns from creatures to creator; yet the status of the consideration is not clear. It is introduced with the claim, presented as a conclusion drawn from what has gone before, that "if God were for us a mere logical abstraction, then all would have to follow from him with logical necessity; he himself would then be only the highest law, from which everything would flow, without personality, and with no consciousness" (7:394). The question is not simply that of what God is; it is that of what God is for us, of what we can know God to be. If we are to avoid viewing all as following from the absolute with logical necessity, we must be able to think or to know the absolute to be the one true and real God and not a mere abstraction. Yet reflection on the absolute *qua* absolute does not reveal that the absolute is God; Schelling insists, as he often has before, that we know that philosophy's highest principle must be absolute, and that the phenomenon of consciousness entails an absolute transcendental unity. As he argues in "On the Ego" and *Bruno*, however, the absolute is not given in such a way that its nature or significance is clear. It can be, for us, more than a logical abstraction—most important, it can be for us God—only if we can succeed in developing from it a world of free individuals. Conversely—and this is the teaching new to the *Freedom* essay—only if the absolute is God can it ground beings whose actions are not fully predetermined.

For philosophy to be the science showing how the experienced world is grounded in the absolute, the absolute must be God, for no other absolute could ground the existence of free individuals. To be God, Schelling continues, the absolute must be personal. This assertion is puzzling, for "personality" is introduced in the essay as "spirit as a self, a particular being (one separate from God)" (7:364), as "selfhood raised to spirituality" (7:370). The attribution of personality to God is justified in that his nature has the same composite character as the nature of human persons: God's nature combines "something self-sufficient with a basis independent of it . . . in such a way that the two penetrate each other and are only One Being [*Ein Wesen*]" (7:394–95). God is the unity of his existence and the ground of his existence, but he can therefore come to be only as the human individual comes to be, only in a primal self-reflective choice: "Creation is no occurrence, but rather an act" (7:396). Confirmation of God's groundedness in a principle distinct from his existence—tantamount to at least partial confirmation of the personality of the absolute—is sought in the world as given:

> Nature in its entirety says to us that in no way is it there by force of a merely geometrical necessity, that it contains not simple, pure reason, but rather personality and spirit; . . . otherwise,

geometrical understanding, which has ruled for so long, would
have long since penetrated it and confirmed its idol of universal
and eternal natural laws to a far greater extent than it has as yet;
it is rather forced with each passing day to more clearly recognize
the irrational relation of nature to itself. [7:395–96]

Were the entire development of nature logically necessary, it
could not contain the irrational elements that it does contain.
It is the task of the philosophy of nature to reveal the nonlog-
ical necessity visible in the natural realm: "the highest striving
of the dynamic mode of explanation is nothing other than this
reduction of natural laws to heart [*Gemüth*], spirit and will"
(7:396; *cf.* 3:341).

Schelling continues his account of the personal nature of
God by confirming divine providence: in the primal reflection,
"there comes to be a reflective image of everything implicitly
contained in the essence, [an image] in which God actualizes
himself ideally or, which is the same thing, knows himself in
advance of his actualization" (7:396–97). This assertion contradicts the earlier claim that the world process must proceed in
stages precisely because what is implicit in the ground is not
immediately accessible to the primal reflection; the new teaching would seem to make possible—for God—"the unravelling
of all in mere thought." Schelling does not acknowledge the
conflict between the two teachings, but continues with another
puzzling account. After introducing the question of God's creative latitude—the question of the multiplicity of possible
worlds, of the ground for actualization of this one, assuming
that it is the only one—he denies the relevance to this problem
of the notion of logical possibility, according to which all is
possible that is not self-contradictory. God is necessitated to
create the world that he created, and no other, but for ethical
rather than logical reasons. In accordance with his general
teaching concerning absolute freedom, Schelling presents the
free creation as requiring nothing like a choice between positive alternatives. God did not choose to create a world containing evil; he rather chose to develop, or to allow the development of, the one system grounded in himself: "There is in the
divine understanding a system, but God himself is no system;
he is rather a life, and therein alone lies the answer to the

question . . . concerning the possibility of evil in relation to God" (7:399). The act of creation itself is, indeed, a victory of good over evil: "Had God, on account of evil, not manifested himself, then evil would have won over good and love" (7:401). The dark or ground principle is aroused by the act of creation, but it is at the same time subordinated to light and understanding and, thus, to the good. The general predominance of good throughout history is illustrated with a second sketch—not completely congruent to the first—of the stages of manifestation and of the final purpose of the process. The final intent appears, however, to be inexpressible; the problem leads Schelling finally to "the highest point of the entire investigation," the consideration of the ultimate unity of ground and existence (7:406).

Urgrund *as* Ungrund: *The "Highest Point" of the Investigation*
Schelling begins his investigation in the *Freedom* essay by simply appropriating the ground-existence distinction from the philosophy of nature; only when nearing the end of the essay is he forced to consider the metaphysical origins of his principles of ground and existence. His outline of history concludes with the ultimate victory of spirit, but, he continues, "even spirit is not yet the highest; it is only spirit, or the breath of love. Love, however, is the highest. It is what was there before even the ground and the existing were (as separate), but it was not yet as love, but—how are we to characterize it?" (7:405–06). With the raising of this question, "we finally meet the highest point of the entire investigation" (7:406). As we did in the *System of Transcendental Idealism* of 1800—the only previously published work in which Schelling develops a philosophy of spirit—we again see at the highest point the highest or most important principle, a principle whose importance has hitherto been ignored. In the 1800 *System,* the introduction of the highest principle, absolute identity, threatens the stability of all that precedes it; we must now determine whether the *Freedom* essay's highest principle is similarly destructive.

The primal unity, the one essence, is *"before* all ground and before all existents, thus before all duality whatsoever"; since it is absolutely first in the order of things, this essence is the

Urgrund, the primordial ground. Since, however, it is fully un-differentiated and therefore cannot serve as the starting point for any explanation of the world process, the Urgrund is the *Ungrund*, the nonground (7:406).[9] Schelling does not concentrate on the Ungrund itself; he asserts that it is the absolute and then, characteristically, he begins to attempt to derive content from it.

It is thus at the highest point of the *Freedom* essay's investigation that Schelling comes to treat the problem that has plagued him throughout his career, that of the introduction of the first duality into the primal unity. He attempts to solve that problem by introducing a new sense of "indifference" to characterize the Ungrund, which, as prior to all duality, cannot be termed an "identity." Since there can be no opposition within the absolute, ground and existence cannot be opposed within the Ungrund; "but nothing hinders their predication as non-opposed, that is, in disjunction, and each *for* itself, whereby the duality (the actual twofoldness of principles) is precisely what is posited" (7:407). The Ungrund does not oppose this positing; since it is indifferent, Schelling argues, it reacts with equanimity.

In so arguing, Schelling moves from logical indifference, or indeterminacy, to psychological indifference, or equanimity; the move gains its superficial plausibility only from the equivocality of "indifference." Schelling's argument is also flawed by the obscurity of his notion of the predication of the principles as "nonopposed." Were the Ungrund both ground and existence, then it would be the absolute identity of the two and would contain an illicit opposition (the true absolute must be beyond all opposition); if, however, the Ungrund is posited as neither ground nor existence, then it is an absolute indifference that is free from opposition. "Duality breaks forth immediately from the neither-nor, from the indifference, . . . and *without* indifference, i.e., *without* an Ungrund, there would be no duplicity of principles" (7:407). Schelling does not explain who or what posits neither ground nor existence in the Un-

9. To the *Freedom* essay's Ungrund compare Bruno's "holy abyss" (*Abgrund*) (4:258; quoted above).

grund, and he thereby enables the Ungrund to respond to their absence with equanimity.

Schelling does not acknowledge that his account of the Ungrund as indifference is either unclear, incomplete, or incoherent; indeed, he asserts that its clarity reveals the profundity of the *Freedom* essay as a whole: "Far from it being the case that the distinction between ground and existence prove itself at the end to have been merely logical, or to have been summoned as an aid that at the end would prove itself to be nongenuine, it has rather shown itself to be a very real distinction, which was confirmed and fully grasped only from the highest standpoint" (7:407). Nevertheless, even after the account seems to have been completed, the Ungrund is treated in the anthropomorphic manner previously reserved for God; Schelling speaks, for example, of its purpose in "dividing itself," that of actualizing the love that is higher even than spirit. This love is characterized in terms, introduced in 1806 in an aphorism, that have in the intervening years not ceased to be contradictory: "This is the mystery of love, that it combines things that are such that each could be for itself, and yet is not, and cannot be without the other" (7:408 *and* 174). This love is the love that is higher than spirit and thus higher than man, higher even than God:

> In spirit, the existent is one with the ground of existence; in it the two are actually together, or it is the absolute identity of them. But higher than spirit is the original Ungrund, which is no longer indifference (equanimity), and yet is not identity of the two principles, but rather the universal unity, alike with respect to all yet grasped by none, the charity that is free from all while working through all, in a word, the love that is all in all. [7:408]

With the account of how content develops from the Ungrund, Schelling's investigation is complete. In the essay's last few pages, he rejects, in advance, several anticipated criticisms. In so doing, he stresses particularly that each of his concepts has, within his system, "its determinate place at which alone it is valid, and which determines its significance as well as its limitation" (7:411). As we have seen, some of Schelling's concepts are introduced and developed incoherently. Perhaps, however, they only appear to be incoherent when they are considered in isolation from the context of the essay as a whole; Schelling insists that readers who analyze his "most universal concepts" out of context will be unable to judge rightly the whole (7:411). Right judgment of the whole is an ideal that cannot be reached through a single reading, an ideal that is likely to remain unreached after many careful readings. Yet such right judgment remains the goal the reader must set, and it is a goal that can be approached only through successive attempts at comprehensive understanding. An introductory study can hope and presume to make no more than an attempt, seeking at least to identify the teachings that must be recognized if Schelling's further development is to be intelligible, at most to trace the lines a comprehensive interpretation of the essay might follow. We have examined the developing argument; we must now turn to the essay as a whole.

Freedom and System

Philosophical Investigations concerning the Essence of Human Freedom and Related Subjects is a strikingly verbose title; *Of Human Freedom* might seem to suffice—as it does for the English translation of the essay—as might, at most, *Of Human Freedom and Related Subjects*. Yet the additional qualifications in Schelling's title are not insignificant. Since Schelling is now normally considered to be a philosopher, it might seem obvious that his work would be philosophical. Yet among his contemporaries were some who believed that he had rejected philosophy for either natural science or theology; they based their opinions, respectively, on his work on the philosophy of nature and his later interest in theosophy, evident in *Aphorisms on the Philosophy of Nature* (1806) and acknowledged in the *Freedom* essay itself. Especially given the essay's concern with God and evil, it might easily be misclassified as theology or theosophy; Schelling's title stresses, perhaps for that reason, that the essay is philosophical. His title also stresses that the essay reports on investigations: the essay is not a system of freedom, not a complete explanation, but is rather an account of developing examinations. According to the title, the investigations concern, not human freedom as such, but rather the essence of human freedom; "essence," as we know, is an important Schellingian

technical term. In "essence," according to the *Exhibition* and
the *Freedom* essay, there is no differentiation; distinction enters
only with form. If the "essence" of the title is read in this technical sense, then the further "of human freedom" is logically
superfluous, for the essence of anything is the essence of
everything. In this case, however, the logically superfluous is
rhetorically significant: the title indicates that human freedom
is grounded in Schelling's "essence," the absolute, and thereby
must be real. If the technical sense of "essence" were stated
explicitly, the title of the essay would be *Philosophical Investigations concerning the Absolute and What Follows from It—
Including Human Freedom.* Though this title appears to be quite
different from the one Schelling provides, it would be equally
appropriate to the contents of his essay, for in addition to considering how human freedom and evil must be understood,
the essay investigates how the absolute principle of Schelling's
system must be thought given the specific requirement that the
system include true freedom and evil.

At least in part, the *Freedom* essay is a reconsideration of the
absolute, and many passages from the essay suggest that this
reconsideration transfigures the system of identity by revealing
that the absolute is God, indeed, a personal God. As personal,
God is a life rather than a system. In the *Stuttgart Private Lectures* (1810), Schelling teaches that God's life is like all others in
"beginning from consciouslessness, from a condition in which
everything that will later evolve individually from it is still in-
separately together" (7:432). The entire process of nature and
history is "nothing other than the process of complete coming
to consciousness, of complete personalization of God" (7:433).
According to the *Freedom* essay, history remains inconceivable
without the concept of a humanly suffering God (7:403), and
while one passage suggests that God enters history as an individual (7:380)—a doctrine no Schellingian principles would
support—Schelling generally maintains that God becomes
manifest in and through mankind as a whole (*see* 7:411). However that may be, Schelling certainly teaches that God is a life,
and that God's life is somehow history; but this means that
God is not unchanging. In a polemic denying that he is an
atheist, Schelling clarifies this doctrine:

I posit God as first and as last, as alpha and as omega, but he is not as alpha what he is as omega, and insofar as he is *God sensu eminenti* only as the latter, he cannot be God, in the same sense, as the former, nor, in the strictest sense, can he then be named God unless it is explicitly stated that he is the non-unfolded [*unentfaltete*] God, *Deus implicitus;* only as omega is he *Deus explicitus.* [8:81]

In a footnote to this passage, he is yet more explicit:

In [the *Exhibition*], to which I must refer again and again, I refrained from naming absolute identity "God" since it was not yet evolved [in that work] to the point designated above. . . . Only in later, less strict exhibitions did I diverge from that course, because I then no longer feared that I would be misunderstood on the point. [8:81n].

Strictly speaking, then, absolute identity is not God until a certain point in its development is reached; that point is not "designated above" in Schelling's polemic—at least not clearly—but since the *Exhibition* covers the development of all of inorganic nature, we may conclude that that much of the system, at least, precedes the introduction of God.[10]

In that the absolute *becomes* God, it is incorrect to say that the absolute *is* God; what then is the absolute? Late in the *Freedom* essay, Schelling argues that the absolute, *qua* absolute, is the Ungrund, which is certainly not God: "In the Ungrund or indifference there is of course no personality" (7:412). God differs from the Ungrund in containing the moments of both ground and existence; only as containing the two moments is God, like the individual human being, a person. God's ground, as real, is not directly accessible; it is visible only through its consequents. The same is true, according to Schelling's analysis of the judgment, of all grounds, and it is certainly true for the grounds of human beings: I am grounded in my primal decision for good or evil, but I cannot become directly conscious of that decision; I can discover what I am— what I have always been—if at all, only through reflecting on

10. According to the 1800 *System,* God will exist only when history reaches its final stage, which still lies in the future; see p. 68 above.

what I have done. I am visible as ground only in my consequents, and, according to Schelling, the same must hold for
God, for he too is a person and he too is a life. God, like man,
is known only through what he does. The divine ground is not
directly accessible; rather, it is induced to unfold, to reveal itself, only by the reflective activity of the divine understanding.
We therefore cannot know from reflection on the absolute
alone that the absolute is God; the absolute *qua* absolute is not
even ground, but is rather the ineffable Ungrund. We can
know the absolute *qua* ground only through observation of
what follows from that ground; that is, only through observation of the fact of the world. Were the world manifestly good,
there would perhaps be no doubt that the absolute is God; yet
observation of the world fosters the impression that the absolute, like most humans beings, is "weak and impotent" rather
than resolutely good or evil.

It is precisely the ambiguous nature of what the absolute
does—of what follows from the absolute—that makes the
problem of evil a problem. The question arises whether we can
possibly envision the absolute as good—thus, as God—given
the apparent imperfection of the world as it is experienced.
The question is crucial, for it marks the reversal that decisively
separates post-Idealistic philosophy from the earlier philosophical tradition: the question is no longer "Since God is good,
how can there be evil?"; it has become "Since there is evil,
how can God be good?" And just as the former question is
generally countered—as Schelling notes—with the denial of
the reality of evil and thus of the legitimacy of the question, so
too is the new question avoided through denial of the existence of God or—and Schelling insists that it must come to the
same thing—denial of the coherent goodness of the whole.
The traditional metaphysical assumption of the intelligibility or
rationality of the whole leads to the denial of the existence—or
at least the importance—of the unintelligible or irrational; contemporary emphasis on the chaotic and irrational often leads
to the nihilistic denial of all rationality. In Schelling's *Freedom*
essay, the metaphysical assumption is confronted with the existential objection: Schelling strives to develop a doctrine of the

absolute that will allow for the presence of the evil and the irrational while preserving the goodness and rationality of the whole.

Throughout most of the *Freedom* essay, Schelling simply refers to the absolute as God; yet his own remarks on the Ungrund, as well as what he says about God himself, reveal that the absolute is not God, or, to be more cautious, that we do not yet know that it is God. The *Freedom* essay thus does not transfigure the system of identity by revealing that its principle is God. Schelling's theological reflections do include arguments for the compatibility of an absolute that is God with a world that contains evil, but they contain no arguments for the existence of God, although they reveal that such arguments are necessary. Schelling does not note the incompleteness of his theological reflections, but that does not mean that he was unaware of it; in 1809, he lived in and was supported by the conservative Catholic city of Munich, and he was well aware that Fichte's career had been virtually ended when charges of atheism were publicly raised against him. If Schelling consciously chose to disguise the implications of his theological reflections, the choice was a prudent one.

Whether Schelling realized it or not, his theological reflections remain inadequate; for that reason, they do not allow the *Freedom* essay to be what Schelling claims that it is, namely, the piece of the system of identity that makes all of the other pieces fit together into a whole. This is not yet to say that the *Freedom* essay fails in this respect, however, for not all of its reflections are theological. Some are anthropological, and there are reasons for supposing that these are the more important. The essay's title suggests that its central teachings are those concerning human freedom, and very early in the essay Schelling tells us why these teachings are so important: philosophy itself stands or falls with the reality of freedom, for if an adequate account of freedom could not be incorporated into a comprehensive system, "philosophy itself would be wholly without worth" (7:338). Perhaps, then, the *Freedom* essay transfigures the system of identity by giving it worth, first by accounting for freedom as real and then by indicating how real freedom can subsist within the world process as a whole.

That human freedom is real is clearly and repeatedly asserted by Schelling: I am free in that I preconsciously decide to
be good or evil and in that all my deeds are determined by that
decision. Yet if my deeds are predetermined, they are not free;
only my primal decision can be free, but it is difficult to comprehend what sort of freedom could be involved in a decision
that I am not, and cannot be, conscious of making. Schelling
does not fully explain either that freedom or the primal decision itself; if his explanations are to be understood, they must
be expanded. I have elaborated on the text already in presenting the doctrine of the choice; I relate it to principles of action
in a way that Schelling does not. I do so because Schelling's
doctrine is incomplete; the adequacy or even the sense of his
notion of real freedom can be determined only through the relating of it to commonsense notions.

According to one commonsense notion, I am free because I
am not like the billiard ball whose every move is the result of
external, mechanical causes. Common sense tells me that I am
free because I do as I please; it tells me that I act freely as long
as I am in full possession of my mental faculties—as long as I
am sane—and as long as others do not compel me to act as
they will rather than as I will. Yet there are various forms of
compulsion, and various degrees of possession of mental faculties; even when no one else chooses for me, I do not always
choose for myself, and even when I retain my sanity, I do not
always know my own mind. In the normal course of my life,
I am thrown into one situation after another, and what I do in
most is determined by the situations themselves, in conjunction with my physical needs and desires and with whatever
habits I have developed and whatever principles I have embraced. I do not consciously choose to do most of what I do
but, rather, allow my acts and choices to be determined by factors deriving from past events and present circumstances;
when I allow this to happen, relatively external factors act on
me as physical forces act on billiard balls, and I do what I do
of necessity. It could be argued that such acts are nevertheless
free, for they are determined in part by my habits and by the
principles that constitute my individuality and make me the
person I am. This argument, however, proves nothing; it

merely changes the question to that of how *I* relate to my habits and principles. The former, of course, arise and subsist only
within me, but that does not mean that I freely rule over them;
as Schelling notes in the *Freedom* essay's introduction, thoughts
can come to dominate the soul. Certainly, my strongest habits
have more power over me than I over them.

What, then, about my principles? If I am determined not to
lie, then that is *my* determination. Yet, if it has resulted from
someone's telling me that I should not lie, then I have not
freely chosen the principle; at most I have chosen to trust the
source who encouraged me to accept it. And if I trust that
source merely from habit, then there would seem to be no freedom at all involved in the resolution. I have freely chosen my
principle only if I have compared it with conflicting principles—that is, only if I have overcome my habits, abstracted
from my own principles, and reflected on principles themselves—and then determined which I should adopt. And if my
decision concerning principles is to be free, it must be based
on reflection on all my principles, or at least on abstraction
from them: if my reflection on lying is guided by other principles, be they ethical or logical or metaphysical, and these other
principles remain unevaluated, then I have not made a decision concerning lying; I have, rather, been blindly determined
by principles that I likely do not even recognize. To be free, I
must reflect on all my principles, and if I am thereafter freely
to adopt all or some of them, I must also recognize their alternatives, for without alternatives there can be no real choice.

All of this indicates that if my acts are to be free, they must
be guided by principles I have freely chosen, and if my choices
concerning principles are to be free, they must be choices
among all principles. I am truly free only if my freedom is
grounded in comprehensive reflection on the highest and most
basic principles. If I have made or were to make such a reflection, I would then be able to make a free decision, a decision
that would be primal: it would be a guide for all my acts and
decisions, and it would determine what kind of human being
I would be. It would determine me as good or evil.

The above reflection on my commonsense understanding of
freedom has led to the denial of the legitimacy of that under-

standing; it has led to the conclusion that most if not all human beings are not truly free, that the truly free are only those who can make truly primal decisions. Schelling too teaches that freedom is grounded in primal decision, but whereas I have been led to the notion of a decision that the philosopher strives to be able to make, Schelling speaks of a decision that all human beings have actually made. In that the decision Schelling describes determines me as good or as evil, it must concern principles rather than specific acts; it is, Schelling teaches, the decision either to recognize the truly good or to attempt to establish what I take to be my private good. According to Schelling, I have chosen my principles—I have made my primal decision—unconsciously; on this point, my reflections on the commonsense notion of freedom partially support Schelling, for those reflections reveal that very few can choose with full consciousness. But even if I am not among the few, even if I have not consciously chosen my principles, I have at least accepted them, and I have accepted them to varying degrees: when I am forced to choose between principles, I sacrifice one in favor of another. It may be my general principle not to lie, but I may nonetheless lie in specific situations, perhaps for the sake of personal gain, perhaps in order to save someone from needless discomfort. If I could reflect with sufficient care, I would discover one principle, or one sort of principle, that I would not sacrifice to any other. My highest principle might demand, in essence, that I protect my life, or preserve my honor, or be a good Muslim or Buddhist—though so simple a formulation would doubtless be inadequate. However that may be, if there is a principle that I will not break—and if there is not, perhaps I am merely "weak and impotent"—if there is a principle to which all my deeds and decisions are subordinate, if I allow that principle to govern my life, then that principle determines whether I am good or evil, and my unconscious adoption or acceptance of that principle, rather than of any alternative, grounds my individuality.

Schelling teaches that human freedom is real, and although the freedom Schelling describes seems at first quite different from the freedom human beings experience, there are lines of reflection that connect the two. Since Schelling's title stresses human freedom, it is surprising that he does not pursue any such reflection. Nor does he develop the most human aspect of his doctrine of freedom, that is, the suggestion that human beings are not bound by their unconscious primal decisions, the suggestion that, with "human or divine aid," it is possible for all save the totally evil to become good (3:389). Schelling does not, in the *Freedom* essay or in his later works, choose to concentrate exclusively on human freedom or on the human realm; he does not because, unlike many later thinkers who make just that choice, he refuses to abandon the quest for a comprehensive metaphysical system. He refuses to acknowledge that there can be no system of freedom; the question remains whether the *Freedom* essay reveals that the system of identity can be that system.

The system of identity can be completed only if the method of philosophical construction can be comprehensive; the *Freedom* essay reveals that it cannot be, for it cannot extend to the human realm or even to the realm of organic nature. The essay draws attention to the irrationality visible in the latter, and points out that irrational elements can be observed, but not rationally derived. The philosophy of nature—of inorganic nature, at least—and the investigations concerning human freedom may nevertheless be parts of one whole, but that whole cannot be the system of identity. If the whole is even possible, Schelling teaches, the absolute must be God; the *Freedom* essay establishes, at most, that the absolute may be God. It indicates in addition that only an empirical science—a science of observation and analysis of what the absolute has done, of the world that has followed from it—could establish that the absolute is God. The pure, constructive method of the system of identity rules out observation of the world; the system of identity must therefore be abandoned.

With his final system, positive philosophy, Schelling attempts to incorporate the requisite empirical element, but he does not begin immediately to work on that system. His first real development following his abandonment of the system of identity is largely the result of a metaphysical application of an existential insight. The insight makes possible the avoidance of the contradiction in the *Freedom* essay between the teaching that the primal decision is binding and the teaching that conversion is possible. The course of reflection followed above suggests that conversion would result from changes in principles. I will be led to change my principles, however, only if I—perhaps with divine or human aid—determine that my current principles should be abandoned, and I can so determine only through reflection on what those principles have led me to do in the past. If that reflection is sufficiently comprehensive, I could even discover my primal decision. I have access to that decision only through reflection on what I have done, on the past, which I cannot change; but through such reflection I may gain access to myself as I am at present, at least potentially free from the past and able to face the future with a new resolve should I decide to do so. If I can free myself from my past, I should be able to reverse my decision.

If the absolute or comprehensive reflective act is seen in this way, its fundamental relatedness to temporality comes into view. The Schelling of the *Freedom* essay may not clearly see that relatedness, but he sees it soon thereafter, and, typically, he extends it from the human to the divine; he attempts to incorporate it into a system entitled *Ages of the World*. The system was never completed, but several drafts of parts of it have been preserved. The drafts reveal that the temporal structure of reflection was to be of fundamental importance to it:

> The past, a serious concept, familiar to all yet understood by few. Most know none save that which increases with every moment, precisely by the moment, always becoming and therefore not existing. Without determinate, resolute present, there is no past; and how many enjoy such a present? The man who has not overcome himself has no past, or rather lives constantly in it. It is admirable and beneficial for a man to put things behind him, as we say, i.e., to posit them as past. Only for him is the future bright, only he can put things ahead of himself. Only the man who has the power to tear himself loose from himself (from that which is subordinate to his essence) is capable of forming a past for himself; he alone enjoys a true present, as he alone may anticipate an authentic future; and it is clear from these ethical observations that no present is possible save that which rests on a decisive past, and no past save that which, as overcome, grounds a present. [8:259]

For the Schelling who wrote this passage, the step into the philosophical world of the twentieth century would have been a short one. Rather than reflecting further on the temporal in relation to the human, however, Schelling turns to a consideration of the temporal and the divine. He plans a system in which the "ages of the world" are grounded in a divine act of reflection; yet that system fails to incorporate the empirical element revealed as necessary by the *Freedom* essay. Schelling forsakes *Ages of the World*, prior to its completion, in favor of the metaphysical empiricism of positive philosophy.

Before we turn to positive philosophy, Schelling's final system, one further question must be raised: Why does Schelling continue to be a metaphysician? Why does he not turn to philosophical anthropology? It would after all have been easy and natural for him to take that turn. As we have seen, Schelling comes by 1809 to a profound understanding of the philosophical problem of human freedom; it is puzzling that his further investigations do not focus on that problem. It is even more puzzling in light of his repeated metaphysical failures. Schelling's project requires him to move from the world to the absolute and back again. From the beginning of his career, the first move causes him no difficulty. The regress from phenomena to their grounds, and then to the grounds of those grounds, leads Schelling unerringly to the Urgrund, the primordial ground; yet he knows the Urgrund to be primordial only because it is also Ungrund: its indeterminacy is essential to its absoluteness. The great and insoluble problem is that the Ungrund is the ultimate *Abgrund* (*see* 4:258), the ultimate abyss.

As early as 1795, in the "Letters," Schelling acknowledges that the emptiness of the absolute excludes the possibility of any constructive move starting from it. Under the influence of Leibniz, he amends his position and attempts a comprehensive construction in the 1800 *System of Transcendental Idealism*. That construction has impressive systematic solidity, yet the ground is cut from beneath it when Schelling is forced to admit that its most fundamental principle, absolute identity, is not the principle with which the construction begins; as in the "Letters," Schelling's reflections draw him from Grund to Urgrund to Ungrund to Abgrund, and the metaphysical system he seeks

to construct is swallowed up in the abyss. The path is different, yet the end is the same, and it continues to be the same in
the works on the system of identity, despite the mathematical
manipulations of As and Bs, and in the *Freedom* essay, despite
the introduction of theosophical terminology.

As of 1809, Schelling's own investigations should perhaps
force him to acknowledge that metaphysical theology is impossible, yet neither earlier nor later failures ever force Schelling
to that acknowledgment. Schelling continues to strive to produce a comprehensive system grounded in God; he does so
not out of perversity or obstinacy, but rather because he is convinced that nothing else can satisfy the demands of philosophy. He cannot turn from theology to philosophical anthropology, because he is convinced that anthropology not grounded
in theology cannot possibly be philosophical. He explains that
conviction most clearly and most eloquently in the lectures introducing his final system, positive philosophy.

5 POSITIVE PHILOSOPHY

For most of the first decade of the nineteenth century, Schelling was the brightest star in the heavens of German philosophy; in the two succeeding decades, that star virtually vanished, outshone by the brilliance of Hegel. From Berlin, the capital city of Prussia, Hegel ruled academic Germany; Schelling, banished to the provincial universities of Erlangen and Munich, was all but forgotten. According to Hegel, Schelling had played his role in the history of philosophy: he had taken the step past Fichte but had been left behind when Hegel himself took a further step and attained absolute knowledge. Particularly during the 1820s, Hegel was remarkably successful in convincing others that his knowledge was indeed absolute; no other philosopher had any public success in opposing his teachings until after Hegel had died. And even after his death, in 1831, no one immediately rose up to counter him. The power of his system began to dissipate not so much because of external attacks as because of internal dissention among those who took themselves to be Hegel's true followers; such is the ambiguity of the implications of "absolute knowledge" that some Hegelians were Christian monarchists while others were atheistic revolutionaries. Understandably, the Prussian king was more disturbed by the latter than by the former, and he was seriously concerned by the right-wing Hegelians' inability to refute their left-wing adversaries. The Prussian state was in need of a critique of Hegel—particularly, of what appears to be leftist in Hegel—presented by one who would command academic respect; consequently, in 1841 the king of Prussia summoned Schelling to the University of Berlin to save the state from the "legions sprung from the teeth of Hegel's pantheistic dragon."[1] Not surprisingly, those of the Hegelian left

1. The phrase *Drachensaat des Hegelschen Pantheismus* is used in the letter offering Schelling the position in Berlin; according to the letter, the phrase was used by the Prussian king. The text of the letter is reprinted in Schelling's *Philosophie der Offenbarung 1841/2*, pp. 408–09.

Schelling never published his lectures on positive philosophy; his lecture texts and notes were edited and published after his death by his son.

were not inclined to be sympathetic to teachings supported—some would say commissioned—by the Prussian king. Arnold Ruge expressed his reaction in a letter to Feuerbach: "Schelling is called to Berlin, Schelling after *Hegel*! . . . how irresponsible it would be if this challenge from the reactionaries were not greeted with bombs and grape-shot."[2] Schelling was not so greeted, at least not by all; Kierkegaard was so impressed by the first two lectures that he records in his journal, "I have set all of my hopes on Schelling."[3] Those hopes were set on Schelling's "positive philosophy."

THE NEED FOR POSITIVE PHILOSOPHY

Philosophy and Life

As he begins to teach in Berlin, Schelling is aware that many in his audience are more concerned with politics than with philosophy. Even nonphilosophers have come to hear him, he insists in his first lecture, because Hegel has brought philosophy to a point of crisis so severe that none can escape its effects:

> Never before has there arisen, in the interest of life, so massive a reaction against philosophy as is visible at present. This proves that philosophy has come to the point of encounter with those questions of life in the face of which it is not permissible—indeed, not possible—for anyone to be indifferent. As long as philosophy is involved with its first beginnings or with the first stages of its development, it is the concern only of those who have made philosophy their lifework. All others await the end of philosophy; it becomes important for the world only in its results. [14:263]

Throughout most of its history, philosophy has been concerned with its "first beginnings," with abstractions that lack obvious practical importance and that are, therefore, ignored by "life" and "the world," that is, by normal human beings. The interest of life is aroused only when philosophy ceases to

2. Letter of 11 February 1841; the quoted passage is included in Hans-Jörg Sandkühler, *Friedrich Wilhelm Joseph Schelling*, p. 79.

3. Journal entry of 22 November 1841; included in *Philosophie der Offenbarung 1841/2*, pp. 452–53.

focus exclusively on the divine and the natural and begins to treat the human realm. Hegel treats that realm, but, according to Schelling, nonphilosophers will reject his teachings regardless of their apparent cogency: those teachings threaten life rather than support it; they destroy mankind's fundamental beliefs rather than ground them. For this reason, human beings will inevitably reject Hegelianism; they may indeed reject Hegel's discipline itself, decreeing, "There shall be no more philosophy at all" (13:364).

Not only will human beings reject Hegelianism; they have, according to Schelling, the right to reject it, even without fully understanding its first principles. Whereas to be consistent a philosophical system need only satisfy its own criteria, to be true it must satisfy the criteria set by life itself; it can do so only by establishing the truth of fundamental human convictions:

> Most study philosophy not in order to become philosophers, but rather to gain those great unifying convictions without which there is no intellectual self-sufficiency and no human dignity. Indeed, in a time when everything else has become questionable, when everything positive is beset with controversies and oppositions of all sorts, then it appears doubly important and necessary that a bold philosophy, one thoroughly acquainted with all the depths of spirit, rebuild and fortify the unsteady foundations of all true human conviction. [9:359]

Particularly in a time when scientific and political revolutions have made questionable all traditional convictions concerning church and state, human beings can look only to philosophy to support "those great convictions that sustain human consciousness, those without which life has no point, without which it would be devoid of all dignity and self-sufficiency" (13:3; cf. GPP, pp. 68–69).[4]

While Schelling's support of traditional convictions may seem to tie him to the Prussian past, his anticipation of positive changes links him also to a utopian, perhaps post-revolutionary future: "The more stridently the dissentions, the dis-

4. GPP signifies Schelling's Grundlegung der positiven Philosophie, ed. and with an introduction and notes by Horst Fuhrmans.

putes, the phenomena that threaten dissolution . . . are presented, the more certainly will he who is truly informed see in all of them only the omens of a new creation, of a great and lasting revival; a revival that, admittedly, will not be possible without grievous misery, a creation that must be preceded by the ruthless destruction of all that has become lazy, fragile, and decayed" (13:10). Though this passage could be cited with approval by Hitler and by some Marxists, Schelling's program is neither fascistic nor communistic; the development presupposed by his utopia is theoretical rather than economic, political, or historical. He anticipates the time when "the striving for wisdom will reach its long-sought goal, when the unrest that has plagued human spirit for many thousands of years will cease . . . when, over all the parts of human knowledge that have before been separate and mutually exclusive, there will flow the spirit of universal mediation, like a balm that heals all the wounds that human spirit has inflicted upon itself in its zealous struggle for light and truth, wounds from which our time still bleeds" (13:10–11).

Schelling thus continues to teach that theoretical must precede practical progress; he insists also that truly adequate theoretical teachings cannot fail to bring with them salutary practical consequences. Such teachings can be found only in "a strong philosophy, one that can measure itself by life, one that, far from feeling powerless in the face of life and its atrocious realities, far from being limited to the sorry occupation of mere negation and destruction, would take its force from reality itself and would then also produce something actual and lasting" (13:11). Schelling promises a new teaching, one that will "measure itself by life" rather than by the abstract criteria of the professional philosopher; his teaching will be metaphysical rather than directly political, but that does not mean that it will be of no concern to nonphilosophers: "True metaphysics is honor, it is virtue, true metaphysics is not only religion, it is also respect for the law and love of the fatherland" (13:27). True metaphysics is not a study of empty abstractions; it "takes its force from reality itself." False metaphysics, which treats the ideal rather than the real, is no more useful to human beings than is the catechism of Shakespeare's Falstaff:

since honor is no more than a word, and words no more than air, "honor is a mere scutcheon" (13:27).

Schelling's references to Falstaff and to the conviction "without which life has no point" reveal his belief that the crucial ills of the age develop from the conclusions that there are no absolute values, that matters of right and wrong are mere matters of opinion, and that nothing is worthwhile except insofar as it serves the momentary interest of the individual. These are conclusions drawn by philosophers; they are not convictions embraced by ordinary human beings. Nonphilosophers look to philosophy, if at all, for support of their beliefs that some things are inherently valuable, valuable enough to be worth fighting and even dying for, and that their lives are not meaningless and their sufferings not in vain. It is because Hegel's doctrines do not support such beliefs that, according to Schelling, they will be rejected "in the interest of life."

To say that philosophy must satisfy these demands of nonphilosophers is to say that philosophy must be edifying; but what if the philosopher's investigations lead him to conclude that life is indeed meaningless, that there are in fact no absolute values? According to Fichte, the philosopher's "highest maxim" requires "that he seek only the truth, however it may be," so that "even the truth that there is no truth would be welcome to him, if that were indeed the truth" (176n). Hegel embraces this maxim, declaring, "Philosophy must avoid wanting to be edifying."[5] Schelling defends his opposing position by insisting that it alone is truly philosophical:

> Philosophy means love of, striving for, wisdom. Thus, not just any sort of knowledge will satisfy the philosopher, but only the knowledge that is wisdom. . . .
>   If man demands a knowledge that is wisdom, he must presuppose that there is wisdom in the object of this knowledge [that is, that the world is wisely ordered]. . . . There is no wisdom for man if there is none in the objective course of things. The first presupposition of philosophy as the striving for wisdom is thus that there is wisdom in . . . being, in the world itself. [13:201–03]

The philosopher demands wisdom, but he thus demands, first, that wisdom be possible. The question of the possibility

5. *Phänomenologie*, p. 14 (*Phenomenology*, p. 10).

of wisdom might initially appear to be a purely epistemological one, that is, one relating only to our intellectual capacities; yet Schelling insists that the question is primarily metaphysical. The true nature of the question is revealed through reflection on the human condition:

> Man finds himself, from the beginning of his existence, thrown into a stream whose movement is independent of him, a stream that he cannot immediately resist and that he must therefore, at first, suffer; yet he is not meant to allow himself to be simply pushed around by this stream like a dead object, and he should learn to grasp the meaning of the movement. . . . Assuming however that man had convinced himself, through the most careful investigation possible, that this movement was completely blind from the beginning, and therefore had no end—that it would proceed infinitely and pointlessly (so that history would have no goal)—or that it had an end that would be reached blindly, resulting from a blind necessity; if man had become convinced of this, . . . he would probably decide to subordinate himself to this inexorable and unavoidable movement and to exclude it as much as possible from his own activities; but this decision would clearly be a clever rather than a wise one. If man is to order his life wisely, that is, with wisdom, he must presuppose that there is wisdom in the movement itself. For only then can he give himself to it of his own free will, that is, as a wise man. . . . "I demand wisdom" means: I demand a [world] that has been posited wisely, providentially, freely. [13:202–03]

These passages indicate why Schelling cannot turn from theology to philosophical anthropology: he is convinced that only metaphysical theology can provide the basis for answers to the questions that are most important to human beings. Those who are convinced that the questions have no answers should not be called philosophers for, having deemed wisdom impossible, they no longer strive for it; they seek, at best, to be merely clever. According to Schelling, Hegel's system provides no answers to the fundamental human questions; it is for this reason that the rejection of Hegelianism by "the world" or "life" is inevitable. Schelling, as philosopher, is not directly concerned with this rejection; he is most concerned with using Hegel's system as a negative example revealing that true philosophy must follow a different path.

The Hegelian Alternative:[6] Negative Philosophy

In bringing philosophy to a point of crisis, in presenting results that human beings cannot accept, Hegel provides the philosopher with an important lesson; from Hegel's failure in the end, philosophers should learn that they must oppose Hegel from the beginning, that is, they should learn that Hegel's approach to philosophy is ultimately self-defeating: "The great service of the Hegelian philosophy is that it is a *negative philosophy* that knows itself in its own nullity, negative philosophy driven to the point of the knowledge of [its own] mere simulation; that it, in the end, negates its own labor" (*GPP*, p. 236). Hegel's philosophy is negative in that it unfolds in pure thought, independent of all real existence, and in that its unfolding is governed by cold, logical necessity. In stressing the importance of necessity, Hegel denies the reality of freedom; in stressing the eternal, he denies the temporal; in stressing unchanging essence, he denies historical existence. These denials are not, of course, straightforward; if Hegel had entirely ignored freedom, time, and history, the limitations of his system would be obvious even to philosophers. Only at the end of the system— after Hegel's treatments of nature and spirit have been completed—are the distinctions among freedom, time, and history dissolved again into the absolute; it is by this dissolution that the system "negates its own labor," that it is "driven to the point of knowledge of [its own] mere simulation."

Were Hegel's name removed from the preceding paragraph, Schelling's critique of negative philosophy might be taken to apply to his own system of identity. In that system, too, all is governed by the logical necessity of the dialectic, and the finite is completely subordinated to—indeed, swallowed up in—the absolute. What this consideration suggests, namely that Hegel's system is similar to the system of identity, would not shock the Hegelian; as has been noted, Hegel acknowledges that he learned from Schelling, indeed, that Schelling's thought

6. The following section summarizes Schelling's critique of Hegel without indicating possible Hegelian lines of defense. For a complete presentation of the critique, accompanied by what I take to be a successful defense, see my *Absolute Knowledge: Hegel and the Problem of Metaphysics.*

represents the penultimate stage in the history of philosophy. Schelling also recognizes that Hegel's doctrines develop from his own, but he views the historical relevance of the development quite differently. Prior to the appearance of Hegel's central systematic works, Schelling relates, he had recognized that his system of identity, which was meant to be the system of freedom antithetical to Spinoza, is in fact a system of necessity, one devaluing the human and real in favor of the absolute and ideal. Schelling's recognition of where the system of identity would end left him, he reports, with the choice of either continuing to reflect on his serene but sterile absolute or returning once again to the point of beginning in order to reconsider how a system of freedom, a true antithesis to Spinoza, could be developed:

> There remained no other choice but either to return to the merely logical unity or to relinquish this entire direction, in order to try to reach by a new way that which I willed, indeed, that which finally is the only thing that is to be willed, a truly *historical* explanation.
>
> It is easy to see that I, faced with this either-or, had to decide in favor of the historical system. The system [of identity], of which I never gave more than the beginnings (because I recognized its limitations), was only an attempt to unite my essential tendency toward the historical with the necessary.
>
> . . . But as soon as the impossibility of this union dawned on me, I strove toward the historical, though I did so in silence. But this other reduction of [the system of identity], with its entire content, to absolutely ahistorical being, to a merely logical relatedness, this other possibility was also chosen; [it was chosen] by Hegel. (*GPP*, p. 216).

In Schelling's view, then, Hegel did no more than travel farther along a path he himself had already, with good reason, forsaken. In clearly showing where that path must end, Hegel provides a service for those less perspicacious than Schelling, those to whom Schelling's early path might otherwise remain attractive. Hegel's system is therefore an "episode" in the history of philosophy, but it is no more than an episode (10:125).

Though Schelling denies that Hegel's system is particularly innovative or important, he recognizes that the general respect it enjoys can be overcome only through a careful critique. A critique of any philosophical teaching can be adequate, Schelling maintains, only if it focuses on the teaching's essence, on its grounding thought *(Grundgedanke)*. Hegel's own grounding thought is that "reason relates itself to the in-itself or essence of things, from which it immediately follows that philosophy, insofar as it is rational science, concerns only the 'what' of things, their essence" (13:60). This grounding thought is developed in the *Science of Logic,* Hegel's account of the absolute in which nature and spirit are grounded. Viewed from Schelling's standpoint in the system of identity, Hegel's *Logic* appears to be an attempt to introduce determinate content into the absolute; Hegel presents a network of determinate forms purported to be dialectically interrelated in a manner allowing them to be mutually distinct without being mutually opposed. Since there is, according to Hegel, no opposition, the distinctness of the forms does not destroy the absoluteness of the absolute; the Hegelian could therefore argue that the *Logic* is precisely the science of ideas demanded by the young Schelling himself. Yet Hegel can interrelate the forms only through relations of negation and negation of negation; the young Schelling was, like Kant, fully convinced that truly absolute ideas must be beyond negation and therefore beyond discursive presentation. In other words, Schelling had concluded from his own investigations, prior to the appearance of Hegel's *Logic,* that a discursive account of the ideas is impossible in principle. Viewed from Schelling's standpoint in the system of identity, Hegel's *Logic* cannot be the science of ideas—of constitutive concepts—it purports to be; it can be no more than a science of derived concepts, a catalog of arbitrary abstractions. In the Schellingian universe, the absolute itself is the highest truth, for it is the source of all being and thinking; it is followed, on a second stage, by the ideas directly grounded in it. The third level is that of finite entities, including human beings. Concepts—notions that can be interrelated through negations—are found only on the fourth and lowest level: human beings perceive finite things and then arbitrarily group them, forming concepts of the groups. Since the concepts are not, in Schelling's view, veridically related to the ideas, their "science" can be of no philosophical importance.

As a mere science of concepts, Schelling argues, Hegel's *Logic* cannot be a science of the absolute. Its development is thus not on the level of the absolute; it is rather a mere movement in thought, and as such, at best, is on the level of Fichtean reflection:

> We can produce everything that comes forth in our experience in pure thought, but then it is *only* in thought. If we wanted to transform this into an objective claim—to say that everything is, in itself, merely in thought—then we would have to return to the standpoint of a Fichtean idealism. [13:164]

If the movement is only in thought, then the determinations are thoughts rather than things; the system can treat only essence and thereby ignores existence. The pure essences would be at best "the mere negative of existence, that *without* which nothing can exist; but from this it by no means follows that everything exists only *through* them." In terms introduced above, Hegel's realm of essence as a whole could be at best the ideal ground, the ground of thinking; it could not be the real ground, the ground of being. Even a comprehensive account of the ideal ground would not satisfy the demands of philosophy: "It can be the case that everything is within the logical idea, without it thereby being the case that anything is thus *explained*, as for example everything in the sensible world is included in number and measure, without it thereby being the case that geometry or arithmetic explains the sensible world" (10:143; *cf. GPP*, pp. 222–23). "We live in this determinate world, not in the abstract or universal world that we so much enjoy deluding ourselves with by holding fast only to the most *universal* properties of things, without penetrating into their actual relationships" (14:332).

The insufficiency of the *Logic* as a mere science of essences is, according to Schelling, recognized by Hegel himself; that recognition is the sole explanation for Hegel's ungrounded transition from the *Logic* to the philosophies of nature and spirit, the parts of the system that seem to treat the world of experience. Since the *Logic* purports to be complete in itself, the motivation for the move to nature must be extrasystematic; Schelling's accusation is that the move is made "just because nature exists" (10:152). The move is made by the human being, not by the absolute: "I, the philosopher, demand more [than the *Logic*] because I am confronted with a real world and am determined to make this nature conceivable" (*GPP*, p. 226). Yet the greatest problem for a merely negative philosophy, one treating only essence, is the transition to positive philosophy, to the treatment of existence:

> Nothing is easier than to displace oneself into the realm of pure thinking; but it is not so easy then to escape from that realm. The world does not consist of mere categories or pure concepts, it does not consist of concrete *concepts*, but of concrete and contingent things, and what must be considered is the illogical, the other, which is *not* concept, but its opposite, which only unwillingly accepts the concept. It is here that philosophy must take its test. (*GPP*, p. 225)

Hegel's attempt to move to nature is, according to Schelling, an attempt to escape from the realm of pure thinking; yet since that attempt represents an afterthought on Hegel's part, it is scarcely surprising that the move should be the "peak of unintelligibility" of the entire system (*GPP*, p. 232). Hegel can account for the move only by first arbitrarily personifying his network of concepts and characterizing it as absolutely free and then explaining nature as developing from a free act, performed by the now-personal absolute. Schelling objects not only to the personification, but also to Hegel's notion of freedom:

> This absolute freedom can be thought only in this way: up to the point of its logical completion, the idea or concept was necessitated to move forward dialectically. To this extent, it was not free. Now that it is finished, it has nothing more to do. While it may not want to stand still, it is in any case not necessitated to move forward any more. Absolute freedom would, according to this expression, be nothing more than the absence of dialectical necessitation. But a mere not-being-necessitated is a far cry from a positively resolute freedom. (*GPP*, p. 226)

Problems do not cease to arise in Hegel's system when the realm of the *Logic* is forsaken. Since the accounts of nature and spirit are also dialectically structured, Hegel's "free" absolute seems to have initiated "a process from which it can no longer escape, against which it has no freedom, in which it is inextricably bound up. [Hegel's] God is not free from the world, but burdened with it" (10:159). In addition, the logical dialectic governs man and world as fully as it governs God. Neither history nor freedom is real, for all events and acts are predetermined. In Hegel's treatment of nature and in most of his treatment of spirit, there appears to be a temporal process, but even this appearance is misleading, for at the end of the system Hegel returns again to his logical absolute: "In the last idea, the entirety of the actual process is sublated, and in the last moment [Hegel's] idealism reverts, manifestly and unashamedly, into a subjective idealism" (*GPP*, p. 234). "In the last thought, all temporality is explained away as sublated. Everything sinks into a colorless nothingness" (*GPP*, p. 236), not to say a night in which all cows are black.

In Schelling's view, Hegel's system is defective from beginning to end. In teaching that all is and remains in the idea, it is a form of pantheism:

> but not the pure, peaceful pantheism of Spinoza, in which the things are pure, logical emanations of the divine nature; this is given up for the sake of the introduction of a system of divine activity and effectiveness in which, however, the divine freedom is lost all the more disgracefully in that there is the illusion that the attempt has been made to preserve and retain it. The region of pure rational science is forsaken, for that expression [i.e., of the absolute in nature] is freely resolved, and yet even this freedom appears again as merely illusory in that one sees oneself forced, in the end, toward the thought that once again sublates everything that has occurred, everything historical; because one must come to one's senses and return to the purely rational. [10:159]

In attacking Hegel's system as he does, Schelling attempts to convince those who hear him in Berlin that they have been seduced by Hegel's claim of comprehensiveness and by the bulk of detail included in his lectures on history and politics. Schelling, primarily a metaphysician, attacks not Hegel's political doctrines—though that is what all Berlin expected—but rather the first principles from which those doctrines purport to develop; in undermining the grounds of Hegel's political teachings, Schelling intends to draw his students' attention away from politics, which do not interest him, to metaphysics, the one science that is truly crucial, the science that is honor, virtue, religion, respect for the law, and love of the fatherland. Hegel of course claims to evaluate all possible forms of metaphysics and of philosophy and to prove that only his is satisfactory. Schelling denies both that Hegel's doctrine is adequate and that his critique of other doctrines can be proved to be comprehensive: "What if, some day, wholly *new* concepts of philosophy were to be found?" (*GPP*, p. 222). Indeed, Schelling insists that a new concept of philosophy has already been found, that his own final system represents a development that Hegel did not foresee: "Positive philosophy is a new discovery that is especially inopportune [for those] who maintain that philosophy had already been completed [with Hegel]" (13:120). It is in presenting his final system that Schelling decisively refutes Hegel:

> Fifty years ago, Kant believed himself to have traversed and exhausted the entire realm of human faculties of knowledge; later, the attempt was made [by Hegel] to circumscribe the entire realm of the concept, and all possible conceptual moments, within a logical circle. Closer observation reveals however that only just those concepts were included that were given in the contingent world-view of the time. Already [in my own lectures], however, many [new] concepts and conceptual movements have come to the fore, ones of which [Kant's and Hegel's] endeavors had no inkling. Those endeavors related themselves to the world as their agents found it before them, the world they knew; in these lectures, a new world has revealed itself to us, one of which they simply knew nothing, which they could in no way take up in the circles of their concepts except through complete distortion. This may serve as warning against premature terminations of philosophy and the swaggering that accompanies them. The fact of a philosophy of revelation shows already that there was an entire

world left over that was not embraced by previous philosophers.
[14:292–93]

Schelling himself recognizes the possibility of a philosophy of revelation—the last part of positive philosophy—only by reconsidering what it is that his own project truly requires.

Spinozist Flaws

Despite the failure of the system of identity and despite the intervention of Hegel, Schelling does not in his final years forsake his lifelong goal; he retains the conviction that "a system of freedom—as great in scope and at the same time as simple as Spinoza's, its complete antithesis—that would really be the highest" (10:36). For the late Schelling, Spinoza's system is—like Hegel's and like the system of identity—a form of negative philosophy, requiring positive philosophy as its antithesis. In his lectures in Munich and Berlin, Schelling continues to maintain that Spinoza was right in attempting to ground his system in the absolute—"the unconditioned," "the necessary being," "that which is absolutely prior"—but he denies that Spinoza fully recognized the problems involved in establishing the absolute as real ground.

In his late lectures, Schelling presents Spinoza's errors as resulting from too complete a reliance on Descartes. Particularly when he first presents the absolute, Spinoza remains too close to his predecessor, "who knew only one way to introduce the concept of the most perfect being, i.e., with the words: *we all have the representation* of a completely intelligent, simply complete being to whose concept it belongs that the being exists" (11:283). The Cartesian-Spinozist introduction of the absolute is, according to Schelling, defective in two ways: first, in that it presents the concept of the absolute as one that we merely happen to have; second, in that it suggests that logical analysis reveals all that need be—or can be—known about the absolute. The problem arising from the first defect is that if a system's highest concept, its first principle, is contingent—if it is a concept that we merely happen to have—then the entire system is contingent; it can show at best what we (we humans?

we rational beings? we seventeenth-century European intellectuals?) happen to think, and it is open to the objection that it shows no more than what its author happens to think. Spinoza does not recognize, according to Schelling, that if the thought of the unconditioned is to ground a necessary system rather than a merely contingent one, then it must first be established as a necessary thought, as a notion standing in relation of necessary logical antecedence or consequence to determinate thought as such. The true first principle of philosophy cannot be what we only happen to think; it is rather what we *must* think.

In not considering the relation of the notion of the absolute to other notions—to thought in general—Spinoza was not sufficiently logical; in introducing determinate content into his system, however, he was overly logical: the second problem arising from Spinoza's absolute is that it leads him to present the finite as following from the infinite with complete logical necessity. Spinoza presents the finite as related to the infinite in the same way that the properties of individual triangles are related to the essence of triangularity; just as the mathematician can derive the properties of all triangles by exhaustively thinking the idea of the triangle—without observing any real triangles—so too, according to Schelling's Spinoza, could any intellect capable of exhaustively thinking the absolute derive from it the fundamental characteristics of finite existence, even without taking notice of any real, finite beings (11:276; *cf. GPP*, p. 75). Spinoza himself admits that no human philosopher can derive the infinitely many modes and attributes of the absolute, but he thereby maintains only that the derivation is impossible in fact, that is, for human beings; he insists at the same time that it is fully possible in principle, and that an infinite intellect would have no trouble making the derivation.

As we have seen, the young Schelling attempts to surpass Spinoza by establishing that the derivation of content from the absolute is possible in fact as well as in principle; the central thesis of the system of identity is that an account of the finite world in its determinacy would follow with complete logical necessity from the thinking of the absolute itself. Schelling is forced to abandon the system of identity because, in its similarity to Spinoza's system, it entails the denial of the subjectivity of the subject: precisely because its development purports to be both necessary and comprehensive, the system is incompatible with at least one essential aspect of the factical world, namely, human freedom. Human freedom can be affirmed, Schelling comes to realize, only if the comprehensive derivation of content from the absolute is possible neither in fact nor in principle: existence cannot follow from ground with complete logical necessity. This consideration clarifies the defectiveness of Spinoza's doctrine of the absolute: to reason that a complete account of all that is would develop from exhaustively thinking of the absolute is to assume that the absolute is nothing more than an idea, an intellectual notion. According to the *Freedom* essay, "if God were for us a mere logical abstraction, then all would have to follow from him with logical necessity" (7:394); since it cannot be the case that everything follows necessarily from it, Schelling reasons, the absolute cannot be a mere idea or logical abstraction, and we, as philosophers, demand that it be more than idea for us. This brings us back to Spinoza's first defect. For Spinoza, the absolute is not even a necessary idea; it is a contingent one, one that we merely happen to have. To be successful, positive philosophy—Schelling's final antithesis to Spinoza—must show first that the thought or idea of the unconditioned is necessary and then that the thought of the absolute is the thought of a being, of a ground that is real rather than merely ideal, one that exists in reality rather than merely in thought. Positive philosophy must finally show that the development of the finite world from the unconditioned is not simply logically necessary, and it must at the same time explain that development. The problems facing positive philosophy are manifold and serious; the way in which these problems may be solved is revealed, Schelling now maintains, through the teachings of Kant.

THE SYSTEM OF POSITIVE PHILOSOPHY

The Kantian Alternative: Metaphysical Empiricism

Schelling's final consideration of Spinoza reveals that the first task of the system of freedom, as a necessary rather than a merely contingent account, is to prove that the concept of the absolute as the necessary being—the being that must exist— "is an idea that follows from the nature of reason itself and that is indispensable to every rational [*verstandesmässig*] determination of things" (11:284). The requisite proof is found in Kant's *Critique of Pure Reason,* in the section on the ideal of pure reason, which has as its partial conclusion, "I can never *complete* the regress to the conditions of existence without assuming a *necessary* being." Schelling endorses this part of Kant's argument, but if he is to put it to positive metaphysical use he must avoid the Kantian conclusion, with which the sentence quoted above ends, that "I can never *begin* from such a being" (A616/B644).

In his doctrine of the ideal of pure reason, Kant argues that conscientious reflection on the nature of knowledge necessarily leads to the idea of God as the absolute being. According to Kant, every real entity must be fully determinate and thus must be, in principle if not in fact, fully conceptually determinable. It must be true that every possible predicate either applies or does not apply to every real entity; this must be true whether or not any intellect is capable of awareness of the application. At the same time, only an intellect that could make the complete determination could attain complete theoretical satisfaction; only such an intellect could develop absolute theoretical knowledge. The intellect that would know which predicates apply to which things would however first have to know—as a logical precondition—"the aggregate [*Inbegriff*] of all predicates of things in general" (A572/B600). This aggregate of all possibility is termed by Kant an *idea:* it is fully concrete in that it must be taken to be fully determinate (A568/B596). In reflecting on the nature of this aggregate, the philosopher is not engaging in arbitrary speculation; he is, rather, considering an essential aspect of absolute knowledge and thus of the wisdom for which he strives.

Kant does not claim that philosophical reflection on the aggregate of possibility will lead to its complete construction; we are not, it would appear, capable of determining all the predicates that would belong therein. We can, however, exclude certain sorts of predicates from it. All concepts that are derived from other concepts can be excluded as can, according to Kant, those "that cannot stand together," that is, those that contradict each other (A574/B602). Further reflection reveals that we can distinguish concepts that "represent a mere nonbeing" from those that express reality. Furthermore, "no one can determinately think a negation without having grounded it in the opposed affirmation"; for this reason, all negative concepts can also be excluded: "all concepts of negations are derived, and the realities contain the data and, so to speak, the matter, or the transcendental content for the possibility and thorough determination of all things" (A575/B603). The aggregate would thus be "the idea of an entirety of reality [*omnitudo realitatis*]. According to Kant, however, that is necessarily the thought of a single perfect being; not merely concrete, it is individual, and thus appropriately named the ideal of pure reason (A576/B604).

The aggregate of highest possible predicates is a thought that reason, considering what would satisfy its demands for knowledge, necessarily constructs; whereas reason necessarily posits the idea, however, it has no warrant for positing that the ideal—the entity to which the idea would correspond—actually exists (A577–78/B605–06). At the same time, it is natural—so natural as to be unavoidable—for reason to hypostatize the idea, thereby thinking God as existent (A580/B608). The hypostatization is not arbitrary, but neither is it justified. Not only is it illicit to move from thinking to being, but furthermore, we are incapable of thinking God as determinate—of fully constructing the ideal—because our concepts are legitimately applicable only to things that are sensibly experientiable, and God is beyond the realm of sensible experience. We are not rationally justified, according to Kant, in claiming either that God exists or that we know what—in a conceptually determinate sense—he is if he does exist. Because reason necessarily strives to unify its knowledge as systematically as possible, however, we are rationally required to reason as if determinate being were grounded in a single perfect, intelligent, personal absolute, for that will facilitate our systematic consideration of the world itself (A672/B700).

Schelling agrees emphatically, from the time of the *Freedom* essay onward, that the thought that the world is a rationally ordered whole entails the thought that the world is grounded in an absolute that is God, and he frequently acknowledges that on this point Kant's influence has been crucial (13:45, 79, 91). As is indicated above, he expresses the point most directly as a demand implied by the name "philosophy" itself: "Philosophy means love of, striving for wisdom. . . . 'I demand wisdom' means: I demand a [world] that has been posited wisely, providentially, freely" (13:203).

Schelling agrees with Kant not only that reason demands God as absolute principle, but also—and again, from the time of the *Freedom* essay onward—that reason alone, unaided by experience, cannot determine whether or not God exists. Both Schelling and Kant reject the ontological proof in all its forms, insisting that no thought or concept can alone establish the reality of an intelligent and benevolent deity.[7] According to Schelling, the ontological determination of the concept "God" reveals no more than that God can exist only as the absolute ground, that he must be that which is absolutely prior, the necessary being, if he exists at all (13:156–57; *cf.* 10:15–16).

The fact that God's existence could, in principle, be proved only *a posteriori*—only through experience—is, in Kant's view, one of three considerations that indicate the impossibility of our grounding a metaphysical system in God. The second difficulty derives from our inability to even think the idea of God satisfactorily. As is indicated above, Kant denies that any of our concepts could legitimately be predicated of the absolute.

---

7. My denial that Schelling accepts the ontological proof is one of several points where I disagree with some other interpretations. Readers interested in other views of how Schelling conceives of his positive philosophy should consult the following works: Horst Fuhrmans, foreword and introduction to Schelling's *Grundlegung der positiven Philosophie* and *Schellings Philosophie der Weltalter*; Harald Holz, *Spekulation und Faktizität*; Walter Kasper, *Das Absolute in der Geschichte*; and especially the extremely influential study by Walter Schulz, *Die Vollendung des Deutschen Idealismus in der Spätphilosophie Schellings*. For my objections to the interpretations developed in these works, and thus a more complete defense of my own interpretation, see *Absolute Knowledge*, chapter 6, footnotes 5, 6, 10, 11, and 13; or "The End of Philosophy," chapter 9, pp. 387–93 and footnotes 3, 4, 7, 10, 13, 16, 17, 19, and 20.

Finally, Kant insists that in even attempting to think the notion of a primordial ground, an Urgrund, we discover only an abyss, an Abgrund:

> The unconditionally necessary [being] that we so indispensably require as the ultimate bearer of all things is the true abyss for reason. . . . The thought is as unbearable as it is unavoidable: that of the being that we represent to ourselves as the highest of all possible beings saying to itself, "I am from eternity to eternity, outside of me is nothing except that which is something through my will; *but from where, then, am I?*" Here, everything sinks beneath us, and the greatest perfection, like the least, wavers unsupported for speculative reason, which can, without losing anything, allow the one as well as the other, without the least hindrance, to disappear. [A613/B642]

From the beginning of his philosophical career, Schelling is little troubled by this third difficulty identified by Kant. Schelling regularly denies that the grounding of God is problematic, that it is difficult to imagine "where God is from": since the absolute is absolute, it must be from itself, it must be self-grounded in a primal reflection. Kant's second difficulty also is of little concern to Schelling. Kant denies that our concepts are applicable to what is not sensibly experienced, but this limitation of our determinative abilities is taken no more seriously by Schelling than by Fichte or Hegel; all were convinced that Kant himself had successfully surpassed it. Kant's trascendental consideration of the intellect is completely dependent on nonsensible access to its object and is expressible only through concepts that, according to the principle that would deny that we can determine the idea of God, should be applicable only within the realm of sensible experience.

In Schelling's view, then, the system of identity already overcomes two of the difficulties that barred Kant's metaphysical progress. The innovation crucial to positive philosophy—that whereby it surpasses the system of identity—relates to the first Kantian objection identified above. Kant, having argued that God's existence could never be proved save through experience, proceeds to limit the scope of experience in such a way that it too is ruled out as a source of evidence relevant to

the problem of God's existence: Kant restricts the experientiable to what may be sensibly experienced, to what may be directly perceived. It is with respect to the experientiable, and
thus to the potential scope of empiricism, that positive philosophy breaks new ground:

> It is a mistake to limit empiricism to the sensibly apparent [*Sin-
> nenfällige*] as though that were its only object, in that, for exam-
> ple, a freely willing and acting intelligence, such as each of us is,
> does not *as such*, as intelligence, encounter the senses, and yet
> each is knowable empirically, indeed *only* empirically; for no one
> knows what is in a man if he does not express himself; with re-
> spect to his intellectual and moral character, he is knowable only
> *a posteriori*, through his expressions and acts. Assuming we were
> concerned with an acting, freely willing intelligence that was a
> presupposition for the existence of the world, that intelligence
> also would not be knowable *a priori*, but rather only through its
> deeds, deeds that would be visible in the realm of experience; it
> would thus, although supersensible, be knowable only through
> experience. Empiricism as such thus by no means excludes all
> knowledge of the supersensible. [13:113; *cf. GPP*, p. 95]

Positive philosophy must satisfy the demands first revealed
in the reflections of the *Freedom* essay: it must prove, by means
of an examination of the world of experience, that God exists.
Positive philosophy is possible only as a "metaphysical empiricism" (13:114). Schelling frequently indicates how metaphysical empiricism is possible by expressing his project in the form
of a hypothetical syllogism. The major premise states that the
finite world can have the specifiable characteristics x, y, and z
only if it is grounded in God.[8] The first systematic task is that
of determining which x, y, and z can be conceived only as following from God; this is the true task of negative philosophy,
negative in that it must be accomplished *a priori*, in thought
alone, and thus has access only to the possible, not to the actual (*see* 11:297–99, 321). The minor premise of Schelling's syl-

8. Schelling generally presents his syllogism in an invalid form: he phrases
the first premise "If the absolute is God, then the world has the characteristics
x, y, and z," rather than "Only if. . . ." The error is trivial, for Schelling's arguments purport to establish the latter form of the premise, the form that
makes the argument valid.

logism asserts that x, y, and z are present in the world as experienced. This premise could be conclusively established as true only if the world as a whole—in the entirety of its historical development—were accessible; since it is not (in part because it has not been completed), analyses of the factical world can only make the premise appear increasingly to be probable. These analyses are clearly *a posteriori*, empirical ones; they are positive in that they deal with the truly existent and are not accomplished in thought alone.[9] The conclusion of the philosophical syllogism is, of course, that God exists as ground of the world (13:129, 169; cf. 14:346; *GPP*, pp. 115–17, 401). Schelling does not claim that his arguments are absolutely compelling: since the syllogism's minor premise cannot be established, neither can its conclusion: philosophy is not to be transformed into wisdom, it will rather remain *philo-sophia*, the philosopher will continue to examine the "fact of the world" as it has unfolded and as it further unfolds, seeking the traces he knows must be visible therein if the world is in fact grounded in God (13:131).

The project of positive philosophy, as expressed in Schelling's syllogism, is structurally identical to that of the *System of Transcendental Idealism* of 1800; in each, *a priori* constructions are developed and then tested against the reality of the experienced world. The tests are, however, intended to serve quite different purposes. In the 1800 *System*, correspondence with the world is the criterion for the adequacy of the constructive method itself; the purpose of the comparison is the determination of whether the philosopher has succeeded in imitating the primal reflection and the process issuing from it. For the finite constructions of that system, such a test would make sense: if I construct, for example, the phenomenon of magnetism, I can then examine the experienced world to determine whether the construct corresponds to the reality.

Within the context of positive philosophy, experience still functions as the control proving that reason's finite constructions are not chimerical—that they do correspond to

9. For various of Schelling's formulations of the distinction between positive and negative philosophy, see especially 13:68, 76, 79, 92–94, 130, 151*ff*., 158, 248*n*; 10:17–18, 109.

structures and entities in the factical world—but that control is, strictly speaking, superfluous; according to Schelling, the philosopher knows in advance that if anything at all exists, then the reality must generally agree with the construction. Experience shows that there is something rather than nothing; reason alone has no access to existence, but it has complete access to essence. The construction, as purely essential, can be adequately tested by reason alone, and to the extent that it satisfies reason's purely logical requirements it would, Schelling insists, be true even if nothing existed (13:162–63, 128–29). The greatest concern of the positive philosopher is not, however, proof of the existence of sensibly experientiable things, but rather proof of the existence of God; it is for this reason that the major parts of the positive-philosophical system are not philosophies of nature and of spirit, but rather philosophies of myth and of revelation. The simple correspondence test of the 1800 *System* is inadequate for the proof of God's existence since God is not directly visible in the world. Thus, Schelling's indirect empirical proof is the only one possible: if the real world corresponds in certain crucial respects to the philosophical construct, then we should conclude, albeit not with certainty, that God exists.

Like the classical physicotheological proof, Schelling's syllogism is an attempt to ground the conviction that God exists by identifying specific sorts of features in the experienced world; it is important, though, that the two proofs not be confused. Not only has Kant argued that the physicotheological proof presupposes the ontological proof, which Schelling rejects; but furthermore, according to Schelling, it is illicit to move simply from that which is actually posterior—the world—to that which is prior. Rather than thus reasoning from consequent to antecedent, Schelling reasons from absolute spirit to the world, first determining—albeit "negatively"—what would follow from absolute spirit as ground. Positive philosophy is, with respect to the world, an *a priori* science, starting from the very beginning—the absolute *prius*—and deriving determinations from it in the original order; with respect to the complete absolute spirit, though, it is an *a posteriori* science, "in that it proves the existence of that spirit, it explains or is the science

of that spirit, only by examining what is posterior to it"
(13:249).

Positive philosophy is not only Schelling's final system, it is
also the final complete metaphysical theology of the Western
philosophical tradition. It is the final one, not because it succeeds, but because it fails: Schelling takes the only theological
path left open by Kant's critique of metaphysical thinking and
inadvertently proves that that path does not lead to the intended goal, that is, to a coherent and compelling first philosophy. That positive philosophy fails might suggest to some
that it is not worthy of consideration; yet if the principle underlying this suggestion is accepted, very little of the history of
philosophy should repay careful study, for few if any philosophical works have been completely successful. At the same
time, few if any have been completely valueless. As Nietzsche
indicates in the passage used as the epigraph for this study,
philosophers often find their most useful building materials in
the rubble of the collapsed systems of their predecessors. In
addition, understanding why and how the system of a great
thinker collapses may protect us from repeating his fundamental error. Schelling's positive philosophy contains the most
complete dialectical theology and the most elaborate doctrine
of creation the history of philosophy provides; though both
complicated and flawed, it is also intriguing and provocative;
it is worthy of serious consideration.

God and Creation

Philosophy must begin at the beginning, with the being that is
necessary to all other beings, the being that is absolutely prior.
Positing that being is, however, no easy task. Anything posited as subject is, according to Schelling, thought as objectifying something; the subject cannot be, as subject, prior to its
object. Similarly, any object is object only in being objectified,
in being for something else that it thus presupposes for its own
being as object. Thus, that which is absolutely prior can be immediately posited neither as subject nor as object; it can be
posited only as the pure, indeterminate being of Parmenides,
the holy Abgrund of Schelling's *Bruno*, the Ungrund of the
Freedom essay. This pure being is neither for itself (it is not sub-

jective), nor is it for anything else (it is not objective); but since
this is so, it has not yet been posited as truly being at all.

The characterization "pure being" is thus misleading; reason
assumes that its first thought will be of the necessary being as
a being, but it discovers that the first thought is of the Ungrund rather than of anything that is. Since, however, the Ungrund is not nothing—that would, according to Schelling,
make it a "nonthought" (see 10:133; *GPP*, p. 244)—it must be
determined as that which can be *(das Seynkönnende)*. It is by so
determining the Ungrund that Schelling attempts to move past
the sterile One of Parmenides (13:224); that which can be
stands in a determinable relation to that which must be if the
possibility expressed in the "can" is actualized, and to the extent that the relation is explicated, the Ungrund is accessible to
conceptual thought (13:226–27). Differently stated, the Ungrund is potentially being, and while if the potential is not
thought as realized there is nothing more to be said, if the potential is taken to be actualized—if, in the broadest sense, the
Ungrund is thought as acting, as doing anything at all—then
it becomes indirectly accessible to thought through its acts
(12:11).

Given the modal determination of what was first posited as
the absolute *prius*—as that which is prior to all else—the question becomes that of how it can be, of how the potential may
be actualized. Since to be, for Schelling, is to be for something—for oneself or for something else—pure being can be
only by objectifying itself. It can come to be only for itself,
since there is nothing else for which it can be or which can be
for it. With self-objectification or self-reflection, two moments
become visible: the absolute is now pure object, the pure being
that has been objectified, and pure subject, pure being as active in the self-objectification. Since the reflection is a self-
reflection, the two moments are not bifurcated, and a third
aspect must be identified: the absolute is subject and object, but
it remains itself in objectifying itself and is thus pure subject-
object.

The moments subject, object, and subject-object are—or, as
we will soon see, can become—the primal "powers" often
symbolized in the system of identity as A, B, and A^2. Schelling

now characterizes and develops the moments in various ways: he occasionally uses the *A*s and *B*s (*see* 13:355*ff*.), but he also names the moments as being "in itself, for itself, and with itself" (*see* 11:289*ff*.) and, in the modal terminology, "that which can be, that which must be, and that which shall be" (*see* 13:267). The moments are also related to the Pythagorean-Platonic principles of unlimited, limited, and determinate being (11:393; 12:12–13; 13:342). The terminological variety indicates a conviction on Schelling's part that his distinctions are essential and, perhaps, a suspicion that they are vague. More immediately enlightening than the abstract terms is Schelling's continuing reliance on the fundamental structure of reflection. This structure is now explicitly related to the traditional notion of God as trinity, most directly to Leibniz's teaching concerning the latter. According to Leibniz, every spiritual nature is necessarily three without ceasing to be one: "The spirit that reflects on itself is that which knows (*id, quod intelligit*), that which is known (*id, quod intelligitur*), and that which is, at the same time, known as knowing and knowing as known" (13:315). In Schelling's words, "the human spirit, in being conscious of itself and thus having itself, is in a sense two, subject and object, but without really being two, in that, despite the duplicity, it remains only one, which is entirely subject and entirely object, without mixing and without mutual limitation or disturbance" (13:254; *cf*. 12:73–74).

Since the thought of the absolute as being is necessarily the thought of its being for itself through a self-reflective act, and since reflection is decidedly spiritual, the absolute—which was first posited simply as the absolute *prius*—must be thought as absolute spirit (13:239). It is therefore structurally similar to human spirit, yet the two are by no means simply identical. The difficulty with Leibniz's presentation of the divine trinity, according to Schelling, is that the moments that Leibniz identifies seem to remain as necessarily united as are the moments within human consciousness as we know it: Leibniz did not realize the extent to which, within the trinitarian structure of the absolute, each moment is distinguished from the others. While the absolute, externally considered, is "fully free and infinite" since there is nothing truly outside of it, it is, within itself, limited against itself: the moments finitize each other without thereby finitizing the absolute. The absolute as trinity is thoroughly determinate in that each moment is placed or determined by the others, but it is at the same time free from determination in that it is not bound to any one of its moments in a way that would force it to exclude the others (13:238).

The development of the thought of absolute spirit is hypothetical: we as philosophers demand, first, the necessary being, and we discover the structure that this being would have to have. Schelling summarizes the development to this point with the cryptic assertion "If there is a being, then the being *itself* is a *necessary thought*" (13:242). In light of teachings already introduced, the statement becomes intelligible. A necessary condition for the being or existence of anything at all is thought: to be is to be for oneself or for something else; there is no true being that is only in itself. There is, furthermore, a logical coherence to reflection on the preconditions of thought itself: there is a necessary regression to the notion of the necessary being, the thought of the being that can be prior to everything else. The regression may follow the lines drawn by Kant in his doctrine of the ideal of pure reason, or it may develop, more simply, from recognition that the thought of anything grounded has as its logical presupposition the thought of "the being itself," the ungrounded. The thinking subject may well be for the most part unaware of the regression, but its object remains, nevertheless, the logical antecedent of all other thought. This is not to say that the absolute exists at all, or that it exists as it is thought; the Kantian Critique establishes that the existential claim cannot follow from the logical one. The claim made by Schelling is, rather, that if a thinking being— any thinking being—fully analyzes the logical presuppositions it makes in thinking at all, it will necessarily come to think the necessary being, and it will come to think it as absolute spirit.

If anything exists, then absolute spirit is a necessary, even if unthought, thought; but "if I go to the limits of all thought, I must recognize it as possible that there were nothing at all. The last question is always, 'Why is there anything at all, why is there not nothing?' " (13:242). Schelling does not hereby question the existence of the world itself: that the question

"Why is there not nothing?" can be asked proves that something exists. Schelling's question concerns not the existence of the factical, but rather the nature of philosophy and of wisdom: the "last question" asks why there is a world, and no teaching that explains merely what the world is can supply an answer. This can be stated differently: we know that there is something, and we know that the things that occupy our finite world do not ground their own existence, that they are possibilities that happen to have been actualized (*see* 10:6). As philosophers, however, we are interested not so much in what merely happens to be as in what determines which of the myriad logical possibilities are privileged or doomed to actualization. We have now discovered, according to Schelling, that the truly actual, that which alone could ground all actualized possibilities in a way that would satisfy the theoretical and practical demands of reason, is absolute spirit (13:243).

Absolute spirit must be thought as that which is absolutely prior; this means, though, that it is prior even to the three moments through which we have constructed it. Spirit is the absolute actuality (if it is at all), and the moments, as powers, are its primal possibilities. There will be, within our logical construct, "something rather than nothing" only if those powers are allowed to actualize. We can therefore think the world as a true whole—as developing from a unitary ground—only by thinking it as grounded in absolute spirit and structured by the powers. Thus, "If there is or is to be a rational [world], then I must presuppose [absolute] spirit" (13:247). This passage suggests that the question of whether absolute spirit exists may be answered not through a consideration of that spirit itself, but rather only through the determination of whether or not the world is sufficiently rational (it has been clear to Schelling, at least since the *Freedom* essay, that the world is not completely rational). The suggestion should not come as a surprise. As the philosophical syllogism expressing Schelling's project indicates, "the entire (positive) philosophy is nothing other than the proof of this absolute spirit" (13:248). As we have now seen, Schelling's proof is dependent in part upon the doctrine of powers, appropriated from the system of identity. The powers are directly discussed only in the negative part of Schelling's final system—they are not, as in the system of identity, the whole story—but without them, the system of positive philosophy is impossible.

The impossibility of purely positive philosophy—philosophy that does not rely at all on Schellingian dialectical necessity—is revealed through the failure of theosophists and of philosophers like Jacobi, all of whom attempt to ground systematic teachings in privileged evidential access to God as existent, that is, in supersensible and ineffable "experience." Schelling rejects theosophy both because this "experience" is questionable (see 11:88–89) and because the adequate philosophical system must rely on information that can become visible only to the negative, that is, the logical, philosopher: only pure thought can discover the "inner organism" of subjective and objective powers crucial both to the determination of what the absolute would be if it were God and to the understanding of how content could issue from the absolute (13:76; 14:350ff.; cf. 12:115).

The doctrine of powers is thus a part of the system of identity that Schelling retains in his final system; in retaining it, he also retains many of the problems that he is unable to solve within the context of the earlier system. Most important is that which plagues him from the beginning of his career, the problem of creation, of the descent from infinite to finite: "if I do not grasp [einsehe] how a being thought as outside of the world and exalted above it could produce a world different from and posited outside of itself, then this presupposition could perhaps arouse my faith, even influence my life, but I would have insight into nothing more than mere words that would not be understood" (13:42). In insisting in his positive philosophy that absolute spirit is complete and fully self-sufficient, Schelling denies that the finite can follow it with any sort of logical necessity. In attempting to develop a teaching that presents the creation as other than necessary, he first suggests that, at the very least, the possibility of creation cannot be excluded from the absolute as it has already been thought (12:39). The account purports to have shown that absolute spirit has no need to create, but not that it is either unwilling or unable to create (13:263–64). It is not impossible, Schelling continues, for this possibility to "show itself" to spirit without thereby being posited by it: the powers would, in this manifestation, become visible as potential principles for a nonabsolute being (13:267). Spirit is in no way bound to actualize the possibility, but the possibility will be attractive in that it provides the opportunity for free expression. Exclusive of this opportunity, spirit is simply as it is, without having willed that it be so. If it wills the actualization of the powers, it will have *acted* as absolute, it will not merely *be* absolute. Indeed, once the possibility arises, spirit must in a certain sense act freely: it must choose either to create or not to create. This recognition that absolute spirit can ground finite being only by choosing to do so marks an important step in our thinking of the absolute: we thereby see that absolute spirit must be thought as positively free rather than as merely noncompelled; having seen this, according to Schelling, we have unwittingly but unavoidably thought absolute spirit as God (13:269).

According to Schelling, we realize that we have thought absolute spirit as God when we realize that we have thought it as making a choice. This signals a radical change in Schelling's doctrine of divine freedom: in earlier works, that freedom is presented as the absolute freedom that is equivalent to absolute necessity, as action in accordance with essence. The late Schelling insists that neither creation nor noncreation is determined by a divine essence: "God is bound to nothing, not even to his own being" (13:305). If God were so bound, creation would have to be envisioned as a logically necessary emanation; but if creation were necessary, God's divinity would be dependent upon the existence of the world and would be relative to it. Schelling agrees with Newton that God is in a sense relative to the world in that he is master of it; for Schelling, though, he is the true master in that he is free to posit the world or not, as he chooses (13:291). Earlier philosophers were, according to Schelling, forced to resort to doctrines of emanation because they could discover no middle term mediating God and his creative act. In Schelling's doctrine, the mediating position is held by God's awareness of the possibility of creation; this possibility is "the first object of divine knowledge" (13:293). In this first vision, God sees "the prologue to the entire future world," he sees the ideas, the "eternal models of things" (13:293–94; *cf. GPP,* p. 448).

In essence, the first claim in Schelling's creation doctrine is that the possibility of creation cannot be simply excluded from the absolute: the absolute could create without disproving its own absoluteness. An account of any actual creation must answer two further questions, that of how creation will work if God wills it and that of why God might will it, of the possible grounds for the decision in favor of existence (13:271). Concerning the second, Schelling begins by asserting that God, in his pure absoluteness, is not yet truly articulated: the three moments have not become persons; they are not truly distinct. Moreover, the unity of the absolute purely as such is so complete that—as Schelling teaches in his earlier works—there is therein no self-knowledge (13:273–74); if God is to know himself, he can come to do so only through the radical self-reflection that will free the first moment, the ground moment, from the bonds of the second (13:274). God creates, according to this first explanation, for his own sake. A second explanation of the reason for creation, "less clever but fully relevant," would hold that God cannot will the finite for his own sake, since he is in need of nothing. He must therefore will it, if at all, for the sake of something finite, a creature (13:277), and if for the sake of a creature, then for one that will be able to appreciate his generosity, a fully self-conscious creature like man (13:287, 12:109, 118; 14:351–52; *GPP,* p. 469).

Whatever the reason, God may create if he decides to do so. Since the creation will not be an emanation—it will not be, initially, logically necessary—it is better described as a begetting or generation *(Zeugung)* (13:312). If the creative possibility is allowed to actualize, the first moment, being in itself (the ground moment of the *Freedom* essay), will become independent of the other two:

> that which [in the abstract idea of the trinity] is merely being in itself can raise itself, can go over into an objective being outside of itself. The peculiarity and the true strength of my idea lies in the claim that that being in itself contains the matter, the occasion [*Veranlassung*], the possibility for a tension [among the three moments]. It is this aspect of my idea that insures its lasting in-

fluence on science; for thereby, that unity becomes living, self-moving, and there becomes visible at least the possibility of moving from it to three powers that exclude each other—to a true *life*. [13:316]

The begetting, the positing, of a tension among the powers is a negation of the primordial unity, but not a permanent one; the purpose of the process is not the negation itself, but rather the eventual negation of that negation (13:325).

The process of purely divine creation is eternal and, although moments are distinguishable as prior and posterior, the relations are logical rather than temporal (14:356), the creation ideal rather than real. The ideal process is complete when there arises a being that shares God's completeness by being the same unity of powers and by being, like God, bound to none; this being with whom the tension is overcome is, as in the *Freedom* essay, man in his primordial form (13:344ff., 118). Man is the point of reconciliation for the ideal creation, but the reconciliation is unstable. Since man is like God rather than like any one of the powers, he is also capable of allowing a tension to arise among the powers. The special status of man and God is best expressed in the terms Schelling at times appropriates from Plato's *Philebus*: the first power is the unlimited, the second the principle of limitation, the third the determinate being that results from the mixture of the first two. God and man alike are transcendent to this complex; they alone can cause the mixing that results in determinate entities. In his primordial form, man is like God in that he is above the powers, he contains them; he is different from God in that he is not yet ruler of the powers, in that they have not yet, for man, become actualized as distinct. Man does not realize that the difference indicated by this "not yet" is crucial: "He imagines that he can be master of the powers in their separation just as he is master of them in their original unity. Precisely therein lies the great if nearly unavoidable illusion [*Täuschung*]" (13:349; cf. 12:119ff.).

Schelling here develops a fundamental teaching of "Philosophy and Religion" and of the *Freedom* essay: in attempting to become fully like God, master of the content implicit in the powers, man falls. He thereby frees the ground moment, losing control over it; it can be subdued, the unity can be restored, only through a temporal process whose major developmental structure is determined by the powers rather than by man, who has lost control of them, or by God, who is fully articulated at the end of the ideal process. Since the development is structured by the powers, it can be rationally reconstructed at least in outline, by negative philosophy (13:359, 359n). The crucial question of positive philosophy is which features of the constructed world would, if correspondent to the existent world, provide evidence that the latter really does have its origin in man's attempt to become fully like God.

Myth and Revelation

From our negative or purely rational consideration of God and creation we have, according to Schelling, already learned that (1) if the absolute ground is God, then man was created in God's image, that is, as unity of the three powers; (2) if the absolute is God and there is a finite world, then that world has resulted from man's attempts to retain mastery over the powers while allowing them to develop individually, that is, from man's attempts to become fully like God; and (3) if the finite world has originated in this manner, then man has failed, at least temporarily, to rule the powers in their independence from each other, and the first and second powers will be fully reconciled into a third only following a temporal process. Schelling continues to insist that the structure of powers is visible in nature (13:379), yet the philosophy of nature is not of central importance within positive philosophy. Negative reconstruction of certain moral, political, and historical features of the human realm is also possible—Schelling sketches such a reconstruction at the end of the "Exhibition of Pure Rational Philosophy" (11:490–559)—but correspondence of these structures to reality would also be irrelevant to the determination of whether the absolute is God. We are supposed to know from the system of identity that we can think the world as structured by the interactions of the powers; but we know that we can do so whether or not the absolute is God.

If the real creation is grounded in man's willful fall—as it is if man is ultimately grounded in God—then the fundamental human desire within the finite realm must be to master the powers by positing them as God, as the primal spiritual unity in and through which all would be made rational; the fundamental human desire must be to regain the paradise that was lost when the powers were freed. The regaining of paradise through the positing of God is not a simply intellectual or purely rational matter: human beings must posit the powers as they are in the world process, not as they are in God, for the latter would be no real mastery or reconciliation of them. This means, however, that the powers must be posited differently in different historical epochs, because the human act that resulted in the fall and in the real creation has involved the powers themselves in the temporal process. God himself is not involved in that process, and the relation of powers in him does not change; yet the powers freed by human action are cosmic rather than divine, and they govern the development of the finite world. The first power, the objective principle or being in itself, attempts to retain its autonomy; it resists the efforts of the subjective principle—being for itself—to know it. Thus, throughout the first part of the historical process, the ruling principle of the world is none other than the dark, irrational power, and early attempts to posit it as such—attempts reflected in myths—result from accurate insight into the state of the world as it is and not from any philosophical, scientific, or religious naiveté.

Until the second power begins to articulate the first clearly, human beings will see the world, if they see it as it truly is, as governed by a single, unintelligible god. As the conflict between powers develops, the original unity of the dark principle is fragmented. The new powers that arise will appear to human consciousness as gods that are related to the first god; they will appear as its offspring, and human accounts of them will develop into systems of theogonic myths. Finally, with the development in which the principle of understanding comes to have real ascendancy over the principle of ground, such that the two are united while remaining distinct, it will become possible for humans to posit the true trinitarian monotheism of the Christian religion. At this point, the cosmic powers will re-

late to each other just as the divine powers do; the positing of
the Christian godhead is thus the positing of the one true, eternal God.

The rational construction of the course of development from
one god through many gods to the God that is three in one is
grounded in the dialectical structures expounded in the system
of identity and in *Ages of the World*. It could thus be said that
positive philosophy is what the *Freedom* essay fails to be,
namely the ideal part of the system of identity, the final part
that fully transfigures what precedes it. This transfiguration
was not foreseen by Schelling: in developing the system, he
was unaware that the ideal part would finally focus on the development of myth and religion (although he was, from his
student days, intrigued by the history of myth). Only in his final system does Schelling argue that the existence of God must
be proved, to whatever extent possible, through man's attempts to posit him, attempts that must, at first, be mythic.

The central contention of Schelling's philosophy of mythology is that the gods of myth are in fact the cosmic powers; his
positive argument for the contention takes the form suggested
by his fundamental syllogism. Before presenting the positive
argument, however, Schelling attempts to give his contention
negative support in the presystematic "historical-critical" introduction to the philosophy of mythology (11:3–252). There, he
purports to demonstrate that traditional theories—some of
which claim that myth is grounded in poetry, others that it is
best understood as a primitive form of either natural science or
rational philosophy—fail to explain the phenomenon adequately. Summarizing the conclusions of that argument in the
Philosophy of Revelation lectures, he insists that "these representations—the mythological ones—cannot be explained in any
other way [save my own], as the results of all previous hypotheses have clearly shown; they cannot be explained as invented [*erfundene*], nor as imagined [*erdichtete*], nor as resulting
either from a merely contingent confusion or from a prior revelation; they are, rather, thinkable only as necessary products
of the fallen human consciousness that is under the domina-
tion of the powers, which themselves, in their separation, have
lost their divine significance, and have become merely cosmic"

(13:378; *cf.* 11:125). The phenomenon of the historical development of systems of myths is possible, Schelling argues, only as a reflection of the theogonic interactions of the cosmic powers. The theogonic process itself will be at once ideal and, in a sense, real:

> In the mythological process, man is not involved with things; the process is rather animated by the *forces that arise within consciousness itself.* The theogonic process through which mythology arises is *subjective* in that it advances within *consciousness* and makes itself known through the production of representations; but the causes and thus also the objects of these representations are the *actual* theogonic forces, the forces *in themselves,* precisely the same ones through which consciousness is existent as positing God. The content of the process is not merely *represented* powers, it is *the powers themselves*—the ones that produce consciousness and, since consciousness is only the end of nature, that also produce nature, and that are thus actual forces. The mythological process has nothing to do with natural *objects,* but with the pure productive powers, whose primordial product is consciousness itself. It is here, then, that the explanation enters the objective realm, and thus itself becomes fully objective. [11:207; *cf.* 13:379, 500–01]

The positive philosopher's understanding of the principles, the powers, allows him to identify the necessity underlying the superficial diversity among the mythic productions of different peoples at different times:

> The principle according to which mythology develops is the principle of a successive stepping forth [*Hervortreten*] of the powers that were united in primordial consciousness and that reunite themselves only successively. . . . The entire mythological process revolves around the three powers. They are what is essential to the process, and insofar as they appear to consciousness as gods, then . . . only *those* gods that enter consciousness successively are the truly *causal,* the *essential* gods. [13:396]

In that it presents only some gods as essential, Schelling's theory allows for contingent aspects within the history of myth; Schelling no longer asserts that absolute necessity rules any part of the factical world process. We are capable of distinguishing essential from extraneous gods in that we know that only the former are interrelated in ways corresponding to the necessary relations among the powers. If essential gods are so identified, though, the basis for their distinction from accidental ones may seem to beg an important question; the positive philosopher is to examine the structures of myths hoping to find certain relations, but he will recognize as essential to those structures only the relations he seeks. Given such a procedure, success might appear to be assured, but of minimal importance; there are enough myths, it would seem, that it would be hard to imagine a structure not reflected in at least some of them. This objection is only partially applicable to Schelling's method. Schelling does not introduce contingency into his account in order to allow himself to explain away insignificant gods, those unrelated to the powers; rather, as he argues as early as the *Freedom* essay, since the ground principle is a principle, irrational and contingent features must be present in the factical world. While the correspondence of gods and powers therefore cannot be complete, Schelling's method does not require that it be complete. Schelling acknowledges that he cannot analytically prove that the world process is theogonic; he need not explain the origins of all mythic gods, but need only reveal enough correspondence between powers and gods to establish his account as superior to the alternatives.

The method of philosophy of mythology corresponds to the structure identified in Schelling's philosophical syllogism. Following the rational determination of what the theogonic process would be and how it would develop, Schelling proceeds to "the philosophy of mythology itself," that is, "the demonstration, through mythology, of the *actuality* of such a (theogonic) movement in consciousness" (14:10). In fact, the negative and positive developments—the rational and the historical investigations—are presented concurrently rather than sequentially; the former does not simply precede the latter, but rather, as each step is developed rationally, it is exhibited historically. Nevertheless, the structure remains that of the syllogism; at various important points in the development, Schelling stresses that the rational is methodologically prior to the historical, that steps are first "derived from the inner workings of the mythological development itself," and then "demonstrated in fact, historically" (12:252; cf. 12:257; 13:464–65, 513). In these derivations and demonstrations, Schelling reveals that he has not lost the attention to detail or the insight into analogous structures that he first exhibited in his philosophy of nature; he presents his investigations of polytheistic myth in twenty-three lectures requiring, when published, 540 pages (12:135–675).

The theogonic process purports to be the process through which the divine powers—which have, as a result of the fall, become "merely cosmic"—reconstruct the articulated but unified configuration in which they stand within the divine unity. The theogonic process visible in myth is thus necessary and true in that it reflects the development of the powers and in that it ends with an accurate image of the triune God: "Polytheism, considered in the totality of its successive moments, is the way to truth and to that extent is itself truth" (11:212). Yet myth, as mere counterpart to the wholly necessary, rationally accessible interplay of the powers, cannot reveal the true relation of the God that it posits to human beings and to the world (11:212). Differently stated, mythic consciousness does not become aware of why there is something rather than nothing. Awareness of the theogonic process cannot explain itself, nor can it explain why human consciousness retains sufficient unity to avoid simple destruction in its own original attempt to become fully like God. According to Schelling, it is intelligible that man is not thereby destroyed only if God himself, having realized that man would fall if given the chance, decided nonetheless to reveal himself to man in the process, despite his certain foreknowledge of the primal sin (14:8–9). Because the truth is finally revealed to man, we can know that God originally decided to create for the sake of man. This, then, is the answer to the question "Why is there something rather than nothing?"—the question that must have an answer for philosophy itself to be possible. If the question had no answer, there could be no true philosophy, for there would be no wisdom "in the world itself":

> There must be a *finis quaerendi et inveniendi,* a *goal* at which the never-resting spirit rests; for otherwise all knowledge would be in vain, i.e., pointless. There must arise something in the devel-

opment of things where human knowledge, which has in itself an infinite drive toward progress and movement, must confess that it can proceed no further, where it thus becomes silent. [14:27]

The truth with which man can rest is revealed in Christian teachings, which enter the historical process only after the theogonic process has been completed. While Christian doctrine represents the highest truth, though, Schelling does not present the Christian Bible as an authority that the philosopher simply accepts.

The reality—this is to be well noted—the reality of the principles that make revelation conceivable [aus welchen sich die Offenbarung begreift] has been confirmed for us, independent of revelation, through the mammoth appearance of mythology. This is the role of the philosophy of mythology within a philosophy of revelation. [13:530]

The status of "revelation" as a source of knowledge distinct from reason is established, according to Schelling, by the prior demonstration that mythic consciousness has accurate but nonrational access to the cosmic powers themselves: "A real relation of the human essence to God is verified by the philosophy of mythology prior to all revelation, and grounded on so broad a base that I may assume it as firmly and unshakably established" (14:29). The fact that pre-Christian mythmakers accurately reflected the relations of the powers in their myths proves that our relation to the divine is real rather than merely ideal: we have access to God, but it is not primarily through reason (see 13:142–43, 150–52). The truth can be revealed at the historical point where the powers themselves have achieved a state of balance correspondent to their balance in the divine unity; at that point, it becomes possible in principle for human beings to grasp the highest truth. At first, it is grasped only by a privileged few; since access to the principles and to God is at this point through revelation rather than through reason, intelligence is not a factor in determining who the few will be (see especially 10:117).

The truth finally revealed in the Christian teaching—or,

more specifically, through the person of Jesus Christ (*see* 14:232)—is that there is something rather than nothing because God decided to allow man to become fully and self-consciously one with him, even knowing that, because man would originally act pridefully, the full oneness could be stably present only following a finite temporal process. In accordance with the doctrine of temporality developed in *Ages of the World*, the stable unity is presented as the state of the "eternal future" that will follow the world process as a whole; the world process is established as a true cosmic "present" through its relation to that future and to the "eternal past," the primordial state of unity posited by man as past in and through his fall from it. Because God did not forsake man when man forsook God, the two will be reunited in the post-temporal future.

The "truth" described in the preceding paragraph is, according to Schelling, the truth of the world, the truth that reveals that there is "wisdom in the world." Schelling devotes fourteen lectures (14:3–334) to developing this truth and to relating it to the person of Jesus Christ, but his presentation seems to require that he assert more than his method and principles allow him to assert. While denying that he desires to establish any sort of religious dogma (14:30, 293) and insisting that his attempt to understand the significance of Christ is methodologically identical to his attempt to grasp the true importance of, for example, Dionysus (14:201; *cf.* 13:133–40), he also seems to assert that Christian doctrine could have arisen historically only if Jesus Christ actually existed as the son of God, sent to earth by God at a specific point in time. While we have no reason to assume or even suspect that the gods of myth were "historical persons," we know, according to Schelling, that Christ existed on earth: "he lived like other men, he was born and he died, and his historical existence is as fully documented [*beglaubigt*] as that of any other historical person" (14:229–30). The birth of Christ, the unique son of God, "at a determinate time" is "a final but fully external event, one entirely within the sphere of other phenomena [*Begebenheiten*]. This fact could not come forth merely in the consciousness of humanity; unlike the facts of myth, it could not have a merely subjectively objective [*subjektiv-objektiv*] truth. For it an absolutely objective truth was necessary; it had to be something that occurred independent of human representations" (14:173).

Schelling at least seems to teach that the appearance of Jesus Christ, as a historical person, is proof of determinate divine intervention within the historical process; yet his principles certainly do not allow such a teaching, for it would draw God himself into time. Schelling's principles would allow no more than the teaching that the representation of the son of God as existent is possible only if God has preserved the unity of human spirit despite the fall that should otherwise have destroyed the unity. This teaching would introduce no inconsistency into the system, but it might not satisfy the system's doctrinal requirements. The development of powers, to which the development of myth corresponds, can lead only to an equilibrium point at which the first two powers are contained in the third; for the introduction of the relation of revelation, Schelling requires a fourth moment over the powers, a higher unity formally identical to what God necessarily is and to what man originally was; he requires a new master of the three powers to inaugurate a new historical epoch. The new transcendent entity must mediate between God and man; in order to do so, it must be both "fully God and fully man" and, for this role, Jesus Christ is the leading "historical" candidate. The question crucial for the complete evaluation of Schelling's final system is whether Christ can be introduced so as to play the role without violating the principles of the system.

The obscurity of Schelling's teaching concerning Jesus Christ weakens the conclusion of his positive philosophy, but it may not indicate an ultimately fatal flaw. Revelation is in any case not accessible to all people, but neither is religion grounded in revelation the final truth; it must be followed by what Schelling calls "philosophical religion," a teaching grounded not in a knowledge or truth revealed only to a few apostles and communicated by them to others who have faith in them, but rather in a knowledge "that would be possible for and accessible to human beings under all circumstances, at all times and in all places, i.e., universally human knowledge, as free, scientific knowledge" (14:296). Schelling's positive philosophy purports to provide the theoretical ground for this "truly spiritual house of God . . . in which all human striving, willing, thinking, and knowing would be brought into complete unity" (14:296). If Schelling does not directly consider the former aspects of this unity, "the practical, the moral [aspects] of Christian life," it is only because "they follow of themselves from the theoretical ideas" (14:293).

THE LEGACY OF POSITIVE PHILOSOPHY

In his opening lectures on positive philosophy, Schelling promises to present "a strong philosophy, one that can measure itself by life, one that, far from being limited to the sorry occupation of mere negation and destruction, [will] take its force from reality itself and . . . produce something lasting" (13:11). The rhetoric of the opening lectures encouraged those in Schelling's audience to believe that even his metaphysical doctrines would have important and immediately obvious practical implications. Schelling's emphasis on reality and existence was welcome to leftists and rightists alike: the former longed for evaluations of existing governments rather than Hegelian descriptions of abstract political forms, the latter for a presentation of God as a personal force acting in the world rather than as Hegel's "absolute idea." Kierkegaard reports that Schelling's second lecture brought him "indescribable" joy, that his spirits soared when Schelling used "the word 'reality' " and spoke "of the relation of philosophy to reality."[10]

The members of Schelling's audience, despite their profound philosophical and ideological differences, agreed with near unanimity that what Schelling promised is extremely valuable; they also agreed that what Schelling delivered as his own teaching is utterly worthless. Expecting to hear discussions bearing on the problems raised either by the failure of the French Revolution to do away with monarchy or by the success of the Enlightenment in doing away with religion, Schelling's audience was subjected instead first to descriptions, pre-

10. Sören Kierkegaard, journal entry of 22 November 1841, included in Schelling, *Philosophie der Offenbarung 1841/2*, pp. 452–53.

sented by the self-professed philosopher of life, of obscure powers and their even more obscure interrelations and then to examinations of archaic myths and the historical Jesus. Kierkegaard concluded, within three months, that Schelling surpassed other philosophers not in profundity but in shamelessness and that "the whole of the doctrine of powers betrays the greatest impotence."[11] Historian Jacob Burckhardt was also appalled by Schelling's presentations:

> Even the students in Berlin will eventually find it impossible to put up with [Schelling's] awful, half-witted [*halbsinnliche*] manner of thinking and speaking. It is dreadful to hear a long, historical analysis of the fate of the messiah, an analysis that is as extensive and involved as an epic but nevertheless wholly lacking in form. Anyone who can still love Schelling's Christianity must have a tender heart.[12]

The disappointed expectations of the members of Schelling's audience led them to judge positive philosophy, and its author, far more harshly than was deserved; those who honestly evaluate Schelling's final system may eventually reject it, but they will do so with admiration rather than with disgust. Be that as it may, the passages quoted above indicate that Schelling's strongest influence was negative; Schelling convinced those who heard him that his is a path the philosopher should not follow. The failure of positive philosophy led many to conclude that metaphysics is impossible as theology, that is, as the science of the highest being, the science that would explain finite entities in terms of their relation to an infinite entity. The abandonment of metaphysical theology is the first part of Schelling's philosophical legacy; the second part of that legacy develops from Schelling's critique of Hegel. Through the apparent cogency of that critique, Schelling established, to the satisfaction of most who were exposed to it (including Kierkegaard, Feuerbach, Engels, Marx, and Bakunin) that metaphysics is also impossible as ontology, that is, as the science of the categories of being, the science that would explain finite enti-

11. Letter of 27 February 1842 to Emil Boesen; ibid., pp. 455–56.
12. Jacob Burckhardt, letter of 14–19 June 1842 to Gottfried Kinkel; ibid., p. 451.

ties in terms of the ideas or concepts that make them intelligible. Schelling convinced his philosophical successors that metaphysics, the fundamental rational science that would ground all other sciences, is impossible as ontology and as theology; he thereby convinced them to abandon the metaphysical quest for rationality altogether.

The conflicting claims of ontology and theology to metaphysical status, and thus to primary philosophical status, begin to develop near the dawn of the Western philosophical tradition; the conflict is visible if Plato's *Sophist* is compared with his *Timaeus*, or if Book 7 of Aristotle's *Metaphysics* is compared with Book 12. Two and a half millennia later, Kant insists that rational theology is impossible and that ontology cannot be the science desired by metaphysicians. In the wake of Kant, Hegel argues that metaphysics can be and must be ontology, and Schelling argues that metaphysics can be and must be theology. The post-Idealistic philosophers, although led in different directions by Kierkegaard and Marx, are convinced by Schelling that metaphysics can be neither, and thus that the philosopher should not be metaphysician.

Kierkegaard and Marx, having abandoned metaphysics, attempt to establish in its place distinct forms of philosophical anthropologies. Kierkegaard focuses on the "sickness unto death" felt by human beings as creatures in need of, but— despite the attempts of metaphysical theologians—deprived of, rational knowledge of their creator; Kierkegaard replaces Schelling's progressive proof of God's existence with an irrational leap of faith. Marx focuses on the alienation suffered by human beings as entities who fail to understand and thus to master the material and economic forces—the real, demonstrable forces—that control their destinies. Both of these turns to anthopology were, again, mediated by positive philosophy in three ways: both Kierkegaard and Marx accept the general demands on philosophy articulated by Schelling in his opening lectures; both accept Schelling's critique of Hegel, at least in its main outlines; and both take positive philosophy as a disastrous failure, one that teaches us only that Schelling's metaphysical empiricism is impossible. Schelling's threefold mediation does not alone fully explain the genesis of philosophical anthropology as a form of first philosophy, but Schelling's influence was of central importance, and no account that ignores it can be complete.[13]

The Marxist and existentialist movements alike are grounded in these three conclusions drawn from Schelling's final lectures. That the conclusions were drawn by the founders of these movements is a significant historical fact; whether they should be drawn is a fundamental philosophical question, a question that remains unanswered. It is questionable whether philosophy can survive in the absence of metaphysics; according to Heidegger, its attempts to do so are like a person's vain attempts to survive his own suicide.[14] Klaus Hartmann has presented powerful arguments against the Marxist alternative to metaphysics,[15] and Stanley Rosen has voiced strong objections to the ways taken by existentialists and by the devoutly antimetaphysical analytic philosophers.[16] I myself have argued that Hegel's ontological option remains viable despite the historical success of Schelling's critique.[17] To argue that metaphysics is necessary is to argue that much of the legacy of positive philosophy should be rejected. Yet even those who would revive metaphysical thinking will do well to attend to a part of that legacy, namely, to the existential questions articulated by Schelling in the *Freedom* essay and in his introductory lectures in Munich and Berlin; these are questions that the future metaphysician cannot simply ignore. It is to Schelling's credit that he recognized them and that he struggled with them.

Schelling struggled with fundamental philosophical questions throughout a career that lasted over fifty years. He devoted that career to an attempt to produce the one system— the antithesis to Spinoza, the system of freedom—that would have satisfied his longing for wisdom. Even if he did not suc-

---

13. A more detailed account of the beginnings of Marx's and Kierkegaard's developments is given in Karl Löwith's *From Hegel to Nietzsche*. Löwith indicates how Marx, who did not attend Schelling's lectures, was influenced by Schelling through the mediation of Feuerbach and Engels.

14. *Schellings Abhandlung*, p. 78.

15. *Die Marxsche Theorie*.

16. See especially *Nihilism*.

17. In "The End of Philosophy" and, more recently, in *Absolute Knowledge*.

ceed, even if he did not surpass Spinoza, the obstinacy with which he held to his project reveals the intensity of his philosophical eros. Schelling demands the philosopher's admiration, for he, like his great rival, "risked everything, desiring either the whole truth, in its entire magnitude, or no truth at all."

SELECTED BIBLIOGRAPHY

Baeumler, Alfred. *Das Irrationalitätsproblem in der Aesthetik und Logik des 18. Jahrhunderts bis zur Kritik der Urteilskraft.* 2nd ed. Tübingen: Max Niemeyer, 1967. Reprint. Darmstadt: Wissenschaftliche Buchgesellschaft, 1975.

Fichte, Johann Gottlieb. *Sämmtliche Werke.* Edited by Immanuel Hermann Fichte. Vol. 1: *Zur theoretischen Philosophie 1.* Berlin: Veit, 1845–46. Reprint. Berlin: Walter de Gruyter, 1971. English translation of *Grundlage der gesammten Wissenschaftslehre* (Vol. 1, pp. 83–328) in *Science of Knowledge with the First and Second Introductions.* Translated by Peter Heath and John Lachs. New York: Meredith, 1970. The translation indicates the German pagination.

Frank, Manfred, and Kurz, Gerhard, eds. *Materialien zu Schellings philosophischen Anfängen.* Frankfurt: Suhrkamp, 1975.

Fuhrmans, Horst. *Schellings Philosophie der Weltalter. Schellings Philosophie in den Jahren 1806–1821. Zum Problem des Schellingschen Theismus.* Düsseldorf: Schwann, 1954.

Hartmann, Klaus. *Die Marxsche Theorie.* Berlin: Walter de Gruyter, 1970.

Hegel, Georg Wilhelm Friedrich. *Briefe von und an Hegel.* Vol. 1. Hamburg: Felix Meiner, 1952.

————. *Phänomenologie des Geistes.* Edited by J. Hoffmeister. 6th ed. Hamburg: Felix Meiner, 1952. English translation published as *Phenomenology of Spirit.* Translated by A. V. Miller. Oxford: Clarendon, 1977.

————. *Wissenschaft der Logik.* Edited by G. Lasson. 3rd ed. 2 vols. Hamburg: Felix Meiner, 1971, 1975. English translation published as *Science of Logic.* Translated by A. V. Miller. New York: Humanities Press, 1969.

Heidegger, Martin. *Schellings Abhandlung über das Wesen der menschlichen Freiheit.* Edited by H. Feick. Tübingen: Max Niemeyer, 1972.

Henrich, Dieter. *Hegel im Kontext.* Frankfurt: Suhrkamp, 1971.

Hölderlin, Friedrich. *Werke und Briefe.* Edited by F. Beissner and J. Schmidt. 3 vols. Frankfurt: Insel, 1969.

Holz, Harald. *Spekulation und Faktizität. Zum Freiheitsbegriff des mittleren und späten Schelling.* Bonn: Bouvier, 1970.

Kant, Immanuel. *Kritik der reinen Vernunft.* Edited by Raymond Schmidt. Hamburg: Felix Meiner, 1926. Cited in the text with page numbers from the 1871 (A) and 1878 (B) editions. English translation published as *Critique of Pure Reason*. Translated by Norman Kemp Smith. New York: St. Martin's Press, 1965. The translation indicates the German pagination.

Kasper, Walter. *Das Absolute in der Geschichte: Philosophie und Theologie der Geschichte in der Spätphilosophie Schellings.* Mainz: Mattias-Grünewald-Verlag, 1965.

Löwith, Karl. *From Hegel to Nietzsche.* New York: Holt, Rinehart and Winston, 1964.

Rosen, Stanley. *The Limits of Analysis.* New York: Basic Books, 1980.

—————. *Nihilism.* New Haven: Yale University Press, 1969.

Sandkühler, Hans-Jörg. *Friedrich Wilhelm Joseph Schelling.* Stuttgart: J. B. Metzlersche Verlagsbuchhandlung, 1970.

Schelling, Friedrich Wilhelm Joseph. *Grundlegung der positiven Philosophie.* Edited and with a foreword and introduction by Horst Fuhrmans. Torino: Bottega d'Erasmo, 1972. Cited in the text as *GPP.*

—————. *Philosophie der Offenbarung 1841/2.* Edited by Manfred Frank. Frankfurt: Suhrkamp, 1977.

—————. *Sämmtliche Werke.* 14 vols. Stuttgart and Augsburg: J.G. Cotta'scher Verlag, 1856–61. Reprint edition of selected works. Darmstadt: Wissenschaftliche Buchgesellschaft, 1974–76. The following listing of works by volume and page number will clarify the references in the text.

1:85–148. "Ueber die Möglichkeit einer Form der Philosophie überhaupt" [On the possibility of a form of philosophy in general] (1794).

1:149–244. "Vom Ich als Prinzip der Philosophie" [On the ego as principle of philosophy] (1795).

1:281–342. "Philosophische Briefe über Dogmatismus und Kriticismus" [Philosophical letters concerning dogmatism and criticism] (1795).

1:343–452. "Abhandlungen zur Erläuterung des Idealismus der Wissenschaftslehre" [Treatises explicating the idealism of the doctrine of science] (1796–97).

2:1–344. *Ideen zu einer Philosophie der Natur* [Ideas toward a philosophy of nature] (1797). "Einleitung" [Introduction], pages 1–73.

2:345–583. *Von der Weltseele* [On the world soul] (1798).

3:1–268. *Erster Entwurf eines Systems der Naturphilosophie* [First outline of a system of philosophy of nature] (1799).

3:269–326. Einleitung to the *Erster Entwurf* [Introduction to *The first outline*] (1799).

3:327–634. *System der transzendentalen Idealismus* (1800). English translation published as *System of Transcendental Idealism*. Translated by Peter Heath. Charlottesville: University of Virginia Press, 1978. The translation indicates the German pagination.

4:105–212. *Darstellung meines Systems der Philosophie* [Exhibition of my system of philosophy] (1801).

4:213–332. *Bruno oder über das göttliche und natürliche Prinzip der Dinge* [Bruno, or concerning the divine and natural principle of things] (1802).

4:333–510. *Fernere Darstellungen aus dem System der Philosophie* [Further exhibitions from the system of philosophy] (1802).

6:11–70. "Philosophie and Religion" [Philosophy and religion] (1804).

6:131–574. *System der gesammten Philosophie und der Natur-philosophie insbesondere* [System of all philosophy and of the philosophy of nature in particular] (1804). Pages 215–574 are omitted from the Wissenschaftliche Buchgesellschaft edition; they are included in the Schröder edition (see below).

7:1–126. "Darlegung des wahren Verhältnisses der Naturphilosophie zu der verbesserten Fichteschen Lehre" [Exhibition of the true relation of the philosophy of nature to the improved Fichtean doctrine] (1806).

7:140–97. "Aphorismen zur Einleitung in die Naturphilosophie" [Aphorisms introducing the philosophy of nature] (1806).

7:198–244. "Aphorismen über die Naturphilosophie" [Aphorisms concerning the philosophy of nature] (1806).

7:331–416. *Philosophische Untersuchungen über das Wesen der menschlichen Freiheit und die damit zusammenhängende Gegenstände* [Philosophical investigations concerning the essence of human freedom and related subjects] (1809). English translation published as *Of Human Freedom*. Translated by James Gutman. Chicago: Open Court, 1936.

7:417–484. *Stuttgarter Privatvorlesungen* [Stuttgart private lectures] (1810).

8:19–136. "F. W. J. Schellings Denkmal der Schrift von den göttlichen Dingen etc. des Herrn Friedrich Heinrich Jacobi" [F. W. J. Schelling's monument to the piece on divine things etc. by Friedrich Heinrich Jacobi] (1812).

8:145–89. "Briefwechsel mit Eschenmeyer bezüglich der Abhandlung 'Philosophische Untersuchungen über das Wesen der menschlichen Freiheit'" [Correspondence with Eschenmeyer concerning the essay "Philosophical investigations concerning the essence of human freedom and related subjects"] (1813).

8:195–344. *Die Weltalter. Erstes Buch* [Ages of the world, first book] (1813).

9:353–366. "Erste Vorlesung in München" [First lecture in Munich] (1827).

10:1–200. *Zur Geschichte der neueren Philosophie* [On the history of modern philosophy].

10:201–224. "Vorrede zu einer philosophischen Schrift des Herrn Viktor Cousin" [Preface to a philosophical piece by Viktor Cousin] (1834).

10:225–86. "Darstellung des philosophischen Empirismus" [Exhibition of philosophical empiricism].

11:1–252. "Historische-kritische Einleitung in die Philosophie der Mythologie" [Historical-critical introduction to the philosophy of mythology].

11:253–572. "Philosophische Einleitung in die Philosophie der Mythologie oder Darstellung der rein-rationalen Philosophie" [Philosophical introduction to the philosophy of mythology, or exhibition of pure rational philosophy].

11:573–90. "Abhandlung über die Quelle der ewigen Wahrheiten" [Treatise on the sources of eternal truths].

12:1–674. *Philosophie der Mythologie* [Philosophy of mythology].

13:1–174. "Einleitung in die Philosophie der Offenbarung oder Begründung der positiven Philosophie" [Introduction to the philosophy of revelation or foundation of positive philosophy].

13:177–530. *Der Philosophie der Offenbarung erster Teil* [Philosophy of revelation, part one].

14:1–344. *Der Philosophie der Offenbarung zweiter Teil* [Philosophy of revelation, part two].

14:335–56. "Andere Deduktion der Prinzipien der positiven Philosophie" [Another deduction of the principles of positive philosophy].

14:357–67. "Erste Vorlesung in Berlin" [First lecture in Berlin] (1841). Note on volumes 10–14: Of the works contained in these volumes, Schelling published only the "Foreword to the Works of Victor Cousin" (10:201–24). The other works are lecture notes and texts from the years 1827–54, edited and published after Schelling's death by his son.

————. *Sämmtliche Werke.* Edited by Manfred Schröter. Munich: C. H. Beck'sche Verlagsbuchhandlung. This is a second reprint edition of selected works. Cited from this edition is the part of the 1804 *System* not included in the edition of the Wissenschaftliche Buchgesellschaft, pp. 215–574.

Schulz, Walter. *Die Vollendung des Deutschen Idealismus in der Spätphilosophie Schellings.* 2nd ed. Pfullingen: Neske, 1975.

Tilliette, Xavier. *Schelling. Une philosophie en devenir.* 2 vols. Paris: Vrin, 1970.

White, Alan. *Absolute Knowledge: Hegel and the Problem of Metaphysics.* Athens, Ohio: Ohio University Press, 1983.

————. "The End of Philosophy: A Study of Hegel and Schelling." Ph.D. dissertation, The Pennsylvania State University, 1980.

Wieland, Wolfgang. *Schellings Lehre von der Zeit. Grundlagen und Voraussetzungen der Weltalterphilosophie.* Heidelberg: Carl Winter Universitätsverlag, 1956.

INDEX

Absolute: as principle, 2, 8, 9–10, 159–60; Spinoza's, 6, 12; necessarily indeterminate, 29, 76–77; as absolute and as ground, 38, 70–71, 73, 82, 129–34, 137–38; as will, 115. *See also* Finitude, origin of; Urgrund and Ungrund
Absolute identity, 68, 69, 71, 76–78
Anthropology, philosophical, 3, 144, 151, 189–90
Aristotle, 87, 124, 189
Art: and the absolute, 29, 34–35; reveals absolute, 69, 92, 100
Augustine, Saint, 57, 116

Bakunin, Mikhail, 188
Barth, Karl, 3
Binswanger, Ludwig, 3
Böhme, Jakob, 119
Boss, Medard, 3
Burckhardt, Jacob, 188

Concepts, 87, 154
Consciousness, 11. *See also* Self-consciousness; Self-reflection, primal
Construction, 51. *See also* Dialectic
Criticism and dogmatism: 14, 17–18, 29–31

Descartes, René, 57, 62, 79, 159
Dialectic: Fichte's, 18–19; Schelling's, 78–79, 99, 119–22, 169–78. *See also* Powers, Schelling's dialectic of
Dialogue form, 81, 92, 93
Dionysus, 185
Divided line, Schelling's, 154–55

Edification and philosophy, 150
Ego, human: in relation to absolute, 11; as absolute, 14, 16, 59; as highest creation, 99, 112, 177

Eleusinian mysteries, 98
Empiricism, metaphysical, 161–69
Engels, Friedrich, 188
Esotericism, intentional, 107, 113, 138
Essence: and form, 134–35; and existence, 155–56
Evil, problem of: 88–89, 116, 137–38; Schelling's solution to, 120–23, 129–30
Existence: and ground, 118–22; and essence, 155–56
Existentialism, 1, 3–4, 137, 189–90

Fall of humanity: in 1804 *System*, 90; in "Philosophy and Religion," 98–99, 100; in positive philosophy, 177–79, 180, 183, 186
Feuerbach, Ludwig, 147, 188
Fichte, Johann Gottlieb: influence on Schelling, 4, 13; and Kant, 13–15, 102; Schelling's divergence from, 24–26, 27, 85, 96, 101, 105, 155: and origin of finitude, 40–41; defective notion of nature, 47, 54, 79, 96; as transcendental idealist, 55; objection to Schelling, 80; and tyranny, 97; and freedom, 116; highest maxim of, 150
Finitude, origin of: in Schelling's early works, 37–42, 48; in system of identity, 75, 76–79, 83–87; in *Freedom* essay, 90, 92, 94, 98–100, 160; in positive philosophy, 177–78
Freedom: beginning and end of philosophy, 27; problem of, 33, 65, 72–73, 86–92, 102–03, 108–09, 161; forms of, 65, 86, 116
Freedom, absolute: as absolute necessity, 12, 65, 124–25; as human goal, 27, 33–34; for Hegel, 156–57; and positive philosophy, 175–76